July
2007

ECONOMIC POLICY

SENIOR EDITORS
GEORGES DE MÉNIL
RICHARD PORTES
HANS-WERNER SINN

MANAGING EDITORS
GIUSEPPE BERTOLA
PHILIPPE MARTIN
PAUL SEABRIGHT

BOARD OF GOVERNORS
GEORGES DE MÉNIL Co-Chairman
RICHARD PORTES Co-Chairman
HANS-WERNER SINN Co-Chairman
MAURICE AYMARD
GUILLERMO DE LA DEHESA
RAY REES
ALFRED STEINHERR
XAVIER VIVES

Published in association with the European Economic Association

Blackwell Publishing Ltd for Centre for Economic Policy Research,
Center for Economic Studies of the University of Munich, and
Paris-Jourdan Sciences Economiques (PSE)
in collaboration with the Maison des Sciences de l'Homme.

STATEMENT OF PURPOSE

Economic Policy provides timely and authoritative analyses of the choices which confront policy-makers. The subject matter ranges from the study of how individual markets can and should work to the broadest interactions in the world economy.

Economic Policy is a joint activity of the Centre for Economic Policy Research (CEPR), the Munich-based Center for Economic Studies (CES) and the Paris-based Maison des Sciences de l'Homme (PSE). It offers an independent, non-partisan, European perspective on issues of worldwide concern. It emphasizes problems of international significance, either because they affect the world economy directly or because the experience of one country contains important lessons for policy-makers elsewhere.

All the articles are specifically commissioned from leading professional economists. Their brief is to demonstrate how live policy issues can be illuminated by the insights of modern economics and by the most recent evidence. The presentation is incisive and written in plain language accessible to the wide audience which participates in the policy debate.

Prior to publication, the contents of each volume are discussed by a Panel of distinguished economists from Europe and elsewhere. The Panel rotates annually. Inclusion in each volume of a summary of the highlights of the Economic Policy Panel discussion provides the reader with alternative interpretations of the evidence and a sense of the liveliness of the current debate.

Economic Policy is owned by the Maison des Sciences de l'Homme, CEPR and CES. An extraordinary Panel meeting was held in February 2007 in New York and was hosted by the Federal Reserve Bank of New York. We gratefully acknowledge this support, without implicating any of these organizations in the views expressed here, which are the sole responsibility of the authors.

PANEL

MANUEL ARELLANO
Centre for Monetary and Financial Studies

LANS BOVENBERG
CentER, Tilburg University

PIERRE CAHUC
CREST-INSEE

WENDY CARLIN
University College London

GIANCARLO CORSETTI
European University Institute

ALLAN DRAZEN
University of Maryland

GILLES DURANTON
University of Toronto

CARLO FAVERO
IGIER, Università Bocconi

NEIL GANDAL
Tel Aviv University

CHRISTIAN GOLLIER
University of Toulouse I

OMAR MOAV
Hebrew University of Jerusalem

PIERRE PESTIEAU
Université de Liège

STEPHEN J REDDING
London School of Economics

HELENE REY
Princeton University

ANNE SIBERT
Birkbeck College

JONATHAN TEMPLE
University of Bristol

REINHILDE VEUGELERS
Katholieke Universiteit Leuven

ERNST-LUDWIG VON THADDEN
Universität Mannheim

VOLKER WIELAND
Goethe Universität Frankfurt

July 2007

CONTENTS

431 Editors' introduction

435 **Will there be a dollar crisis?**
Paul Krugman
DISCUSSANTS: Kevin O'Rourke and Giancarlo Corsetti
Panel discussion

469 **The missing dark matter in the wealth of nations and its implications for global imbalances**
Ricardo Hausmann and Federico Sturzenegger
DISCUSSANTS: Anne Sibert and Cédric Tille
Panel discussion and appendixes

519 **Europe and global imbalances**
Philip R. Lane and Gian Maria Milesi-Ferretti
DISCUSSANTS: Paolo Pesenti and Federico Sturzenegger
Panel discussion and appendixes

575 **Assessing China's exchange rate regime**
Jeffrey A. Frankel and Shang-Jin Wei
DISCUSSANT: Linda Goldberg
Panel discussion and appendix

Editors' Introduction

On rare occasions, *Economic Policy* publishes an issue in which all articles have a particular focus. This is one such special issue which focuses on global imbalances. The issue of global imbalances, in particular the US current account deficit, has generated widespread concerns about sustainability as well as about its exchange rate and macroeconomic consequences. The four papers published in this issue address these concerns with different angles and different answers. They were presented in draft form at a special Panel meeting hosted in February 2007 by the Federal Reserve Bank of New York.

A DOLLAR CRISIS?

Between 1997 and 2006, the US current account deficit rose from $140 billion, or 1.7% of US output, to over $840 billion, or 1.7% of world output. Most economists believe that the current imbalance is unsustainable and adjustment is on the cards. From this starting point, Paul Krugman asks two questions: First, how will the decline of the dollar come about? Will it be an *abrupt* fall – a dollar plunge? Second, if such a dollar plunge occurs, will it be a source of major macroeconomic problems? The answers to both questions are given in the form of a reduced-form analysis that helps to clarify the main issues and mechanisms at work. The analysis on the form of the dollar fall draws on a classic piece in the international finance literature, the portfolio-balance model by Kouri (1976). The required ingredient for a plunge (since the current account deficit cannot be the news that triggers a shift in expectations) is some form of investors' myopia, in the sense that 'markets are not taking the prospective long-run decline in the dollar into account'. Krugman builds up his case by comparing returns that investors obtain holding dollar assets with the estimated annual dollar depreciation required to deliver sustainability. At some point investors will realize that they are not sufficiently compensated for the future depreciation. At that moment, the 'Wile E. Coyote' moment as Krugman calls it, the dollar will plunge.

To analyse the second question – the macroeconomic consequences of a dollar plunge – Krugman suggests a simple framework. The main concern here is that the compression of domestic demand caused by a reduced foreign willingness to buy dollar assets may happen quickly, while the increase in net exports will happen slowly. Any economic contraction in the short run will therefore be the result of differences in adjustment speeds, and in particular of a rapid fall in real housing prices. Hence, Krugman concludes that there is more uncertainty on the macroeconomic consequences of the dollar plunge than on the plunge itself.

The paper generated a great deal of interest and discussion at the Panel. The Panel discussion centred on the fact that Wile E. Coyote has been running in mid-air for several years now. We understand neither what accounts for his continuing successful challenge to the law of gravity nor what will trigger the fall. Several hypotheses on possible triggers were offered but Krugman reminded the Panel that even after currency crises it is often difficult to pinpoint one specific event that triggers the crisis. Not surprisingly, the Panel was also uncomfortable with the implications of the paper on investors' myopia as it suggests that markets do not pay any attention to what most economists have been saying for some time on current account deficits and the dollar. Or maybe they have been biased and listened to more optimistic (or more complacent) views on the sustainability of the US current account deficit.

DARK MATTER AND INTERNATIONAL IMBALANCES

The next paper focuses on a truly essential piece of the global imbalances sustainability puzzle, namely the definition and measurement of country-level external positions. In 2006, as the widening US current account imbalance attracted much attention and concern, Ricardo Hausmann and Federico Sturzenegger attracted even more attention by pointing at hidden balancing forces. Just as the cosmos appears to be prevented from exploding into infinity by the gravity attraction of invisible 'dark matter', they argued, so the global financial system's stability may be enhanced by the unmeasured foreign assets of countries that, like the US, earn positive net foreign capital income in spite of very large current account deficit accumulations. Their proposed measure of US dark matter assets, based on capitalization at a constant interest rate of officially measured net foreign investment income, was greeted with keen interest and some enthusiasm by journalists and by financial market practitioners, who were perhaps relieved by the comforting message given by those computations to any portfolio containing US assets. But it was met by puzzlement and pointed criticism by policy-makers and by researchers, who pointed out the dangers of complacency regarding global imbalances and the many pitfalls of such simple computations.

We decided to consider for publication a version of their paper that, while based on the same intriguing ideas, would aim at addressing the justified criticism of its quick and dubious first application. After much revision work (and heated discussion at the Panel), the paper we publish in this issue does take the basic idea as seriously as it deserves, considers a variety of possible explanations for evidence of an unusual borrowing capacity on the part of the US and a few other countries, and offers an appropriately qualified assessment of the results' implications for sustainability of external imbalances. The consensus view is that dark matter has very little to do with sustainability of the current US situation, both because new matter would need to be generated continuously, and because the capital income balance has been changing recently. As an accounting concept, however, capitalization of 'dark' assets is a methodologically useful complement to other simple and potentially misleading measures of imbalances. The wider perspective offered by the paper's analysis of yield differentials offers interesting insights into the workings of the international financial system, and complements nicely related existing work and the paper's own original dark matter computations. Over the next few years, as global imbalances unwind, the intriguing approach based on capitalization of observed income flows and on adjusted valuations of foreign direct investments, and the critical remarks of the discussants and Panel members, will be highly relevant references for all researchers and policy-makers.

EUROPE AND GLOBAL IMBALANCES

Currently, large external deficits in the United States are matched by large surpluses in Asian emerging markets, Japan and oil producing countries. Only a few European countries have large surpluses and the *euro area* as a whole is close to external balance and is not a major contributor to the US current account deficit. Shall we then conclude that the adjustment of global imbalances will affect Europe only marginally, since the heart of it will consist in rebalancing the position of the US vis-à-vis the surplus regions, especially Asia? In their paper, Philip Lane and Gian Maria Milesi-Ferretti provide evidence that Europe will not be a bystander of the global adjustment process. The growth in trade and financial linkages between Europe and the rest of the world means that the spillover impact on Europe of a contraction in the US deficit is now larger than 20 years ago. The dollar depreciation that will likely accompany a reduction in the US trade deficit would have a non-negligible negative wealth effect on European investors, by reducing the value of their dollar-denominated claims. However, this effect should be smaller than in China and Japan, that hold larger net dollar positions. Also, an interesting result of the paper is that there is considerable heterogeneity across Europe in terms of exposure to this valuation effect of the adjustment.

But the paper goes further, as it considers different rebalancing scenarios with different degrees of economic stress. Using the Global Economy Model (GEM), the multi-country model developed at the International Monetary Fund, it uses these scenario projections to forecast paths of financial variables and valuation effects excluded from GEM. The paper generated a lot of interest at the Panel and discussion on some methodological points related to GEM and its use in this context. The assumption that the projected paths for exchange rates are invariant to the extent of valuation effects mean that the estimated capital gains and losses as well as the depreciation of the dollar may be biased upward. These methodological issues notwithstanding, this paper will certainly attract attention as the first quantification of this important issue.

CHINA'S EXCHANGE RATE

The next paper focuses on the bilateral relation between the US and China, which has great bearing on the way global imbalances may unwind in the future. It is both an assessment of China's currency policies vis-à-vis the dollar and of the US Treasury's decision whether to name a country like China as a currency manipulator. The paper brings clarity to these two issues that are politically charged. Jeffrey Frankel and Shang-Jin Wei find first that despite China's announced shift to a managed floating rate regime with reference to a basket of currencies that includes many currencies, the US dollar still receives an overwhelming weight. Neither the euro nor the yen has had any *de facto* positive weight in China's implicit basket. Hence, not much has changed since the announcement of an exchange rate reform by the Chinese authorities in July 2005. On the second question, the US Treasury decisions to name a country as a currency manipulator could be determined either by legitimate economic variables (such as the trading partner's multilateral balance, reserve accumulation, and real exchange rate) or by domestic political considerations (such as the US unemployment rate and the bilateral balance). Frankel and Wei find that both types of determinants matter but that the most consistently significant variable is the bilateral balance which should not be a legitimate economic determinant of the decision of the US Treasury. Given the importance that the bilateral relation between China and the United States has acquired in the global trading system, the clarification that this paper provides attracted a lot of interest at the Panel. The Panel's main questions focused on whether there were any real consequences on the exchange rate policy of the country named as a manipulator by the Treasury and whether economics had much to say on the concept of 'manipulation' for exchange rate policy. It was widely felt that these are questions on which more research remains to be done.

Will there be a dollar crisis?

SUMMARY

Almost everyone believes that the US current account deficit must eventually end, and that this end will involve dollar depreciation. However, many believe that this depreciation will take place gradually. This paper shows that any process of gradual dollar decline fast enough to prevent the accumulation of implausible levels of US external debt would impose capital losses on investors much larger than they currently expect. As a result, there will at some point have to be a 'Wile E. Coyote moment' – a point at which expectations are revised, and the dollar drops sharply. It is much less clear, however, whether this 'crisis' will produce macroeconomic problems.

— *Paul Krugman*

Will there be a dollar crisis?

Paul Krugman
Princeton University

1. INTRODUCTION

The United States has a remarkably large current account deficit, both in absolute terms and as a share of GDP. At the moment the country is not having any difficulty attracting capital inflows sufficient to finance this deficit, but many observers nonetheless find the deficit worrisome. The worriers see an ominous resemblance between the current US situation and that of developing countries that also went through periods during which capital flows easily financed large current deficits, then experienced 'sudden stops' in which capital inflows abruptly ceased, the currency plunged, and the economy experienced a major setback.

Yet there does not seem to be a clear consensus about how to think about the risks of a dollar crisis. Most of a 2005 issue of *Brookings Papers on Economic Activity* (issue 1) was devoted to the question, and contained excellent, stimulating discussions. Yet the papers seemed, in many ways, to be talking past each other – answering different questions, without being clear about their differences. The purpose of this paper is to sort out the major issues. The idea is to figure out where the various arguments fit, whether they really mean what their proponents claim, and – to the extent possible – how they add up given the available numbers.

I would like to thank participants in the Economic Policy meeting at the Federal Reserve Bank of New York for helpful comments. The Managing Editor in charge of this paper was Philippe Martin.

Although there are some analysts arguing that the US current account deficit is either sustainable or a statistical illusion – arguments discussed briefly below – for the most part the crucial debate is not whether the dollar and the US current account deficit must eventually decline; even if the unorthodox views are given the benefit of the doubt, it is hard to argue that the current levels are indefinitely sustainable. Instead, the debate is or should be about two questions. First, will there be an *abrupt* fall in the dollar – a dollar plunge? Second, if there is a dollar plunge, will it be merely embarrassing or a source of major macroeconomic problems?

This paper does not offer a full model. Instead, it carries out a reduced-form analysis of the possibility of a dollar plunge, followed by a sketch rather than a model of the ways in which such a plunge might cause macroeconomic trouble. As we will see, there are some conceptual problems in linking the question of whether the dollar will plunge to the question of what will happen if it does. But this paper tries to tell a consistent story.

The remainder of the paper is in five sections. The next section argues that investor myopia is key to the question of whether a dollar plunge is likely: it is reasonably clear that the dollar must eventually fall, but that fall only needs to happen abruptly if investors have failed to factor the long-run need for dollar decline into their portfolio decisions. Section 3 offers an analytical treatment of the question of investor myopia and a potential dollar plunge. The fourth section introduces some caveats and qualifications to that analysis. Section 5 suggests a framework for thinking about the macroeconomic effects of a dollar plunge, if that is what is going to happen. A final section suggests some conclusions and directions for research.

2. THE CASE FOR A PLUNGE: A WILE E. COYOTE APPROACH

There is little doubt that the dollar must eventually fall from current levels. Trade deficits on the current scale cannot continue forever – and we are all fond of quoting Stein's Law: 'If something cannot go on forever, it will stop.' Closing the trade deficit will require a redistribution of world spending, with a fall in US spending and a rise in spending abroad. One occasionally hears assertions that this redistribution of world spending can lead to the required change in trade deficits without any need for a change in real exchange rates – a view John Williamson once felicitously described as 'the doctrine of immaculate transfer'. In fact, however, a redistribution of world spending will require a fall in the relative prices of US-produced goods and services, because US spending falls much more heavily than the spending of other countries on those US-produced goods and services. So there must, eventually, be a real depreciation of the dollar. But this depreciation could be gradual, a few percent per year or less. Why should it take the form of a discrete drop?

There has actually been surprisingly little discussion of this question, even in papers that can seem, on a casual reading, to be about the prospects for a dollar plunge. For example, the widely cited work of Obstfeld and Rogoff about dollar adjustment, continued in their 2005 *Brookings* paper, is often cited as reason for alarm.

But their framework is designed to estimate the size of the dollar decline needed to eliminate the current account deficit; it sheds little light on whether that decline will happen quickly, as opposed to a gradual adjustment over the course of a number of years.

The closest any paper in the 2005 *Brookings* symposium came to addressing that question directly was Edwards (2005), whose view is echoed less clearly in a number of discussions. The basic idea can be summarized as follows: there has been an upward shift in the proportion of US assets that foreign investors want to hold in their portfolios. As long as foreign investors are still in the process of moving to this new, higher share of dollars in their wealth, their actions generate a large capital flow into the United States. But the capital flows needed to *maintain* an increased dollar share in portfolios are much smaller than those required to *achieve* that share. So once the desired holdings of US assets have been achieved, the argument goes, capital flows into the United States will drop off sharply, leading to an abrupt decline in both the current account deficit and in the dollar.

There are a number of questions we could raise about this story, but one that seems particularly germane is that of expectations: won't investors see this coming? If they do, the dynamics will be very different. The initial shift into dollars, and hence initial capital inflows, will be damped by expectations of future depreciation. On the other hand, capital inflows will be sustained much longer, because dollar assets will become more attractive over time as the dollar drops toward its long-run sustainable level, reducing the need for further depreciation. So the whole process will be smoothed out. In fact, that is the adjustment process described by another paper in the same conference, by Blanchard *et al.* (2005), which does *not* imply a dollar plunge. So to get the kind of sudden stop envisaged by Edwards and others, investors must be myopic: they must fail to understand the unsustainability of the current exchange rate.

Once we have introduced the possibility of investor myopia, however, we have also introduced the possibility that this myopia will eventually be cured by events: at some point it will become obvious to investors that the dollar must decline – and at that point it will, suddenly. And this brings us to an approach I and others took to the question of prospects for a dollar plunge more than 20 years ago.

Two decades ago the United States was in a position that resembled the present in some important respects. The country had a large current account deficit, although it was only half as large relative to GDP as the deficit today. Then as now some people argued that this deficit could be sustained indefinitely. Others, myself included, argued that the dollar was in for a fall (Krugman, 1985). And some argued that this fall would have dire consequences (Marris, 1985). Fortunately, although the dollar did fall, the predicted evil effects failed to materialize.

At the time I suggested an approach to thinking about the prospects for a dollar plunge that I believe is once again useful, although the modelling framework here is different. The key to this approach is arguing that the real question is not whether the dollar must eventually depreciate. It is whether the dollar must eventually depreciate at a rate *faster than investors now expect*. That is, the only reason to predict a plunge is if we believe that today's capital flows are based on irrational expectations – that the future path of the exchange rate that investors expect is inconsistent with a feasible adjustment path for the balance of payments. If markets are failing to take the required future fall of the dollar into account, they will eventually have a 'Wile E. Coyote' moment,[1] when they look down and realize that nothing is supporting the currency. At that point the dollar will plunge. That is, we are looking for evidence that investors are not properly forward-looking, and that an abrupt exchange rate adjustment will occur when reality bites.

Some form of Wile E. Coyote analysis is implicit in many dire warnings about a dollar plunge, such as those of Roubini and Setser (2005). The International Monetary Fund's 2006 *World Economic Outlook* (IMF, 2006) offers, in guarded terms, what appears to be a Wile E. Coyote warning: after laying out a benign 'No policies scenario' for the adjustment of external balances, it goes on to point out two problems with this scenario:

> 'First, foreigners are assumed to be willing to accommodate a further very substantial buildup in U.S. foreign liabilities, from currently less than 30 percent to ultimately around 85 percent of U.S. GDP. This would represent a very high level of external indebtedness, even for a large industrialized country. Second, foreigners would be willing to allocate an increasing share of their asset portfolios to U.S. assets without demanding a large risk premium, even though they may face continued foreign exchange losses ... [T]hese assumptions may not be realistic, and it is relevant to explore alternative scenarios based on more pessimistic assumptions.' (p. 26)

It is, however, useful to make the Wile E. Coyote analysis explicit: doing so both highlights the significance of key economic observations, such as the absence of clear real interest rate differentials between major economies, and helps us sort out the relevance of various seemingly related arguments, such as the alleged emergence of a 'Bretton Woods II' system of exchange rates.

3. WILE E. COYOTE ANALYTICS

What constitutes a feasible adjustment path for the dollar? I would argue that the key criterion for feasibility is that the dollar must fall sufficiently rapidly to avoid an unsustainable level of US external debt. I will not try to define at this point how high a level of debt is unsustainable; as we will see, that may be the crucial question.

How should we model the relationship between the path of the exchange rate and the path of external debt? Those who have been involved with exchange rate models since the early days of floating rates have seen a sudden jump in the value of some old intellectual capital: portfolio-balance models of the exchange rate, drawing on

---

[1] For those not familiar with the classics: there were often scenes in *Road Runner* cartoons in which the ever-frustrated Wile E. Coyote would run off a cliff, take several steps on thin air, then look down – and only after realizing that there was nothing under him, would he plunge.

early work by Kouri (1976) in particular, are back in fashion. As we will now see, a 'generic' portfolio balance model, which glosses over many details, lets us get quite directly at the question of whether investors are properly anticipating the necessary future fall in the dollar.

Our generic model contains only two equations. The first is the portfolio balance equation, which determines the real dollar exchange rate given US net external debt – measured as a share of GDP – and expected dollar depreciation:

$$x = x(D, \dot{x}^e) \tag{1}$$

where x is the real exchange rate, D is US net external debt as a share of GDP and $\dot{x}^e$ is the expected rate of real dollar appreciation. (We measure x so that up is up: a rise in x is a real appreciation of the dollar.)

D has a negative effect on x for at least one and possibly two reasons. First, there is the usual portfolio balance effect: a larger net external debt requires some combination of foreigners holding a larger share of US assets in their portfolios and US residents holding a smaller share of foreign assets in their portfolios. Both changes in portfolio require a lower dollar, other things equal. Second, there may be concerns about US ability and/or willingness to service its debts as the debt-GDP ratio grows large.

Meanwhile, the expected rate of appreciation affects the current exchange rate through its effect on portfolio choice. Consider a simple two-asset model, in which investors allocate their wealth between dollars and euros, which are in fixed supply. Other things equal, expected appreciation of the dollar will make dollars relatively more attractive, inducing investors to hold a larger share of dollars in their portfolio. Since the quantity of dollars is fixed, this share increase occurs through an appreciation that increases the euro value of the dollar stock. Similar logic applies to more complex models; hence the reduced-form inclusion of expected appreciation as a determinant of the exchange rate.

The other equation describes debt dynamics:

$$\dot{D} = B(x, D, \dot{x}) \tag{2}$$

The rate of change of the debt-GDP ratio is not identical with the ratio of the current account deficit to GDP, because it must also take account both of changes in the denominator due to growth in GDP and of capital gains and losses. As Gourinchas and Rey (2005) show, these capital gains and losses loom large in some years. Because the United States tends to hold real assets or equities abroad, while its liabilities consist to a large extent of dollar-denominated debt, dollar depreciation tends to reduce the US net external debt position.

Here is how to interpret the effects of the three variables on the right side of Equation (2). The effect of the real exchange rate is fairly straightforward, although it is important to understand that we are not talking about a naïve 'elasticities' approach. Instead, it should be understood as a reduced form of a general equilibrium calculation: given a redistribution of spending from the United States to the rest of the world that has as its counterpart a rise in B, we ask how the real exchange rate changes as part of the adjustment. (A well-known recent example of this kind of calculation is Obstfeld and Rogoff, 2005.)

The effect of D on its own rate of change works through two channels. On one side, higher net debt reduces net investment income. On the other side, the debt-GDP ratio tends to fall, other things equal, due to GDP growth, and the size of this effect depends on the initial ratio. Which effect predominates depends on whether the marginal rate of return on foreign debt is greater or less than the rate of GDP growth. At the moment, with the US external deficit mainly financed by sales of bonds whose real interest rate seems to be less than the rate of potential growth, the numbers seem to suggest that an increase in debt *reduces* the rate of debt accumulation, a disturbing conclusion. Perhaps this condition will be reversed when foreign investors begin to earn a higher rate of return on their US assets. In any case, as we will see, in the reduced-form approach of this paper we do not need to take a position on the sign of R-g.

Finally, the effect of changes in the real exchange rate on the rate of debt accumulation reflects valuation effects. The United States has very little external debt denominated in foreign currency; its liabilities, consisting overwhelmingly of dollar bonds, foreign-owned stocks, and direct foreign investment, can to a first approximation be considered a claim denominated in terms of US goods and services. On the other hand, the bulk of US external assets consist of foreign stocks and direct investment, both of which can to a first approximation be considered claims denominated in terms of foreign goods and services. So a real depreciation of the dollar raises the value, in terms of US GDP, of US external assets without increasing the value of US external liabilities. As a result, dollar depreciation reduces net external debt.

Figure 1 illustrates the familiar dynamics associated with this model. The line DD shows the relationship between D and x that would apply if $\dot{x}^e = 0$, that is, if investors did not expect any future real depreciation of the dollar. The line BB shows the locus of point at which the debt-GDP ratio is stationary, given zero change in the real exchange rate. BB is drawn as downward-sloping, which corresponds to a marginal rate of return greater than the growth rate. If $R < g$, BB is upward-sloping, but the qualitative behaviour is unchanged. With rational expectations, the economy will follow the saddle path SS. (Ignore points 1 and 2 for now.) Notice what happens if investors are forward-looking: when D is below its long-run equilibrium level, the value of the dollar is held down by expectations of future decline, but as D rises, the decline in the dollar is cushioned by rising demand as expected depreciation falls off. That is, forward-looking behaviour by investors works against the possibility of a dollar plunge.

But are investors, in fact, forward-looking? Does the current situation look as if investors are fully taking into account the prospects for future dollar decline? Or does staving off an unsustainable accumulation of debt require a rate of dollar decline that will come as a surprise to investors, setting off a dollar plunge?

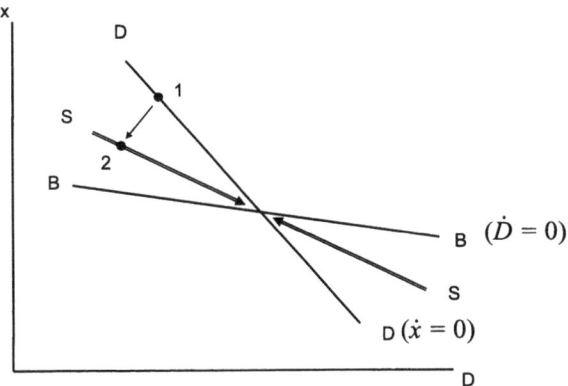

Figure 1. Investor myopia and the Wile E. Coyote moment

One way to approach these issues is to note that if we linearize the model, it implies that both the real exchange rate and the adjusted current account will converge exponentially to their long-run levels:

$$\ln x = \ln \bar{x} + (\ln x_0 - \ln \bar{x})e^{-\kappa t} \tag{3}$$

$$\dot{D} = \dot{D}_0 e^{-\kappa t} \tag{4}$$

where $\bar{x}$ is the long-run equilibrium value of the real exchange rate, and κ is the rate of convergence. Equation (4) also implies that the long run debt to GDP ratio will be:

$$\bar{D} = D_0 + \frac{\dot{D}_0}{\kappa} \tag{5}$$

What Equation (5) tells us is that the eventual debt accumulation depends on the rate of convergence, κ. If we believe that there are limits to how high the debt-GDP ratio can realistically go, that sets a lower bound on the rate of convergence. But from Equation (3), the higher the rate of convergence, the faster the rate of real dollar decline. So we can now rephrase our question: if we assume that the economy converges on long-run equilibrium sufficiently rapidly to lead to a feasible level of debt, is the implied rate of dollar decline consistent with what we know about investor behaviour?

To answer this question, we need to put in some specific numbers. US net external debt at the end of 2005, with direct investment assessed at market value, was 20% of GDP in the fourth quarter of 2005, so we can set the initial value of the debt-GDP ratio, D_0, at approximately 0.20.

The initial value of $\dot{D}$ may seem straightforward, but it is actually a bit tricky. As I have already pointed out, it is not simply the ratio of the current account to GDP, currently approximately 7% of GDP. Instead, we need to make two adjustments.

First, we need to take account of the erosion of the debt-GDP ratio due to the growth of GDP. Let us assume real growth at 3%, and an inflation rate of 2.5%, giving us 5.5% nominal growth. With net external debt of 20% of GDP, this subtracts 1.1 percentage points of GDP off the current account deficit.

Second, we need to take account of valuation effects. Since we are measuring D as a share of US GDP, we are in effect using US-produced goods and services as a numeraire. To a reasonable approximation, we can assume away valuation effects in terms of this numeraire on US external liabilities. However, a substantial part of US external assets, consisting both of private holdings of securities and of foreign direct investment, can to a good approximation be considered denominated in foreign goods and services. Then we have:

$$A = A^*/x$$

where A^* is the value of these external US assets in terms of foreign goods and services; when the real exchange rate changes, we have:

$$\Delta A = -A\frac{\Delta x}{x}$$

This tells us that the initial value of $\dot{D}$ depends on the value of selected US assets abroad and on the rate of real depreciation along the assumed equilibrium path. US holdings of foreign securities at the end of 2005, plus foreign direct investment at market value, were equal to 59.7% of fourth-quarter 2005 GDP – call it 60%. With foreign-goods-denominated assets equal to 60% of GDP, real depreciation of 4% per year will cause valuation effects that subtract 2.4 percentage points from the adjusted current account. If real depreciation is only 2% per year, valuation effects will subtract only 1.2 percentage points, and so on.

Finally, how much must the real dollar fall in the long run? In principle, this depends on the steady-state level of external debt relative to GDP, and thus needs to be simultaneously determined along with the adjustment path. For the purposes of this paper, however, it seems possible to take a shortcut, by assuming that the required depreciation needs to be just sufficient to bring the US balance of payments on goods and services to zero. As long as the long-run rate of return on net US liabilities is greater than the growth rate – which is not true in current data, but will probably be true in the long run – this is a lower bound on the real depreciation necessary.

But how large a depreciation would be needed to bring US trade in goods and services into balance? A simple model assumes that the United States and the rest of the world each produce a single composite good, that preferences are Cobb–Douglas, and that the current situation can be viewed as one in which the rest of the world is making a transfer to the United States equal to the US goods and services deficit. If we assume that the rest of the world has a combined GDP equal to three times US GDP, and calibrate the model to US data from the second quarter of 2006, we find that eliminating the transfer would lead to a 42.6% rise in the relative price of rest-of-world products, or a 35% logarithmic real depreciation of the dollar. This is close to the estimate of required dollar depreciation by Obstfeld and Rogoff. Both estimates

Table 1. Implications of different rates of convergence

κ	Initial value of $\dot{D}$	Long-run value of D	Initial rate of real depreciation
0.05	0.049	1.18	0.0175
0.10	0.038	0.58	0.035

of required depreciation are considerably less than those indicated by fitted trade equations, which suggest that the dollar might have to fall by as much as 20% to reduce the external deficit by 1% of GDP. For current purposes I will assume that:

$$\ln x_0 - \ln \bar{x} = 0.35$$

that is, that the dollar must eventually experience a logarithmic 35% real depreciation; it is unlikely that this is a serious overestimate, and quite possible that it is a serious underestimate.

An aside: as Obstfeld and Rogoff and others have pointed out, a realistic model of future trade adjustment should, at minimum, portray a three-cornered world, since the counterpart of the US external deficit lies in Asia, with Europe roughly balanced. The details of any attempt to model this three-cornered adjustment depends on what we assume about the European balance of payments: would a reduction in the US deficit come partly via a European move toward deficit, or entirely via a counterpart adjustment in Asia? What is clear is that Asian currencies can be expected to appreciate more than average, and the euro less. Lane and Milesi-Ferretti (2007) analyse in this issue how Europe may be affected by an adjustment of the US deficit.

We can now look at the implications of different hypothetical rates of convergence for debt accumulation and rates of real depreciation. Let us be clear: these are not intended as predictions, they are thought experiments. As a result, the assumed rates of convergence here should not be compared with empirical estimates of convergence following exchange rate shocks.

Instead, what we are doing here is a feasibility test: we are trying to determine whether there is any rate of convergence consistent both with market expectations and with plausible end levels of D. Table 1 shows the results of such a calculation. We consider two hypothetical values for κ. A low value, 0.05, implies an initial rate of depreciation of 1.75% per year – 0.05 times the logarithmic long-run depreciation of 35%. After taking account of the growth and valuation adjustments, this implies an initial value for $\dot{D}$ of 0.049, and an eventual net debt-GDP ratio of 118%. As Eichengreen (2006) has pointed out, debt level that high would imply foreign ownership of at least a third of the US capital stock, and more if the US continues to have substantial gross assets abroad. A higher value, 0.10, implies an initial 3.5% real rate of depreciation, an initial value for $\dot{D}$ of 0.038, and an eventual debt-GDP ratio of only 58% – still high by historical standards for a large, relatively closed economy, but perhaps plausible given financial globalization.

Table 2. Interest rates and inflation, August 2006

	Long-term interest rate	Break-even inflation rate on index bonds
United States	4.7	2.5
Euro zone	4.2	2.1
Japan	1.7	1.4

Source: ECB *Monthly Bulletin*, April 2007.

This exercise suggests that a plausible path for long-run adjustment requires real depreciation at more than 2% per year, and possibly as much as 4%. This need not be implausible, if investors were being compensated with higher real returns on dollar investments. But they aren't.

As Table 2 shows, long-term nominal interest rates in the United States are higher than in the euro area, and much higher than in Japan. However, these differentials are partly offset by differences in expected rates of inflation. With well-known caveats (markets for inflation-indexed bonds are relatively thin), we can use the break-even inflation rate on inflation-indexed bonds (BEIR) as an estimate of expected inflation. As of April 2007 the long-term BEIR in the United States was approximately 2.5% per year; that in the euro zone was approximately 2.1%; that in Japan only 0.4%. Thus there was essentially no real interest rate differential between the United States and the euro zone, and only a 0.9% real differential versus the yen.

Nonetheless, private investors are not only holding substantial quantities of US debt, they are continuing to purchase that debt at a substantial rate. (Setser, 2006, argues that a substantial part of apparent private purchases of US debt are actually central bank purchases routed through intermediaries, but even he acknowledges substantial private buying.)

Because we are assuming that bonds in different currencies are imperfect substitutes, expected real returns do not have to be equalized – or to put it differently, the real interest differential is not necessarily an implicit forecast of changes in the real exchange rate. If, however, a realistic path for the exchange rate involves dollar depreciation at 2–4%, this implies large gaps in real rates of return. In fact, investors in Japan and the euro zone are buying US bonds that offer a low or even negative real rate of return in terms of their own consumption baskets. Do they know this?

It seems plausible to argue that they don't: that markets are not taking the prospective long-run decline of the dollar into account. The anecdotal evidence suggests that investors are purchasing US debt not merely for the purpose of diversification, but because they perceive the expected yield on dollar-denominated debt as higher than that on euro- or yen-denominated debt. Thus in the 21 November 2005 issue of *Business Week* an article on the rising dollar declared, 'Behind the dollar's allure: Investors love the higher inflation-adjusted yields on U.S. securities. "Real" rates on 10-year government bonds are around 2% in the U.S., vs. 1.5% in Europe and 1% in Japan.' Notice that the *Business Week* quotation describes the higher real rate on dollar bonds as a reason for the dollar's 'allure'. That suggests that investors' decisions are based on the expectation that the real exchange rate will remain essentially unchanged over time.

If markets are not taking future dollar decline into account, the world economy is not on the rational-expectations saddle path. In terms of Figure 1, the world economy is at a position like point 1, on the curve that corresponds to zero expected real depreciation, rather than on the saddle path.

And now we can see what a Wile E. Coyote moment would look like: after a period of real dollar decline, or some kind of economic or political shock, investors would take a closer look at the prospects for dollar-denominated assets – and the world economy would jump from DD to the saddle path SS, from a point such as 1 to a point such as 2. (Notice that the jump is to the southwest, not the south; this reflects the valuation effects of a dollar depreciation, which will reduce net external debt.)

On the face of it, then, there is a pretty good though not ironclad case for believing that markets are failing to take account of the needed future real depreciation of the dollar; that at some point investors will realize that they are being insufficiently rewarded for holding dollar-denominated assets; and that the dollar will drop steeply as a result. But the intensive discussion of the US current account deficit over the past few years has turned up several influential arguments often interpreted as implying that the current value of the dollar is more sustainable than I have suggested.

4. NOVEL ARGUMENTS REGARDING CAPITAL FLOWS AND THE DOLLAR

Any sustained deviation of an economic variable from historical norms raises the question of whether we are seeing a temporary aberration – perhaps a bubble – or a structural change. At least four influential arguments suggest structural reasons why the US current account deficit and hence the dollar may be more sustainable than previous experience would seem to indicate. On the other hand, there is one important argument, which has received surprisingly little attention, suggesting that the dollar is even less sustainable than the previous analysis indicated. Let's look at these arguments in turn.

4.1. Global savings glut

In a widely quoted speech, Ben Bernanke (2005) argued that there is a global excess of savings over investment outside the United States, in effect attributing the US current account deficit to high savings abroad rather than low savings at home. Follow-up analyses have tried to assess world savings and investment rates: are savings really exceptionally high, or is investment demand unusually depressed? Either way, a savings glut could explain why the United States is running such a large current account deficit, and could provide support for the view that a large deficit for an extended period makes sense in economic terms.

But even if there is a global savings glut, the net indebtedness of the United States as a percentage of GDP must eventually stabilize, which means that the dollar must eventually fall in real terms. If investors take this into account, a capital inflow produced by a global savings glut should have the same signature as a capital inflow produced by a US savings shortfall: a real interest differential between the United States and other countries. That is, the sign that the United States offers higher investment opportunities than other economies ought to be high US investment relative to savings *in spite of* a real interest differential that compensates investors for necessary eventual US real depreciation.

So Bernanke's hypothesis does not, at least in any obvious way, offer comfort against concerns about a dollar crisis. There may well be a global savings glut, and that glut may explain why real interest rates are low everywhere. But real rates are nearly as low in the United States, with its huge current account deficit, as in surplus economies. This suggests that markets are not taking into account the long-run need for dollar decline, which implies that at some point the dollar will plunge.

4.2. Return differentials

In recent years economists, starting with Gourinchas and Rey (2005), have drawn attention to an important point, which we have already mentioned, about the US position as a debtor nation: US investors abroad earn substantially higher rates of return than those earned by foreign investors in the United States. This explains why the US balance on investment income is still slightly positive, even though the US net international investment position is strongly negative.

The explanation of this gap lies largely in the low rates of return foreign investors earn on direct investment in the United States. These low returns seem odd; they may reflect either an initial period of 'breaking in' to the US market, or they may be a statistical illusion created by tax shifting. If either of these explanations is correct, the US current account deficit may, in a fundamental sense, understate the accumulation of future debts. But suppose that for some reason the return differential is permanent, that it reflects some form of what Gourinchas and Rey call 'exorbitant privilege', using DeGaulle's term for the alleged ability of the United States to force the world to accept dollars and low-return dollar-denominated securities because of the dollar's key currency status.

Exorbitant privilege is already reflected, in two ways, in the calculations reported in Section 3 of this paper. First, the yield differential, coupled with low real interest rates everywhere, leads to a low, perhaps negative value of $R\text{-}g$. This low value means that the impact of debt build-up on the adjusted current account is basically negligible, a point that does undermine more apocalyptic views of the consequences of today's deficits.

The second effect of exorbitant privilege is its effect on the initial value of $\dot{D}$, the rate at which the debt/GDP ratio is changing. Even though the United States is a net debtor, its balance on investment income is still approximately zero, and it is probably significantly positive if you adjust for inflation. So the rate of debt accumulation is actually lower than the deficit on goods and services.

Does exorbitant privilege have any further impacts on prospects for a dollar plunge beyond those already taken account of in these calculations? We will get to that later.

4.3. Bretton Woods II

In a now famous phrase, Dooley, Folkerts-Landau and Garber (2003) declared that the international monetary system has entered 'Bretton Woods II', a new era in which major central banks, mainly in Asia, can be counted on to buy dollars in order to maintain more or less fixed exchange rates. A lot of the debate over this work has focused on their analysis of central bank motives and their implications: can we really count on the Reserve Bank of China, in particular, to seek ever-larger dollar hoards over the long term? But before we get to that, let's ask what it takes before reserve holdings can matter in the first place.

The answer, of course, is that assets denominated in different currencies must be significantly imperfect substitutes. China is engaged in very large-scale sterilized intervention that supports the dollar; sterilized intervention only affects exchange rates to the extent that bonds in different currencies are imperfect substitutes. Imperfect substitution means both that Chinese reserve acquisition can have an impact on the value of the dollar, and that interest rate differentials cannot be interpreted as implicit forecasts of future exchange rates. So the data in Table 2 could, in principle, be consistent with the view that everyone expects the dollar to decline by 2% or 3% per year in real terms. And Dooley, Folkerts-Landau and Garber in effect argue that capital is still flowing in the United States, in spite of the low rate of return, because central banks believe that they need dollar assets to provide liquidity, act as escrow for direct investment, and so on.

But if central bank intervention was really supporting the dollar in spite of a fairly high rate of expected real depreciation, one would expect to see private capital outflows at least partly offsetting official capital inflows. That is, official inflows should not merely be financing the current deficit, they should be overfinancing it (as they do, in reverse, for China's current account surplus).

In fact, however, official data seem to indicate that while central bank reserve accumulation plays a substantial role in financing the US current account deficit, private bond purchases also play a large role. Even estimates like those of Setser, which suggest that true official inflows to the United States are larger than reported, show significant private inflow, not the outflow we would expect if official inflows were maintaining the dollar's value in spite of realistic private expectations about the dollar's future evolution. As a result, Bretton Woods II seems a doubtful way to resolve the puzzling fact that investors seem to regard a modest real return differential, well short of reasonable estimates of the rate at which the dollar must fall, as sufficient to attract private funds into the United States.

4.4. Dark matter

In an analysis that made a substantial media splash, Hausmann and Sturzenegger (2005) argued that the positive US balance on investment income, despite a large net debtor position, reflects measurement error. In particular, they argued that US assets overseas are drastically understated by official statistics (see their contribution in this issue, Hausmann and Sturzenegger, 2007), probably because US-based multinationals are exporting hidden assets, such as reputation, stability know-how and marketing expertise. They argued that this 'dark matter' not only implies that the United States is not a net debtor, but that the true current account balance is much less in deficit than the measured number.

There have been many discussions of this claim. Let me summarize what I believe to be the three key points.

First, much of the 'dark matter' puzzle reflects the failure of flows to be fully reflected in stocks – that is, large cumulative current account deficits have not made the United States as much of a debtor nation as one might expect. There is, however, a prosaic explanation for this divergence: unanticipated capital gains and losses. The difference between the cumulative current account balance and the actual net investment position is largely explained by US capital gains on its assets abroad, primarily because of the long-term decline in the dollar, but also to some extent because the past quarter-century, which has been a time of persistent US deficit, has also been a secular bull market that has worked to the advantage of the United States, a country that in effect borrows and invests proceeds in foreign equities and real assets.

Second, the puzzle of the roughly zero investment income balance given the negative net US investment position seems to reflect low returns on foreign investment in the United States rather than high returns abroad. As Brad Setser puts it (using bad physics but good economics), to explain the numbers using the Hausmann–Sturzenegger approach we need 'dark antimatter', not dark matter; rather than having US firms export good reputations to overseas markets, we need foreign firms bringing bad reputations to US markets, which does not seem to make sense.

Third, the *level* of dark matter, if it exists, is not very important to sustainability calculations. What we need to refute the argument made in Section 3 of this paper is a rapid increase in dark matter and/or dark antimatter, so as to reduce the value of the adjusted current account deficit. And that is a much harder case to make.

4.5. Secular dollar decline

One last point actually strengthens the case for a dollar plunge: the argument that any long-term dollar decline must chase a moving target.

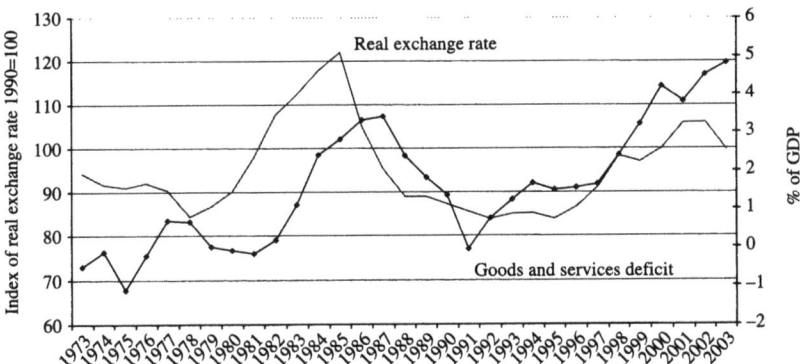

Figure 2. Real exchange rates, external balance, and the secular dollar trend
Source: OECD Economic Outlook database.

Figure 2 shows the US real effective exchange rate and the deficit on goods and services as a percentage of GDP since 1975. The data strongly confirm the impact of the real exchange rate on the trade balance, especially during the dollar cycle of the 1980s, while indicating a significant lag in that relationship, which as we will see may play an important role in the adjustment to a dollar plunge. But they also suggest a significant secular downward trend in the real dollar: over time, the real dollar associated with any given level of trade deficit seems to have declined.

Old hands often refer to such secular trends with the term 'Houthakker–Magee', after the early work showing large differences in the income elasticities of demand for US exports and imports. At a deeper structural level, the secular decline in the dollar may reflect technological catch-up by emerging economies; the data hint at an accelerated trend as China's exports have soared. Whatever the source, a downward trend in the equilibrium real exchange rate reinforces the case that markets are not properly taking future declines in the dollar into account.

5. MACROECONOMICS OF A PLUNGE

Suppose that there is a dollar plunge. What will this do to spending, income, and output?

There is broad consensus about what a fall in capital inflows would mean in the medium run. The dollar would depreciate in real terms, leading to a rise in net exports. At the same time, domestic demand would be compressed, possibly via a rise in interest rates. Overall aggregate demand should be roughly unchanged, with higher net exports and reduced domestic spending cancelling each other out.

The question is whether the transition to this new equilibrium would be smooth or rocky – whether it would involve a recession or at least a slowdown along the way. Mainly this comes down to the question of whether the squeeze on domestic demand will get ahead of the rise in net exports. Let me deal briefly with two possible reasons for a temporary slump in aggregate demand, before turning to what I believe is the central issue for the United States.

In many sudden stop crises in the developing world, balance sheet effects of depreciation seem to have played a crucial role. Indonesia 1997 and Argentina 2002 are the classic examples. In each case external debts were denominated in foreign currency, so that when the domestic currency fell the net worth of many economic agents was compressed, in a sort of open-economy version of Fisherian debt deflation. Advanced countries are less susceptible to this effect because they tend to be able to borrow in their own currency. The United States, of course, is especially secure. In fact, the nature of its international investment position means that depreciation tends to reduce net indebtedness and raise net worth.

The United States is less secure against a surge in consumer prices as a result of a sharp dollar decline, although even there pricing to market by foreign firms may limit the effect. If the Federal Reserve feels that it must respond to an increase in headline inflation by raising short-term interest rates – perhaps because it believes that wages and other factor costs are indexed, at least implicitly, to inflation – this could indirectly be contractionary. The Fed's recent response to a spike in energy prices suggests that there may be something to this. In fact, precisely this sort of response underlies IMF concerns about a disorderly unwinding of global imbalances. But it is not the main channel most of those fearing a dollar plunge have in mind.

The main concern, instead, is that the compression of domestic demand caused by a reduced foreign willingness to buy dollar assets will happen quickly, while the increase in net exports will happen slowly. But this can seem a bit puzzling. If we expect net exports to rise in the future, that is the equivalent of saying that foreign savings available to finance domestic investment will dry up at some future date. But what is the channel through which the expectation of a future fall in savings reduces demand today?

Discussions such as DeLong (2005) emphasize the effect of future savings on long-term interest rates. I find it clearer, however, and perhaps more accurate, to focus on Tobin's q: the price of capital in place relative to replacement cost.

Consider the following stripped-down representation of the savings-investment balance:

$$S(q) - I(q) = B(x) \qquad (6)$$

I include an effect of q on saving because of wealth effects. In fact, in the United States today surely the most important component of q is housing. Rising house prices have led both to high residential investment spending and, via refinancing, high consumption and low spending. Equation (6) defines an upward-sloping locus, as shown by GG in Figure 3.

Meanwhile, investors are comparing returns at home and abroad. Let's write the arbitrage equation as follows:

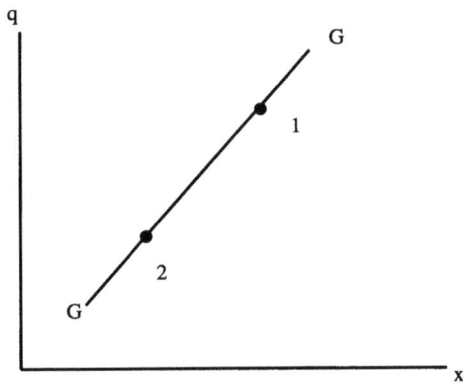

Figure 3. Internal balance and the adjustment problem

$$\frac{n}{q} = r^* + \rho \tag{7}$$

where n is the rental per unit of capital and r^* is the rate of return on foreign bonds. Here, ρ is a catch-all term that includes risk premia and expectations both about future exchange rates and future values of q. The case for a dollar plunge can be represented in this framework as a claim that ρ is low right now compared with its medium-run value, and can be expected to jump. This would have the effect of moving the economy along the curve GG from a point like 1 to a point like 2, causing a real depreciation together with a fall in q.

Why might we argue that ρ is low and must rise? First, as argued above, we can argue that investors have unrealistic expectations about future exchange rates, because they have failed to take proper account of the prospective decline in the real value of the dollar. Second, we can argue that investors have unrealistic expectations about future values of q. In practice, this amounts to saying that there is a bubble in housing prices, which in real terms are vastly above historical experience. This does not prove the existence of a housing bubble, a question that is much debated, but it explains why those so inclined may see high housing prices as a very big issue – quite possibly bigger than the current account deficit.

The possible excesses in housing are the reason it may be a mistake to focus on long-term interest rates in analysing the possible effects of a dollar plunge. Suppose that we have double bubble trouble, and the crisis takes the form of a more or less simultaneous downward revision of expectations about the future value of the dollar and expectations about the future price of houses. In that case, long-term interest rates could move either way.

Now, finally, we can ask whether the medium-term adjustment shown in Figure 3 would involve a recession or at least a slowdown in the short run. The answer depends on the relative speed of adjustment to changes in x and in q. To put it crudely, if the contractionary effect of a burst housing bubble arrives more quickly than the expansionary effect of a dollar depreciation, a dollar plunge will be associated with an overall slump.

In fact, at the time of writing a serious slump has already developed in the US housing market, while the dollar, despite some weakening, remains in the same range as recent experience. Because the bursting of the housing bubble is already underway, issues of dollar sustainability cannot play the leading role in driving an economic slowdown. However, a dollar plunge, by heading off what might otherwise be a substantial fall in long-term interest rates, may extend and deepen the housing-induced slump.

A weaker dollar would eventually be expansionary through its effect on net exports. But standard estimates indicate a lag of more than two years before depreciation has its full effect on trade flows. Moreover, the size of the trade deficit is unprecedented; this suggests that a major increase in net exports may take longer than usual, because resources need to be shifted on a large scale back into tradable sectors.

Can the Fed offset the contractionary effects of a dollar plunge-cum housing slump by cutting interest rates? There are two possible limitations to the Fed's ability to act. One is that the Fed, concerned about inflation, might be reluctant to cut rates in the face of a plunging dollar. The second is the zero bound on the Fed funds rate. Bear in mind that the principal channel through which Fed policy affects domestic demand is via housing. If a burst housing bubble is part of the economic problem, the Fed's leverage over the economy will be greatly reduced, and even a zero Fed funds rate might have only a modest stimulative effect. So there is a plausible, but far from conclusive, case that the initial impact of a dollar plunge will be contractionary, and that the Fed will find itself unable to offset this contraction.

Are we missing something here? Quite possibly. The history of crisis modelling in international macroeconomics reveals that each successive wave of crises exposes possibilities for crisis that were overlooked in earlier analysis. There may be risks of a hard landing – perhaps in the form of financial disruption – that are overlooked by our models. On the other hand, there are cautionary tales on the other side: currency plunges, from the dollar in 1985 to Brazil's *real* in 1999, that were widely expected to bring recession in their wake but didn't.

6. SUMMARY AND CONCLUSIONS

Concerns about a dollar crisis can be divided into two questions: Will there be a plunge in the dollar? Will this plunge have nasty macroeconomic consequences?

The answer to the first question depends on whether there is investor myopia, a failure to take into account the requirement that the dollar eventually fall enough to stabilize US external debt at a feasible level. Although it is always dangerous to second-guess markets, the data do seem to suggest such myopia: it is hard to reconcile the willingness of investors to hold dollar assets with a very small premium in real interest rates with the apparent necessity for fairly rapid dollar decline to contain growing foreign debt. The various rationales and rationalizations for the US current account deficit that have been advanced in recent years do not seem to help us avoid the conclusion that investors are not taking the need for future dollar decline into account.

So it seems likely that there will be a Wile E. Coyote moment when investors realize that the dollar's value doesn't make sense, and that value plunges.

The case for believing that a dollar plunge will do great harm is much less secure. In the medium run, the economy can trade off lower domestic demand, mainly the result of a fall in real housing prices, for higher net exports, the result of dollar depreciation. Any economic contraction in the short run will be the result of differences in adjustment speeds, with the fall in domestic demand outpacing the rise in net exports.

The United States in 2007 isn't Argentina in 2001: although there is a very good case that the dollar will decline sharply, nothing in the data points to an Argentine-style economic implosion when that happens. Still, this probably won't be fun.

Discussion

Kevin O'Rourke
Trinity College, Dublin

The basic argument of this paper is simple and intuitive. It is easy to derive crisis-like behaviour in cases where exchange rates are fixed, as Krugman himself and others have shown us over the past quarter of a century. One of the points of floating exchange rates, therefore, is that they help you avoid such crises. So how on earth could there be an exchange rate crisis in the context of a floating exchange rate regime? Where is the elastic band that can be stretched up to a certain point, but eventually snaps? Krugman's answer is that for such a story to hold, there has to be investor myopia, and this seems to me to be entirely sensible.

However, I wonder whether Krugman has made his life unnecessarily difficult, if what he wants to do is convince us that there may be a dollar crisis, by his choice of where to draw the line (in the balance of payments, that is). He has drawn it under the current account, and thus his argument depends on the current account being unsustainable (which is what implies that the dollar will have to fall, which is why the absence of significant real interest rate differentials in favour of the United States suggests investor irrationality). History, however, tells us that very large current account deficits are in fact sustainable for very long periods of time, as one glance at Figure 4 will indicate. The late 19th century, in particular, saw very large and sustained current account imbalances, with countries such as the United Kingdom exporting vast amounts of capital, and countries such as Argentina, Australia and Canada importing equally vast quantities. As is the case today, these flows were interpreted in a number of different ways at the time. Some observers worried that UK investors were irrationally lending money overseas, despite inadequate foreign

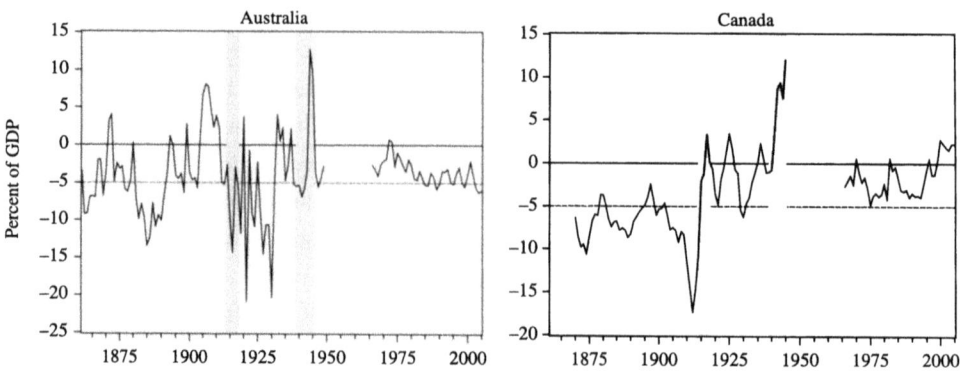

Figure 4. Current account as a percentage of GDP, Australia and Canada, 1861–2005

Note: The shaded areas refer to the two world wars.
Source: Jones and Obstfeld (2001), *World Development Indicators*.

returns, an argument that was eventually debunked by Michael Edelstein (1982). Others explained the flows in terms of savings and investment, at home and abroad. Like Ben Bernanke, J.A. Hobson believed that a UK savings glut was responsible for the outflows, while a lack of good domestic investment opportunities was pointed to then by Vladimir Lenin as the root cause, as it is today by commentators such as Backus *et al.* (2006). Today's new economy boosters are the 21st century counterparts to frontier enthusiasts such as Horace Greeley, arguing that it is outstanding investment opportunities in the United States that are driving the deficit, just as 19th century frontiers drove lending to the New World. Meanwhile, cliometricians such as Taylor and Williamson (1994) have found evidence that New World savings were insufficient 100 years ago, just as Larry Summers (2004) argues they are today.

Once you start posing things in savings–investment terms, large-scale flows start to seem rational and stable (though Hobson and Lenin would disagree!), and in fact the late 19th century experience *was* relatively stable. While the events of August 1914 mean that we will never know how sustainable these flows really were, many observers will surely regard Figure 1 as being reassuring from a US point of view. Moreover, when there *were* current account reversals in the late 19th century, these tended to be sustained, with adjustment being relatively smooth (Meissner and Taylor, 2006), facilitated by real exchange rate changes (Catão and Solomou, 2005), with real depreciations of the order of just 2–8%, as well as by migration flows. Only 3 out of 33 reversals were associated with currency crises (or 7 out of 33 if a 5-year currency crisis window is used) (Meissner and Taylor, 2006).

So, does history suggest that there is no problem? It may depend on where you draw the line. Draw it further down, and we fast-forward from the 1870s to the 1960s, with its many arguments about what constituted a sustainable balance of payments, a context-specific issue if ever there was one (Despres *et al.*, 1966; Cooper,

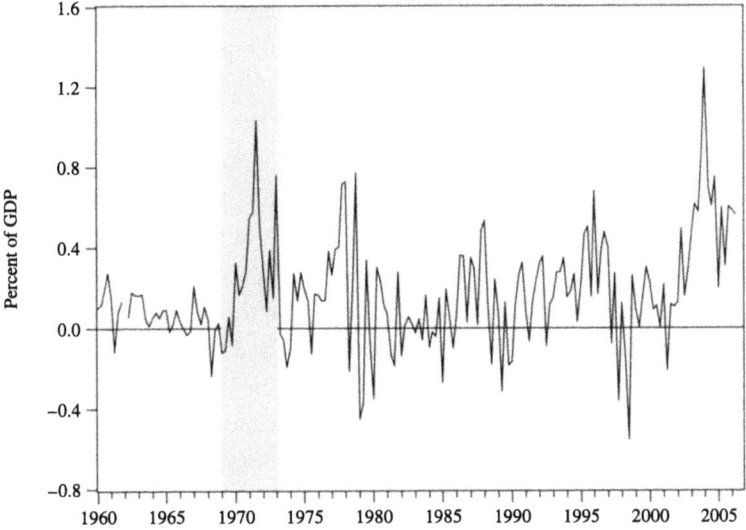

Figure 5. Increase in foreign official assets in the United States as a percentage of US GDP

Note: The shaded area refers to the quarters 1969:1 through 1973:1 inclusive.
Source: BEA.

1966; Kindleberger, 1969; and so on). If you draw the line just above official reserve transactions, for example, the case for pessimism may be easier to sustain, even in the absence of a gold-backed dollar and the Triffin paradox (Roubini and Setser, 2005; Eichengreen, 2004). Central banks may not always be consenting adults, and collective action problems may make it difficult for the rest of the world's central banks to prop up an overvalued dollar (with non-Chinese central banks playing the 'spoiling' role of the 1960s *Banque de France*). If one lesson of history is that large current account imbalances are sustainable over the long run, a second is that there may be a limit to the willingness of the rest of the world to accumulate dollar reserve assets. And as Figure 5 shows, foreign accumulation of official dollar assets is now at a historically high level when expressed as a percentage of US GDP, higher even than during 1969–73, when the Bretton Woods regime was in its death throes.

The dollar may well plunge for the reasons Krugman outlines. But even if investors are more rational than he thinks they are, the dollar may *still* plunge. This 'probably won't be fun' for the United States, as he says, and it risks being a great deal worse than that for Europe.

Giancarlo Corsetti
European University Institute

This intriguing piece by Paul Krugman (what else can you expect from Paul Krugman but an intriguing piece?) addresses a crucial question. Taking for granted that the correction of US imbalances requires (further) dollar depreciation in real terms, the adjustment is likely to take the form of a dollar plunge: under what conditions will the dollar plunge create a macroeconomic crisis?

The argument is developed in three steps. First, the text clarifies the meaning and the analytics of a dollar plunge, defined as a fall of the dollar at a much faster rate than the markets have so far anticipated. The plunge is essentially attributed to investors' myopia: waking up from a state of denial, at some point people realize that the dollar must fall, and this makes it happen. To study the dynamics of a dollar plunge, Krugman uses a reduced-form model which directly draws on the portfolio model developed by Kouri (1976). Admittedly, this is a vintage model (a good vintage though). But portfolio theory is an area in which the ongoing micro-founded reconsideration of international economics has only recently started to deliver. So at the time of the writing there is no well-established alterative.

Second, the text inspects the main interpretations of the causes underlying the current imbalance. Here the main issue is where the recent literature provides any convincing argument that the US current account deficit is 'more sustainable than previous experience seems to indicate', and that adjustment will occur without substantial dollar depreciation. The answer is a qualified 'no'.

Finally, the text sketches a model of possible macroeconomic consequences associated with a dollar plunge, distinguishing between mild and more worrisome scenarios.

In what follows, I will develop my discussion starting from an essential premise to the main argument: the need for a large dollar depreciation in real terms. I will then discuss the logic underlying popular estimates of the magnitude of the adjustment. I will make some comments on the interpretation of the results from the portfolio model in the text. I will conclude with some observations pointing to issues left open in the piece.

On the need for dollar depreciation

The task of writing this comment gave me a golden opportunity to read once again Paul Krugman's previous piece on a similar topic, 'Has the adjustment process worked?', written for the Institute for International Economics in 1991, after a conference with the same title held in November 1990. The question on the table was: 'Has [the adjustment problem] worked more or less as we thought it would? . . . And in ways that we find acceptable?' (Krugman, 1991, p. 3). The answer is positive and articulated in three main conclusions: (a) exchange rate changes work; (b) exchange rate changes are necessary; and (c) the relation between trade and exchange rate is stable. To a large extent, these three points summarize well Paul Krugman's (and the mainstream) view today.

In the 1991 piece, the mainstream view was shaped by the 'Mass. Ave. Model,' i.e. a macro model derived from the Mundell–Fleming framework, as opposed to a portfolio model in the current text. Notably, the 1991 text did not have any chapter on financial issues: these were only discussed in the appendix.

The discussion of challenges to the mainstream view focused on three competing schools of thought. The first is the 'schmooist view', according to which relative prices do not matter in the adjustment (this is true if all national goods are highly substitutable, i.e. there is a single 'schmoo' traded across borders). This view questions the necessity of exchange rate adjustment.

Some traces of this view can be found in current analyses placing a large weight on expectations of large income and productivity gains in the United States in the future, as the main determinants of the US current account deficits. For this channel to be strong, the relative-price movements associated with higher future output cannot be expected to be too large. If future prices are expected to fall a lot with an increase in quantities, the effects on current consumption and investment of anticipation of future growth in output are necessarily contained. In other words, the higher the substitutability of domestic and foreign goods, the stronger the short-run macroeconomic implications of expectations of high productivity in the future. The mechanism underlying this point, stressing the interaction of shock persistence and trade elasticities, is analysed in detail in related work of mine joint with Luca Dedola and Sylvain Leduc, where we also discuss its implications on the dynamics of the real exchange rate and the terms of trade (see Corsetti et al., 2007a).

The second view at odds with the mainstream is the structuralist view – casting doubts on the effectiveness of adjustment through exchange rate movements, per effect of changes in the economic environment. Interestingly, Paul Krugman concedes that 'we are all a little bit structuralists', observing that 'at least in the short run, and possibly for a little longer, the real exchange rate changes needed to achieve substantial trade adjustment are simply too large to be tolerable' (p. 16). As I argue below, in my opinion this observation applies to the possibility of macroeconomic costs of turmoil in the financial and currency markets – a possibility the above text abstracts from.

The last view listed in the 1991 piece is the secularist view, questioning the stability of the transmission mechanism, because of trend depreciation of the dollar. Interestingly, in 1991 secular dollar depreciation was attributed to the 'declining relative US technology and quality, . . . as a result of poor US education, deteriorating infrastructure or whatever'. Today, Paul Krugman espouses the same secular view of the dollar, but by using quite different arguments!

As in the 1991 piece, the current text also discusses theories (in part different from the one listed above) which could potentially challenge the mainstream view. Section 4 of the text is devoted to an analysis of recent popular interpretations of global imbalances, including: 'Global savings glut', 'Return differentials' 'Bretton Woods II,' and 'Dark matter', in addition to the new version of the 'Secular dollar decline' (my own analysis of these interpretations is included in Chapter 3 of the EEAG's Annual Report on the European Economy 2006). The analysis of these interpretations is important, because one's view of the causes underlying the US current account deficit is likely to shape one's view of the modalities of adjustment of global imbalances. However, on the specific question of exchange rates and relative prices, Krugman argues that none of the competing views of the origin of global imbalances casts doubt on real dollar depreciation as an essential element in the coming adjustment. So, in 2007, as in 1991, there is no disagreement on this point. Or is there?

The required magnitude of dollar depreciation

The essential premise to Krugman's analysis is that dollar depreciation is necessary to close the US current account deficit. The reason is rooted in the economics of the 'transfer problem' – as defined in the well-known debate between Keynes and Ohlin. Krugman refers to a recent reconsideration of this problem provided in a popular set of pieces written by Obstfeld and Rogoff (2004, 2005, henceforth OR) on the US current account imbalance.

It is instructive to reconsider in some detail the logical structure of the OR reasoning step by step. Reducing the US trade deficit requires a redistribution of world spending – spending must fall in the United States, must increase abroad. This redistribution of demand is essentially a 'transfer'. Now, consider a world economy with four goods: US traded (T) goods and non-traded (NT) goods; foreign traded and non-traded goods. The value of total domestic demand (commonly referred to as 'absorption') plus the transfer must be equal to the total value of output. Using a simple accounting scheme, and normalizing the price of foreign goods to 1 (i.e. $P_F = 1$), we can write:

$$\underbrace{P_N C_N + P_H C_H + C_F}_{absorption} + Transfer$$
$$P_N C_N + P_T C_T + Tranfer$$
$$= P_N Y_N + P_H Y_H$$

where P_T denotes the price of tradables, including both domestic and imported.

Now, assume that *output is fixed* (an upper bar will denote variables which are constant by assumption). Then current account adjustment (i.e. an increase in transfer from the United States to the rest of the world) requires a fall in the relative price of US tradable goods ($P_H/P_F = P_H$), to raise foreign demand for US exports, and discourage US demand for imports. However, note that, other things equal, cheaper US tradables would also increase the US demand for them. Hence adjustment also requires a fall in the relative price of US non-tradables (P_N/P_T), to redirect US demand away from tradables, towards US non-tradables (whose quantity is fixed by assumption).

These relative price movements – corresponding to real effective depreciation of the dollar – reduce absorption. Seen from the 'income' side, they lower the value of US output (both traded and non-traded) relative to foreign output:

$$P_N \downarrow \bar{C}_N + P_H \downarrow C_H \downarrow + C_F \downarrow + \text{Transfer} \uparrow$$
$$= P_N \downarrow \underbrace{\bar{C}_N + P_T \downarrow C_T \downarrow}_{\text{absorption}} + \text{Tranfer} \uparrow$$
$$= P_N \downarrow \bar{Y}_N + P_H \downarrow \bar{Y}_H$$

A striking result by OR concerns the relative magnitude of these price adjustment. Namely, the equilibrium adjustment in the relative price of tradables ($P_H/P_F = P_H$) – i.e. adjustment in the terms of trade – accounts only for a relatively small portion of the overall required depreciation: it can explain a real exchange rate depreciation between *5 and 15%*. It is the relative price of non-tradable which plays the leading role: adjustment in P_H/P_T can explain a real exchange rate depreciation between *20 and 30%*. This is 3 to 5 times larger than explained by terms-of-trade movements!

To summarize, adjustment requires a large fall of US non-traded goods prices, but a relatively contained adjustment of US export prices. It is worth stressing that the limited movements in international relative prices of US exports is an equilibrium outcome, totally independent of pricing to market.

As mentioned above, the OR estimates are derived from fixing output quantities, checking robustness for different values of elasticities of substitutions across goods. Most adjustment margins – including employment, sectoral labour allocation, investment etc. – are shut down. Many see this as a very strong assumption.

Notably, some debate has focused on whether rebalancing of the current account would require a prolonged recession (see e.g. Edwards 2005, and the discussion in Faruquee *et al.*, 2007). Using the scheme above, we can easily see that if Y_N falls *persistently*, the quantity of non-tradables which need to be consumed by US residents in equilibrium is lower, and US demand falls with US relative income:

$$P_N \downarrow C_N \downarrow + P_H \downarrow C_H \downarrow + C_F \downarrow + \text{Transfer}$$
$$P_N \downarrow \underbrace{C_N \downarrow + P_T \downarrow C_T \downarrow}_{\text{absorption}} + \text{Tranfer}$$
$$= P_N \downarrow Y_N \downarrow + P_H \downarrow \bar{Y}_H$$

Then, it is clear that the dollar depreciation required to close the current account imbalance is lower than in the case of fixed output.

The same logic underlies the idea, stressed by OR, that 'growth in nontradables' in the United States is 'bad for the dollar'. Given prices, an increase in NT output translates into an increase in US income: the dollar needs to fall more to correct the trade imbalance. By the same token, an increase in European exports raises competition in the world markets: in order for US producers to export, they need to reduce their prices more (see Corsetti *et al.*, 2007b for an empirical assessment).

However, the logic of the transfer problem goes through also in models with tradable goods only – a point which is well understood since the controversy between Keynes and Ohlin. The important difference with the above scheme is that, with only one relative price, adjustment is entirely carried over through movements in the terms-of-trade adjustment (the relative price of non-tradables plays no role).

Indeed, looking at the evidence on the episode of dollar depreciation and current account adjustment in the mid-1980s, movements in domestic relative prices are strikingly contained: the relative price of non-tradables did not fall significantly, and definitely much less than the terms of trade.

Specifically, I calculate the average quarterly rate of real depreciation based on the multilateral real exchange rate for the United States from the beginning of 1985 to the end of 1987; then I calculate the average quarterly rate of change of the US PPI relative to the US CPI for services. This is arguably a good proxy for the relative price of non-tradables.

Now, over these years, average real depreciation (2.4% on a yearly basis) is three times as large as the change in the domestic relative price of non-tradables (0.8%). The relative magnitude of these relative price adjustment is the opposite of what is suggested by the OR estimates mentioned above.

It is quite likely that, in practice, the adjustment faced by the US involves much less domestic price movements than implied by the OR baseline scenario. This is not to say that dollar depreciation in real terms is not necessary. But the weight placed on adjustment of non-traded prices may not be as large as suggested by the OR calculations.

Moving from this observation, Philippe Martin, Paolo Pesenti and I have developed a model of transfers which differs from the above in two respects: first, there is almost no movement in the price of non-tradables; second, labour supply is elastic and mobile across sectors (Corsetti *et al.*, 2007c). Running the same exercise as OR, we find that the rate of real dollar depreciation required to close a current account deficit as high as 5% of GDP is of the order of 20%. From a macroeconomic vantage point, this is achieved through a combination of lower consumption (−6%), and higher employment (+3%).

We also have a version of the model with entry and exit of firms and product varieties – drawing on another contribution by Paul Krugman (Krugman, 1989). The exchange rate predictions change quite a bit in this case, and the dollar depreciation can actually become much smaller than 20% – even close to zero.

The exercise we perform is quite informative in at least two respects. First, our results show that the magnitude of price adjustment is not necessarily an indicator of macroeconomic pain. In our calculations, we find that the welfare consequences of adjustment are equally harsh, whether there is a large adjustment in prices, or the adjustment is mainly through the flow of new firms and products in the market.

Second, it is important to recognize that there is quite a bit of uncertainty as regards the 'required real exchange rate adjustment'. This is not to deny that 'adjustment will be!' As Krugman stresses: 'Keynes may have been wrong in theory, he was right in practice' (1991, p. 19). But ultimately, the issue is an empirical one. As in the 1980s, we are now living through another important field experiment in the area of exchange rate economics. We may well run into some interesting surprises regarding the relative role of different margins of adjustment.

Portfolio models and the analytics of dollar plunges

The core of Paul's model of dollar plunge is the analytics of the portfolio and macroeconomic consequences of what one can dub a 'RE-ality check' on investors' beliefs about the dollar – where RE stands for Rational Expectations. The model in the background is similar to the one developed by Blanchard et al. (2005), except that US debt is measured in ratio to GDP.

The main elements are well explained in the main text of the article. In what follows, I just summarize the essential passages, and provide a slightly different reading of the main results.

In the model economy, US and foreign bonds are imperfect substitutes; return differential R and R^* depends on both a risk premium (in turn depending on the outstanding supply plus other things) and expected devaluation δ.

The dollar exchange rate X depends on US foreign debt D (because of portfolio balance effects and other considerations), and the expected rate of depreciation:

$X = x(D, \delta^e)$

The dynamics of US foreign net debt (to GDP) D depends on X, D, and the rate of actual and expected depreciation, dx/dt and δ^e:

$dD/dt = B(X, D, \delta^e, dx/dt)$

The accumulation of net foreign liabilities (in percentage of GDP): (a) *slows down* with a weaker dollar (in real terms), as well as with *ex post* valuation effects from current depreciation (note that uncovered interest parity is assumed to hold in this part of the model); (b) *rises* with D as a function of R-g.

Now, putting some flesh on the bare bones of this model, Krugman posits that the initial current account deficit (growth-, valuation-adjusted) is 5% of GDP; the logarithmic real depreciation of the dollar required to achieve trade balance is 35%.

Based on these pieces of information, the model provides a simple framework to assess the rate of debt accumulation and dollar depreciation along the saddle path in the presence of fully rational agents. Specifically, the speed of adjustment depends on the elasticity of foreign (US) demand for US (foreign) assets, i.e. the degree of substitutability between US and foreign bonds (see Blanchard et al., 2005). The logic is straightforward:

High elasticity → high substitutability → low speed of adjustment along the saddle path
Low elasticity → Low substitutability → high speed of adjustment.

In equilibrium, the rate of exchange rate convergence along the saddle path k and the long-run foreign debt level are linked to each other by the formula:

$D_{LR} = D_0 + CA/k$

Set $k = 0.05$ and 0.1, corresponding to relatively *high and low US-foreign bond substitutability*. It is easy to see that, with a 35% dollar depreciation required in the long run to ensure trade balance: (a) the initial US annual real depreciation is between 1.7 and 3.5%; (b) the half life of 35% depreciation is between 15 and 8 years; and (c) the long-run (sustainable) level of US foreign debt D_{LR} is roughly between 120 and 60% of GDP.

Observe that, to the extent that market integration affects bond substitutability, it also affects exchange rate dynamics in response to shock.

Now, suppose investors do not expect any depreciation: the economy is initially on point 1 of figure 1, a point which is not stable. In principle, the forces of the model should generate high debt dynamics, with a stable or even an appreciating dollar in real terms. But assuming that investors are myopic, there is no particular harm in thinking that the economy lingers around it.

Starting from point 1, the 'RE-ality check' experiment consists of a sudden injection of rational expectations into markets. From point 1, the economy cannot but jump onto point 2 in the graph.

Here is a second important point. Not only the speed of adjustment, but also the initial exchange rate jump depends on elasticity of substitution between bonds. In the high elasticity case ($k = 0.5$), the exchange rate adjustment is large on impact, but the rate of depreciation along the saddle path is small. In the low elasticity case ($k = 0.1$), the adjustment is smaller on impact, but the adjustment along the saddle path is faster.

Observe that the RE-ality check is not at all a liquidity run. Sure enough, when it happens investors will not be willing to hold US liabilities at the current exchange rate. But this will just accompany the change of market rates consistent with equilibrium relative prices.

I emphasize this point: the reader should avoid interpreting the 'dollar plunge' as a financial crisis. In the model, there is no macroeconomic cost associated with it. Actually, there is a cost in maintaining the dollar at a disequilibrium high rate. This is not to deny the possibility of liquidity runs involving liquidation costs and macro stress, if the exchange rate swings widely and suddenly: as Paul Krugman puts it in 1991, we are all a little bit 'structuralists'. But the paper analyses a benign scenario in which the dollar jumps towards equilibrium. Namely, despite (or thanks to) a large dollar fall, the world keeps financing the United States.

So, where can stress come from? The crucial point is that RE-ality check may involve a strong correction of other prices in disequilibrium, namely, housing prices. Stress in the housing markets is worrisome not only because of its direct contractionary effect on demand; but also because it may weaken an important channel through which monetary policy can effectively stabilize the economy: housing market stress may jeopardize the effect of interest rate cuts on aggregate demand. The paper rightly stresses that corrections in housing prices need not coincide with an increase in real rates.

The analysis in the text is quite clear, and I have little to add. I just observe that a correction in the price of housing plays the same role of the contraction in Y_N in the analysis of OR, as regards its effect on US income and absorption. I also observe that the reduced impact of monetary policy on long-term rate in both directions (contraction and expansion) is a concern for central banks already, independently of housing market stress.

Concluding comments

So, what is the main message of this paper? I try to summarize it as follows: the economics and policy of soft-landing does not rule out large dollar correction. It may actually need 'more correction': by how much is, however, an open issue.

An *equilibrium* correction of the dollar cannot be painful almost by definition. Macroeconomic stress may nonetheless come from elsewhere. The analysis emphasizes the consequences of a strong correction in the housing market.

Yet, the analysis somewhat shies away from possibly important international dimensions of the dollar crisis. If and when the dollar plunge will come, it is possible that the world at large will experience financial and macro stress. Sizeable changes in the currency composition of international portfolios are likely to have relevant international financial and macro ramifications.

Where can we look for inspiration? The analysis of emerging markets crises (say, Thailand in 1997) can hardly provide guidance and insights into the global risks faced by the United States. The breakdown of Bretton Woods fits the bill in one dimension, namely, the crisis resulted from the unravelling of tension generated by US policies inconsistent with the current international monetary arrangement (the gold exchange standard), as well as with inflation preferences in the other major player in the world economy (Germany). However, the size and importance of international financial markets at the time was pathetically smaller than today.

It would be quite interesting to hear more from Paul Krugman on this question.

Panel discussion

Many of the panel questions focused on the event(s) that could trigger a dollar crisis. Roubini argued that the exact nature of the event that triggers the moment matters for the kind of landing. It could be a trade war with China and a stock market crisis, as in 1987, or a foreign policy announcement like the one of Japan in 1998. The exchange rate crisis could lead to a hard landing, or in the opposite direction, a housing crisis could trigger a sharp fall of the dollar. The mechanics that follow are different in terms of flight to safety, credit crunch, and so on. Krugman replied that even *ex post* it is not as easy to determine which event(s) triggers an exchange rate crisis. In fact, hundreds of explanations were polled by Shiller in 1987! It is not fully obvious today whether the baht devaluation, the Russian default really triggered the 1997 crisis.

Milesi-Ferretti pointed out that risk management strategies matter in this type of situation. There is a complex web of financial instruments and it is not clear who would bear the brunt of the crisis.

REFERENCES

Backus, D., E. Henriksen, F. Lambert, and C. Telmer (2006). 'Current account fact and fiction', mimeo.

Bernanke, B. (2005). 'The global savings glut and the U.S. current account deficit'. Sandridge Lecture, Virginia Association of Economists, Richmond, Virginia. http://www.federalreserve.gov/boarddocs/speeches/2005/20050414/default.htm

Blanchard, O., F. Giavazzi, and F. Sa (2005). 'International investors, the U.S. current account, and the dollar', *Brookings Papers on Economic Activity*, 1, 1–49.

Catão, L.A.V., and S.N. Solomou (2005). 'Effective exchange rates and the classical gold standard adjustment', *American Economic Review*, 95, 1259–75.

Cooper, R.N. (1966). 'The balance of payments in review', *Journal of Political Economy*, 74, 379–95.

Corsetti, G., L. Dedola and S. Leduc (2007a). 'International risk sharing and the transmission of productivity shocks', *Review of Economic Studies*, forthcoming.

Corsetti, G., L. Dedola and S. Leduc (2007b). 'Productivity, external balance and exchange rates: Evidence on the transmission mechanism among G7 countries', in L. Reichlin and K. West (eds.), *NBER International Seminar on Microeconomics 2006*, forthcoming.

Corsetti, G., P. Martin and P. Pesenti (2007c). 'Varieties and the transfer problem: The extensive margin of current account adjustment', European University Institute, mimeo.

DeLong, J.B. (2005). 'Divergent views on the coming dollar crisis', *The Economists' Voice*, vol. 2, iss 5, article 1.

Despres, E., C.P. Kindlerger, and W. Salant (1966). 'The dollar and world liquidity: A minority view', *The Economist*, 5 February, 526–29.

Dooley, M., D. Folkerts-Landau, and P. Garber (2003). 'An essay on the revived Bretton Woods system', NBER Working Paper No. 9971.

Edelstein, M. (1982). *Overseas Investment in the Age of High Imperialism: The United Kingdom, 1850–1914*. Columbia University Press, New York.

Edwards, S. (2005). 'Is the U.S. current account deficit sustainable? If not, how costly is adjustment likely to be?', *Brookings Papers on Economic Activity*, 1, 211–71.

EEAG at CESifo (2006). *The EEAG Report on the European Economy 2006*, CESifo.

Eichengreen, B. (2004). 'Global imbalances and the lessons of Bretton Woods', NBER Working Paper No. 10497, May.

— (2006). 'Global imbalances: The new economy, the dark matter, the savvy investor, and the standard analysis', *Journal of Policy Modelling*, 28, 645–52.

Faruqee, H., D. Laxton, P. Pesenti and D. Muir (2007). 'Smooth landing or crash? Model-based scenarios of global current account rebalancing', in R. Clarida (ed.), *G7 Current Account Imbalances: Sustainability and Adjustment*, University of Chicago Press, Chicago, IL.

Gourinchas, P. and H. Rey (2007), 'From world banker to world venture capitalist: U.S. external adjustment: the exorbitant privilege', in R. Clarida (ed.), *G7 Current Account Imbalances: Sustainability and Adjustment*, The University of Chicago Press, 11–55.

Hausmann, R. and F. Sturzenegger (2005). 'Dark matter makes the U.S. deficit disappear', *Financial Times*, 8 December.

— (2007). 'The missing dark matter in the wealth of nations and its implications for global imbalances', *Economic Policy*, 51, 469–518.

IMF (International Monetary Fund) (2006). *World Economic Outlook*.

Jones, M.T., and M. Obstfeld (2001). 'Saving, investment, and gold: A reassessment of historical current account data', in G.A. Calvo, R. Dornbusch and M. Obstfeld (eds.), *Money, Capital Mobility, and Trade: Essays in Honor of Robert Mundell*, MIT Press, Cambridge, MA.

Kindleberger, C.P. (1969). 'Measuring equilibrium in the balance of payments', *Journal of Political Economy*, 77, 873–91.

Kouri, P. (1976). 'The exchange rate and the balance of payments in the short run and in the long run: A monetary approach', *Scandinavian Journal of Economics*, 78, 280–304.

Krugman, P. (1985). 'Is the strong dollar sustainable?', Federal Reserve Bank of Kansas City, Proceedings.

— (1989). 'Differences in income elasticities and trends in real exchange rates', *European Economic Review*, 33, 1031–54.

— (1991). 'Has the adjustment process worked?', *Policy Analyses in International Economics*, 34, September.

Lane, P. and G. Milesi-Ferretti (2007). 'Europe and global imbalances', *Economic Policy*, 51, 519–73.

Marris, S. (1985). *Deficits and the Dollar: The World Economy at Risk*, Institute for International Economics, Washington.

Meissner, C.M. and A.M. Taylor (2006). 'Losing our marbles in the new century? The great rebalancing in historical perspective', paper prepared for the session 'Global Imbalances: Lessons from History' Federal Reserve Bank of Boston Conference Chatham, MA, June.

Obstfeld, M. and K. Rogoff (2004). 'The unsustainable U.S. current account position revisited', *National Bureau of Economic Research Working Paper*, No. 10869 (November).

Obstfeld, M. and K. Rogoff (2005). 'Global current account imbalances and exchange rate adjustments', *Brookings Papers on Economic Activity*, 1, 67–123.

Roubini, N. and B. Setser (2005). 'Will the Bretton Woods 2 regime unravel soon? The risk of a hard landing in 2005–2006', presented at a Symposium on the 'Revived Bretton Woods System: A New Paradigm for Asian Development?' organized by the Federal Reserve Bank of San Francisco and UC Berkeley, San Francisco, 4 February.

Setser, B. (2006). 'So, just who is financing the U.S. deficit?', *RGE Monitor*, 13 September.

Summers, L.H. (2004). *The U.S. Current Account Deficit and the Global Economy*, Per Jacobsson Foundation, Washington DC.

Taylor, A.M., and J.G. Williamson (1994). 'Capital flows to the new world as an intergenerational transfer', *Journal of Political Economy*, 102, 348–71.

Dark matter and international imbalances

SUMMARY

Current account statistics may not be good indicators of the evolution of a country's net foreign assets and of its external position's sustainability. The value of existing assets may vary independently of current account flows, so-called 'return privileges' may allow some countries to obtain abnormal returns, and mismeasurement of FDI, unreported trade of insurance or liquidity services, and debt relief may also play a role. We analyse the relevant evidence in a large set of countries and periods, and examine measures of net foreign assets obtained by capitalizing the net investment income and then estimating the current account from the changes in this stock of foreign assets. We call dark matter the difference between our measure of net foreign assets and that measured by official statistics. We find it to be important for many countries, analyse its relationship with theoretically relevant factors, and note that the resulting perspective tends to make global net asset positions appear relatively stable.

— *Ricardo Hausmann and Federico Sturzenegger*

The missing dark matter in the wealth of nations and its implications for global imbalances

Ricardo Hausmann and Federico Sturzenegger

Kennedy School of Government and Center for International Development, Harvard University; Kennedy School of Government, Harvard University and Universidad Torcuato Di Tella

1. MOTIVATION

Economists pay attention to the current account as a way of keeping track of the change in net foreign assets for any given country over time. Large deficits signal that a country is running up its foreign liabilities, and if the countries experiencing such imbalances are themselves large, the resulting 'global imbalances' may require major changes throughout the whole international financial system. In fact, the current state of affairs, with large measured imbalances in the United States, has been a source of concern for a large number of academics and analysts.

In a nutshell, the point of our paper is that global imbalances are not as evident if the analysis is done on the basis of trends in the income flows paid by countries' net foreign assets, which appear to be significantly more stable than what could be inferred by current account dynamics. There is a reason to focus on income payments. Current account deficits are worrisome because they are the prelude to higher payments in the future. But if repayment does not need to occur then current account trends need not motivate strong concerns.

Why would the dynamic of income flows diverge from what should be expected from current account dynamics? The literature has stressed two main reasons: valuation effects that change the value of the assets independently of the current account, and return privileges that allow some countries to obtain abnormal returns (positive or negative). Of course, to have an impact on the way we perceive current imbalances these valuation effects or yield privileges must not only be large enough but should be expected to persist going forward.

To discuss whether such a claim can be made, this paper shows that for some countries these abnormal returns respond in a fairly stable manner to some key underlying economic fundamentals and as a result appear to be quite persistent. For example, poor countries may systematically benefit from debt relief allowing them to run deficits without increasing their payments abroad. Stable countries like Switzerland may be able to pay less for their liabilities because investors associate their assets with an extra sense of security, which lets it earn larger net income from foreign assets than what would be expected from its current account surpluses. Other countries may run deficits without accumulating liabilities because their currency is used by other countries, or may earn income from unrecorded services that multinationals' headquarters supply to their affiliates around the world.

To the extent that these factors are fairly stable it makes sense to factor their effect on income flows into the analysis of global imbalances. One, albeit imperfect, way of doing so is to use the income flows to compute a notional stock of assets. This has problems of its own but provides an alternative to the traditional computation, one that puts the focus on the income data. Because this may deliver a valuation of net foreign assets that is different from traditional valuation, there is a difference, that we call 'dark matter'. Dark matter is a way of measuring the difference between what income flows are and what they should have been as inferred from current account dynamics and is an object of interest in its own right. To the extent that the sources of dark matter are systematic, they may shed new light on the current account dynamics of each country.

The paper is organized as follows. Section 2 describes the inconsistencies between stock and flow data and documents the existence and persistence of yield differentials.

Section 3 discusses whether these differences are systematic or not, and provides empirical evidence relating them to a few underlying fundamentals. In Section 4 we suggest a measure of these discrepancies by introducing the concept of dark matter. Section 5 looks at global imbalances under the light of dark matter. Section 6 concludes with suggestions for further research.

2. TWO PUZZLES IN THE CURRENT ACCOUNT STATISTICS

The purpose of this section is to characterize the 'typical' yield countries make on their net foreign assets, and then to document the evolution of 'return privileges', i.e. the systematic differences in the return to net foreign assets from the typical yield.

We are not the first to study this issue. In a recent paper Meissner and Taylor (2006) estimate these return privileges by regressing the net investment income (NII) on the amount of net foreign assets (NFA):

$$\frac{NII_{it}}{GDP_{it}} = r\left[\frac{NFA_{it}}{GDP_{it}}\right] + \alpha_i + \varepsilon_{it}. \qquad (1)$$

The normalization by GDP is intended to reduce the heteroscedasticity problems arising from different country sizes. The model is estimated for a panel of G-7 countries. A constant slope coefficient r approximates the 'typical yield' obtained on net foreign assets. The fixed effect is an estimate of the return privilege. Meissner and Taylor find that the United States, the United Kingdom and Japan benefit from returns privileges relative to other G-7 countries, while the opposite is true for Canada and Italy. They also find small return differentials in favour of France and Germany but these appear not to be statistically significant.

To run this regression, we have to restrict the sample to countries with net foreign asset data. This reduces significantly the number of observations and makes it necessary to simplify the specification if the aim is to estimate return privileges for a larger set of countries. To do so, we start from the typical equation that describes the evolution of net foreign assets. As discussed in Lane and Milesi-Ferretti (2006a), the change in the net foreign asset position (B) of a country can be written as:

$$B_t - B_{t-1} = CA_t + KG_t + KA_t + E_t \qquad (2)$$

where CA is the current account balance, KG is the capital gain or loss on net foreign assets (equal to the change in stocks minus the underlying flows), KA includes factors such as capital account transfers (the so-called capital account balance) and E stands for errors and omissions.

An alternative representation of Equation (1) can be obtained by multiplying (2) by the interest rate and then by dividing by GDP. Using the fact that the return on net foreign assets times the net stock provides a measure of net investment income we can write:

Table 1. Typical returns on net foreign assets

	All countries	Industrial countries	Non-industrial countries	Emerging countries	Non-industrial non-emerging countries
Since 1980s	0.052***	0.044**	0.052***	0.034*	0.054***
	(0.017)	(0.018)	(0.018)	(0.018)	(0.019)
Observations	2466	597	1869	635	1234
R-squared	0.074	0.141	0.068	0.039	0.080
Since 1990s	0.057***	0.084***	0.056***	0.021	0.059***
	(0.019)	(0.031)	(0.020)	(0.021)	(0.019)
Observations	1431	348	1083	369	714
R-squared	0.097	0.137	0.094	0.061	0.109

Notes: Estimated with fixed effects. Robust standard errors in parentheses.
* Significant at 10%; ** significant at 5%; *** significant at 1%.

$$\frac{r(B_t - B_{t-1})}{GDP_t} = \frac{\Delta NII_t}{GDP_t} = r\left[\frac{CA_t}{GDP_t}\right] + r\left[\frac{KG_t + KA_t}{GDP_t}\right] + \frac{rE_t}{GDP_t} \quad (3)$$

The advantage of this specification is that we have investment income and current account for many countries. We can thus run (3), assuming the second term in the right-hand side to be a fixed country effect, for a large sample of countries:

$$\frac{\Delta NII_{it}}{GDP_{it}} = r\left[\frac{CA_{it}}{GDP_{it}}\right] + \alpha_i + \varepsilon_{it} \quad (4)$$

Here $\varepsilon_{it} = rE_t/GDP$ is the error term, and α_i represents the return privileges as in Meissner and Taylor (2006) except that, as (3) makes it clear, it may include capital gains and capital account transfers in addition to return privileges. Table 1 shows the typical yield obtained on net foreign assets as estimated by an OLS estimation of Equation (4). The regressions are run for different subsamples and for different time periods. Column (i) includes all countries in our sample (see Appendix A for a list of countries included in each group, and Appendix B for data sources), column (ii) includes industrial economies, column (iii) non-industrial countries, column (iv) includes only emerging countries – defined as countries in the J.P. Morgan Emerging Market Bond Index Global (EMBI Global)[1] – and column (v) the rest of the non-industrial countries.

The results are presented for data since 1980, as well as for a subsample since 1990 in order to verify the stability of the results over time. The results of all the specifications are fairly similar, and the typical yield, if anything, higher during the 1990s. The results for the full sample indicate a return of 5.2% since 1980 and 5.7% since 1990. For other subsamples we obtain somewhat lower values. In what follows we will consider 5% to be a reasonable proxy for the 'typical yield'.

---

[1] To be included in the EMBI Global a country must have a bond of large enough size and sufficient liquidity, two conditions that signal an effective integration in international financial markets.

Table 2. Return privileges for selected countries

	1980–2004	1990–2004
Positive		
Nicaragua	1.117* (0.642)	1.244 (0.761)
Malawi	0.785*** (0.278)	0.701** (0.312)
Laos People's Dem. Rep	0.533** (0.256)	0.467 (0.298)
Tanzania	0.459** (0.230)	0.874*** (0.326)
Madagascar	0.307 (0.188)	0.597*** (0.215)
Senegal	0.275* (0.161)	0.310* (0.178)
Benin	0.241 (0.222)	0.422** (0.215)
Nepal	0.215* (0.114)	0.207 (0.152)
United Kingdom	0.211* (0.125)	0.345* (0.184)
Guatemala	0.141 (0.114)	0.240* (0.139)
Haiti	0.141* (0.079)	0.130 (0.116)
Kenya	0.135 (0.088)	0.269** (0.107)
Sri Lanka	0.130 (0.118)	0.210* (0.109)
United States	0.120** (0.048)	0.150** (0.065)
Ethiopia	0.083* (0.043)	0.137** (0.056)
Negative		
Italy	−0.077* (0.044)	−0.026 (0.053)
China P.R.: Mainland	−0.123 (0.081)	−0.225* (0.124)
Dominican Republic	−0.263 (0.208)	−0.598* (0.309)
Venezuela, Rep. Bol.	−0.355 (0.224)	−0.507** (0.231)
Singapore	−0.437 (0.411)	−1.264** (0.576)
Ireland	−1.455*** (0.276)	−1.636*** (0.440)
Observations	2466	1431
R-squared	0.074	0.097

Notes: Robust standard errors in parentheses.
* Significant at 10%; ** significant at 5%; *** significant at 1%.

In addition to this 'typical yield', the specification also provides an estimate of the return privileges as in Meissner and Taylor. The estimated return privileges are similar when the different subsamples of countries are used so that in Table 2 it is sufficient to show the results corresponding to the full sample. Table 2 shows the value of the fixed effects in specification (4) for those countries where it was significant at least at the 10% level in at least one of the samples, and splits the countries in two groups, those with positive yield differentials and those with negative differential. One immediate point that is made by the table is that return privileges (positive and negative) are not a widespread phenomenon, with only a handful of countries managing to obtain them in a systematic fashion. The diversity of countries that are able to sustain a privilege also suggests that it may originate for a variety of different reasons. For example, it is likely that the factors underlying privileges for very rich countries, such as the United Kingdom and the United States, are not the same as those that are relevant for very poor countries such as Tanzania or Laos. The same should hold for the countries with unusually low returns among which we find rich countries such as Ireland, Italy and Singapore as well as very poor countries such as

China and Dominican Republic. The explanations for why the return privileges differ for each sub-group will be the focus of our discussion below.

Having established that there are differences in the returns that countries obtain from net foreign assets, we move to the question as to whether these return differentials present any systematic patterns. In the next section we do this by exploring the relationship between return privileges and country characteristics. Before that, however, we address two issues that can be analysed with the aggregate data. First, we discuss whether the return differentials are persistent. Second, we address a feature that is critical to evaluate the potential danger of global imbalances: whether there is a systematic relationship between return privileges and registered imbalances or, in other words, whether the size of the yield privilege is systematically different for those countries that run a current account surplus relative to those that run a current account deficit.

To analyse the first issue we cannot rely on the fixed effect, so we compute a time series for the privilege by looking at the difference between the changes in the net income payments of a country, and the changes one would have expected on the basis of current account dynamics. This expectation is computed by applying the 'typical yield' on foreign assets that we estimated in (4) to the cumulative current account during this period. Specifically the definition of abnormal returns between any two years, t and $t + j$ is

$$AR_{t,t+j} = \Delta NII_{t,t+j} - 0.05 \left(\sum_{i=t-1}^{t+j-1} CA_i \right) \tag{5}$$

The fixed effect estimated in Equation (4) and the abnormal return defined in Equation (5) will be the two measures of yield privileges we will use throughout the paper. To test for the persistence of return privileges we estimate for each country this privilege as in (5), except that in building our series we compute the cumulative privilege since 1980. The reason we look at the persistence of the cumulative return privilege is because we want to test if previous abnormal returns are likely to be reversed or not. In other words, we want to test if deviations in net income from what would be expected from current account dynamics are likely to persist over time. If a country runs a deficit (surplus) but seems not to pay (earn) for these deficits (surpluses), we want to know if this advantage (disadvantage) may disappear over time. For the case of the United States, for example, this is tantamount to asking whether the large abnormal returns obtained in the past are likely to be reversed in the foreseeable future.[2] This is tested by checking if the cumulative return privilege is persistent.

To do so, we run both an autoregressive specification as well as a random walk test on these cumulative returns. The autoregressive coefficient is close to one, and typically

---

[2] As an alternative example consider a country that has benefited from debt relief. The year the debt relief is granted the country has a large return privilege. This large privilege will not repeat itself in future years (so that the measured privilege year after year may not show a high degree of persistence), but the effect of this shock on net income payments will not be undone, allowing the country to pay less relative to what it would have otherwise paid for the indefinite future, leading to persistence in the abnormal cumulative return.

the DF-GLS test fails to reject the random walk hypothesis, indicating that these privileges appear to exhibit substantial persistence over time. These results are shown in Table 3 to hold both when the abnormal return is measured as a share of GDP (series denoted a) as well as when it is expressed in nominal terms (series denoted b).

Figure 1 explores the second issue, by showing the scatter plot relating the yield privileges estimated by the fixed effects of regression (4) with the cumulative current account.[3] Table 4 shows that the relation appears to be negative, though not statistically significant either for the industrial and emerging group. However, as can be seen from the scatter plots, the lack of significance may result from one or two big outliers as there is a clear negative relation for the rest of the group. The coefficients of the regressions between these two variables shown in Table 4 indicate that, when using the abnormal return over the last 23 years as a measure of return privilege, an increase in the accumulated current account deficit of 1% is typically associated with an increase in the privilege of between 0.033% and 0.04%. Somewhat larger results are obtained when using the fixed effect (the point estimate is now smaller because the fixed effect provides an estimate for the effect per year rather than over the whole sample). For this measure of yield privilege a 1% current account deficit appears related to an increase in yield privileges of between 0.046% and 0.069% over the sample period 1980–2004 (obtained by multiplying the coefficients for the sample that includes all the countries by 23).

We believe that the fact that the relation is negative may be indicative of two things. First, that large imbalances are to some extent self-correcting. For example, if a country over-borrows it may be with the expectation (validated later on) of obtaining a sufficient amount of debt relief that make its accounts sustainable. Alternatively, it may be an indication that the current account may not be a good indicator of the changes in the net asset position of the country. For example, consider a country where absorption appears to be high, leading to a current account deficit, but where income flows remain stable over time. This may be signalling that the current account is not properly reflecting the true asset position which may be larger than measured. Because the value of assets is appropriately perceived by its owners the consumption levels are consistent with this true asset position and therefore fail to build into a problem over time. This anticipates one of the main implications of our work: to the extent that countries that have surpluses tend to have lower returns than the typical return, and those with deficits higher returns, global disequilibria must be *smaller* than those reported by official numbers. This will be the reason why we will find below more stability in net foreign positions than that usually derived from official numbers.[4]

---

[3] The scatter plots using the abnormal return over the whole 24 years look very similar and are omitted for brevity.

[4] This is reminiscent of the 'financial adjustment channel' described in Gourinchas and Rey (2005), except that we show it applies to many countries – they focus only on the United States. The sources for the financial adjustment channel may be different in different countries.

Table 3. Tests of persistence of the yield differential

	Autoregression coefficient (a)	Autoregression coefficient (b)	DF-GLS test statistic (a)	5% critical value for DF-GLS (a)	DF-GLS test statistic (b)	5% critical value for DF-GLS (b)
Benin	0.992***	1.058***	−1.014	−2.612	−0.224	−2.602
China, P.R.: Mainland	0.954***	1.022***	−0.779	−2.617	−0.307	−2.602
Dominican Republic	0.967***	1.094***	−0.970	−2.612	−0.022	−2.602
Ethiopia	1.058***	1.110***	−0.608	−2.612	0.287	−2.602
Guatemala	0.958***	1.042***	−0.257	−2.612	0.421	−2.602
Haiti	0.995***	1.039***	−1.470	−2.612	0.240	−2.602
Italy	1.003***	1.028***	−0.984	−2.612	−0.610	−2.602
Ireland	1.046***	1.173***	0.628	−2.612	1.497	−2.602
Kenya	1.029***	1.067***	−1.054	−2.612	0.128	−2.602
Laos People's Dem.Rep	1.001***	1.054***	−1.017	−2.604	0.581	−2.602
Madagascar	1.053***	1.085***	0.083	−2.612	−0.108	−2.602
Malawi	1.002***	1.043***	−1.348	−2.612	0.175	−2.602
Nepal	1.010***	1.032***	−0.653	−2.612	−0.519	−2.602
Nicaragua	0.602*	1.084***	−4.599	−2.612	0.334	−2.602
Senegal	0.995***	1.048***	−0.857	−2.612	0.024	−2.602
Singapore	1.023***	1.164***	0.565	−2.612	0.983	−2.602
Sri Lanka	1.003***	1.077***	0.354	−2.612	0.793	−2.602
Tanzania	1.028***	1.086***	−0.772	−2.612	0.020	−2.602
United Kingdom	1.003***	1.147***	−0.552	−2.612	0.577	−2.602
United States	1.098***	1.165***	2.206	−2.612	1.559	−2.602
Venezuela, Rep. Bol.	0.999***	1.069***	−2.184	−2.612	0.837	−2.602

Notes:

[a] β in $\frac{AR_{80,t}}{GDP_t} = \alpha + \beta * \frac{AR_{80,t-1}}{GDP_{t-1}} + \varepsilon_t$ see appendix for variable definitions.

[b] β in $AR_{80,t} = \alpha + \beta * AR_{80,t-1} + \varepsilon_t$ see appendix for variable definitions.

* Significant at 10%; ** significant at 5%; *** significant at 1%.

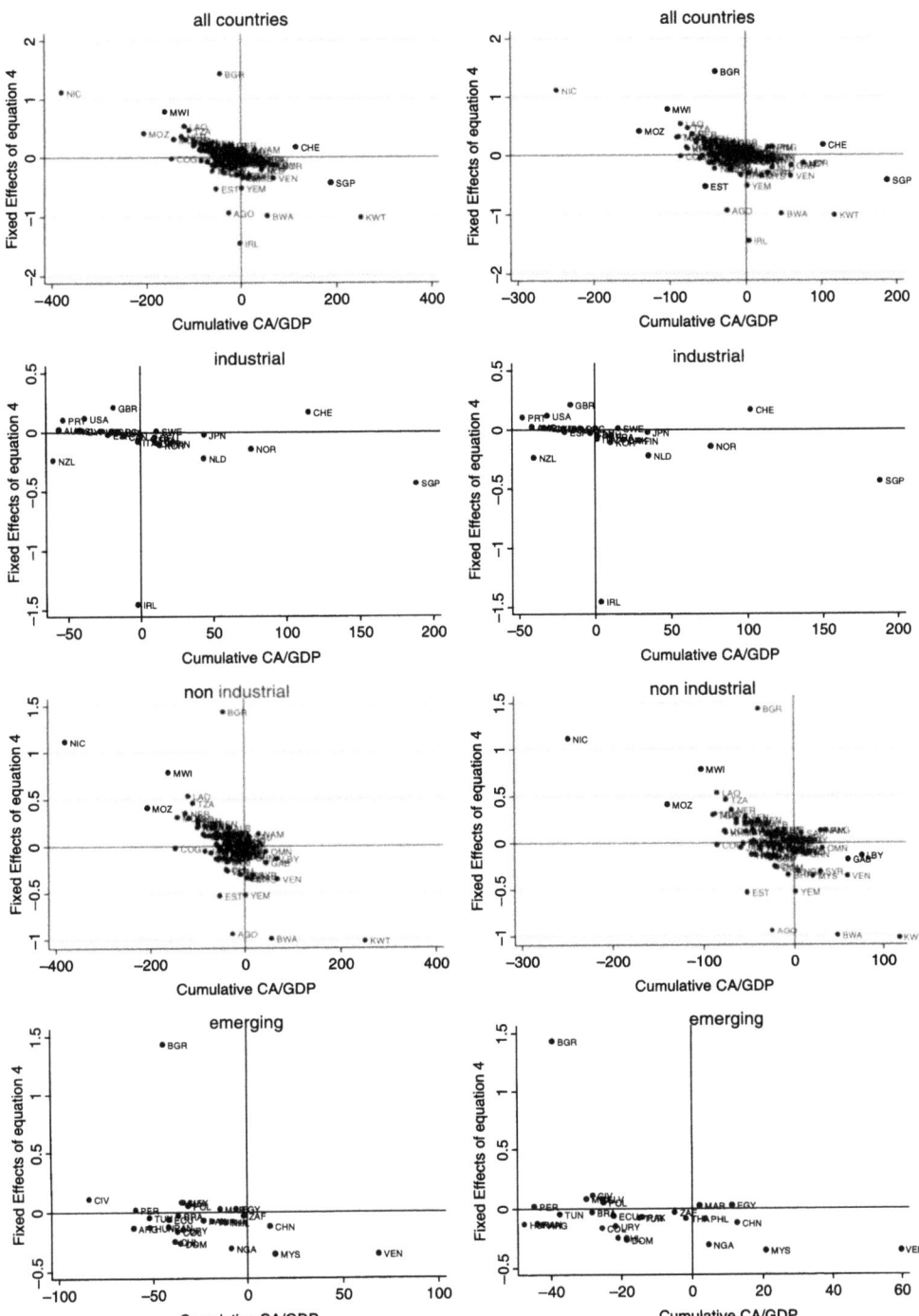

Figure 1. The current account and the level of privilege

Notes: Left side: 1980–2004. Right side: 1990–2004.

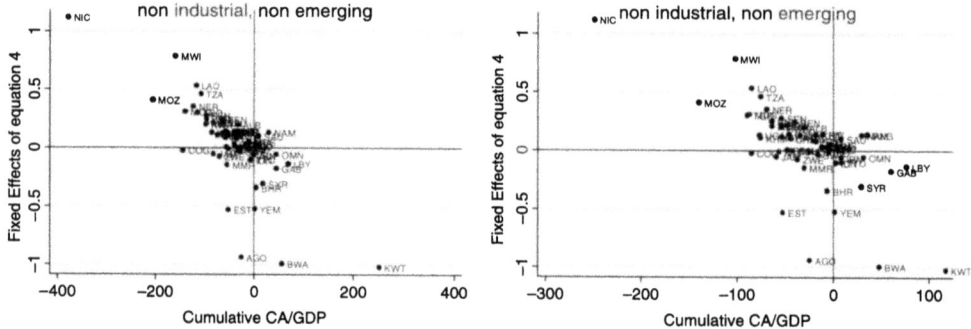

Figure 1. *Continued*

Table 4. The current account and the return privilege

	All countries	Industrial	Non-industrial	Emerging	Non-industrial non-emerging
	Using fixed effects as measure of return privilege				
1980–2004					
Change in current account	−0.002***	−0.001	−0.003***	−0.001	−0.003***
	(0.000)	(0.001)	(0.000)	(0.002)	(0.000)
Observations	109	25	84	27	57
R-squared	0.283	0.040	0.359	0.021	0.498
1990–2004					
Change in current account	−0.003***	−0.002	−0.004***	−0.003	−0.004***
	(0.001)	(0.001)	(0.001)	(0.002)	(0.001)
Observations	109	25	84	27	57
R-squared	0.256	0.060	0.331	0.054	0.439
	Using abnormal returns as measure of return privilege				
1980–2004					
Change in current account	−0.033***	−0.028*	−0.034***	0.004	−0.037***
	(0.004)	(0.014)	(0.004)	(0.013)	(0.004)
Observations	109	25	84	27	57
R-squared	0.377	0.143	0.445	0.003	0.557
1990–2004					
Change in current account	−0.040***	−0.039***	−0.041***	−0.006	−0.044***
	(0.005)	(0.013)	(0.006)	(0.017)	(0.006)
Observations	109	25	84	27	57
R-squared	0.361	0.272	0.394	0.004	0.503

Notes: Robust standard errors in parentheses.
* Significant at 10%; ** significant at 5%; *** significant at 1%.

3. STUDYING THE DETERMINANTS OF INCOME FLOWS – ASSET STOCK DISCREPANCIES

Why would the dynamic of income flows diverge from what we should expect from current account dynamics? As we mentioned above the literature has stressed two main reasons: valuation effects that change the value of the assets independently of the current account, and yield privileges that imply that some countries exhibit abnormal returns. The first has received substantial attention, as it is potentially relevant for explaining the US current account imbalance. Because the US economy can issue liabilities in its own currency, a dollar depreciation implies a capital gain by diminishing the value of net foreign liabilities (see, for example, Blanchard *et al.*, 2005) thus easing the burden of an adjustment. But, of course, that channel plays only a limited role when explaining the discrepancies for a much wider range of countries as we do here, many of whom cannot issue debt in their own currency. There are multiple other reasons why income flows may not track current account dynamics closely. Some of these reasons have been the object of a recent and intense debate, and therefore deserve a brief review here.

A first channel involves the notion that foreign direct investment (FDI) abroad is a vehicle for two income flows that are very imperfectly captured in official statistics. First, the valuation effects that are associated to the fact that FDI allows for the dissemination of ideas, blueprints and knowledge. The valuation effects are not picked up because market value adjustments to FDI assets that do not have visible market prices occur at best on the basis of the host (not source) country characteristics, and these are not likely to be strongly related to the earnings potential of the firm.[5] Second, the return to unrecorded exports of services from headquarters to their affiliates around the world. These are missed simply because there is no registration of the services shared across national borders within the firm.

A second channel may come from the underlying stability or instability of a given economy that may allow some economies to sell some of this stability to the rest of world, and charge for it, while other countries pay to diversify away some of their own instability. This is just the standard risk premia argument (dating back to Frankel, 1982), which will persist in equilibrium. The payments corresponding to this risk premia are akin to the trading of insurance services. Some of the most innovative recent interpretations to explain the US current account imbalance rely on this channel. Mendoza *et al.* (2006) provide a story where agents in financially sophisticated markets can insure their local and worldwide claims, something that agents in less financially developed countries cannot do. In equilibrium assets in the less financially developed country must earn a higher return, because local agents are unable to fully insure their claims there.[6]

The Mendoza *et al.* (2006) approach directly derives the risk premia resulting from financial backwardness. The related perspective of Caballero *et al.* (2005) focuses on financial backwardness in some fast-growing countries, such as China. Underdeveloped financial systems can prevent agents in those countries from writing claims on their

---

[5] For a description of the methodological approach see Kozlow (2002) on US data, and Simard and Boulay (2006) on Canadian data.

[6] In fact there are three main reasons why assets in equilibrium may be discounted at different rates: surprises, risk premia and embedded services. Surprises refer to the fact that assets may turn out to have a lower rate of return if faced with expropriation, restructuring or unexpected negative business conditions, and this risk requires an *ex ante* higher discount rate to compensate for these expected losses. But the net income flows already take this into account because they are *ex post* returns. Because they average out over a large number of assets it seems implausible (though not impossible) that realized returns may differ significantly and for very long periods from expected returns. This leaves the risk premia and embedded services as drivers of *ex post* return differentials.

own productive assets. This forces residents in those countries to use their savings to buy foreign assets while allowing foreign companies to own their productive assets. The superior financing/corporate governance technology provides a return differential. In their interpretation financially developed countries sell financial services and charge for them.[7]

Another explanation, though focused on the United States, is provided by Dooley *et al.* (2004) who argue that current imbalances are sustained by peripheral countries adopting export-led strategies with undervalued pegged exchange rates and capital controls. In this approach, dubbed Bretton Woods II, some countries are willing to purchase specifically US assets at lower (*expected*) returns as part of an implicit contract with the United States, whereby they are guaranteed access to its domestic market. To the extent that this is a 'purchase' of the access to the US market, it is another reason for a yield differential.

Alternatively a yield differential may arise from the provision of liquidity services, basically through the use of a foreign currency or by paying a premium for purchasing instruments in liquid financial markets. The simplest example is when people around the world need liquid assets and choose to hold a particular currency, dollars, pounds or euros in cash, that earns them a zero interest rate. By having foreigners accumulate this currency, and by paying no interest on this, the source country can accumulate current account deficits, in the amount of the demand of this currency, without deteriorating its net investment income account. But liquidity services do not only originate from seignorage. Deep financial markets may also carry a liquidity premia advantage that allows paying lower returns for the issuers in those markets. This is likely relevant for the few countries that issue vehicle currencies for global or regional markets (the dollar, the pound, the euro, the Swiss franc and the rand are natural examples).

Finally, the empirical results that identify very poor countries that have been the target of debt relief as showing high return privileges suggests that an additional channel is debt relief that also allows large deficits to be accumulated but never repaid.

Some of these mechanisms have been studied and quantified in previous work. In what follows we first discuss mismeasurement problems for FDI, which has received less attention in the literature, and then provide a systematic analysis of the relevance of the different stories based on cross-country evidence.[8]

3.1. Mismeasurement of foreign direct investment

We suggest that one explanation for the existence of yield differentials may be the result of measurement problems with FDI.[9] There are three basic methodologies for estimating FDI assets. The most traditional is the use of book value estimates. This,

---

[7] Ju and Wei (2006) provide a similar story.

[8] See also Cooper (2005) who mentions most of these channels.

[9] Yield differentials in FDI has been extensively studied for the US. However, the evidence appears inconclusive. Higgins *et al.* (2005) provide supporting evidence in favour of large yield differential in FDI. In contrast, Gourinchas and Rey (2006), compute a more comprehensive gross returns figure (i.e. including capital gains) and when comparing foreign assets in the US with US assets abroad find that there are large differences in the returns of debt, equity, bank loans and trade credit in favour of the US, but virtually no difference in FDI.

while commonly used, is a fairly poor measure of the value of investments abroad. An improved version uses the current cost method, which adjusts book value by estimated changes in the value of the underlying investments (usually exchange rate and inflation adjustments). A third alternative is to adjust the values by using stock market data, to approximate market valuations for the underlying assets. As described in Lane and Milesi-Ferretti (2006a), in recent years a wider range of countries have implemented market valuation methodologies, but book value remains the method of choice for a large number of countries.[10] To obtain the market value estimate, current methodologies start from the book value declared by companies and update it with the evolution of the stock markets of the country where the investment is located (the US follows this procedure, see Kozlow, 2002) or with capitalization ratios that compare market to book value (for example in Canada, see Simard and Boulay, 2006, though they explain that this is done for investments in Canadian firms, with no adjustments made on the investment of Canadian firms abroad). Updating by the stock market of the host country makes sense to the extent that *host* markets capture the profitability, tax, expropriation risks, and similar types of constraints faced by firms in those markets. However, it is also equally reasonable to think that the productive capacity of a multinational may be somewhat captured by the conditions in the source country, and, eventually, its stock market. An example may help illustrate the point. The S&P 500 may better capture the profitability of Intel-Costa Rica, than the San Jose stock market. In fact, we believe the San Jose stock market probably has no relation to the profitability of Intel's factory in Costa Rica. But how large of an adjustment would this lead to? One alternative is to recompute the FDI using the source country stock market data rather than that of the host country. One way of doing this is taking the book value of FDI abroad and multiplying it by the market to book ratio in the home country. We do this exercise for the United States, where sufficient information is available to perform the exercise and assess its potential relevance. Table 5 goes through the computations. For US FDI abroad this exercise is fairly simple because it boils down to revaluing assets abroad by using the S&P 500 market to book (rather than foreign stock markets). This is done in the left half of the table and suggests a potentially massive revaluation of foreign assets. By the end of the sample the adjustment is close to $2.7 trillion.[11]

---

[10] For the specific case of the US it has been long since the Bureau of Economic Analysis (BEA) introduced a market value alternative to the original measure, and updated the book value alternative by its improved current cost method. For a careful (and official) description of the two methodologies see Kozlow (2002). The original book value is no longer published though still being reported in the BEA's website.

[11] This computation is done with 2004 data, the latest available at the time of writing. We thank Willem Buiter and Gian Maria Milesi-Ferretti for suggesting this calculation. One of our discussants shows that an alternative way to perform the exercise is to use BEA's market to book ratio for foreign FDI assets in the US to reassess the value of US assets abroad, under the presumption that this adjustment is similar to the one we are proposing. He shows, however, that our procedure delivers much larger adjustments. The answer lies in the fact that FDI series use the stock market index to value only those assets that do not have market prices, thus the discrepancy would come to confirm that foreigners' investments in the US have taken place in firms that have done particularly poor relative to the S&P. This may be because foreigners invest in low risk low return activities, i.e. that they purchase insurance through FDI investments. It also reveals that in our adjustment of FDI abroad we are assuming these assets deliver a general equivalent to that of the S&P, an assumption that also may not be correct.

Table 5. Foreign direct investment of US abroad, and FDI of Japan in the US

End of the year	Estimation of FDI investment of US abroad					Estimation of Japanese FDI in the US				
	FDI abroad at market value (a)	FDI abroad at historical cost (b)	Ratio market to book value S&P (c)	Adjusted FDI abroad (d)	Adjustment (e)	FDI of Japan in US, at historical cost (f)	Ratio market to book value BEA (g)	Ratio market to book value Nikkei 500 (h)	Adjusted FDI of Japan in US (i)	Adjustment (j)
1982	226 638	207 752	1.22	252 447	25 809	9 677	1.05			
1983	274 342	212 150	1.37	291 000	16 658	11 336	1.12			
1984	270 574	218 093	1.31	286 767	16 193	16 044	1.05			
1985	386 352	238 369	1.58	377 531	−8 821	19 313	1.19			
1986	530 074	270 472	1.74	471 836	−58 238	26 824	1.24			
1987	590 246	326 253	1.67	544 740	−45 506	34 421	1.20			
1988	692 461	347 179	1.73	602 164	−90 297	51 126	1.24			
1989	832 460	381 781	2.09	797 455	−35 005	67 268	1.45	5.67	381 410	−283 908
1990	731 762	430 521	1.84	790 693	58 931	83 091	1.37	2.87	238 471	−124 937
1991	827 537	467 844	2.24	1 048 820	221 283	95 142	1.60	2.71	257 835	−105 934
1992	798 630	502 063	2.40	1 204 194	405 564	97 769	1.65	2.02	197 493	−36 634
1993	1 061 299	564 283	2.53	1 430 177	368 878	100 721	1.64	2.23	224 608	−59 028
1994	1 114 582	612 893	2.38	1 455 672	341 090	98 513	1.58	2.40	236 431	−81 109
1995	1 363 792	699 015	2.85	1 995 108	631 316	104 997	1.88	2.43	255 143	−57 967
1996	1 608 340	795 195	3.13	2 486 524	878 184	116 144	2.06	2.35	272 938	−34 227
1997	1 879 285	871 316	3.87	3 368 327	1 489 042	125 041	2.40	1.93	241 329	58 950
1998	2 279 601	1 000 703	4.55	4 557 423	2 277 822	134 340	2.80	1.80	241 812	134 248
1999	2 839 639	1 215 960	5.00	6 085 599	3 245 960	153 815	2.93	2.60	399 919	50 424
2000	2 694 014	1 316 247	4.05	5 333 992	2 639 978	159 690	2.21	2.02	322 574	31 047
2001	2 314 934	1 460 352	3.39	4 954 934	2 640 000	149 859	1.90	1.58	236 777	48 704

Table 5. *Continued*

	Estimation of FDI investment of US abroad					Estimation of Japanese FDI in the US				
End of the year	FDI abroad at market value (a)	FDI abroad at historical cost (b)	Ratio market to book value S&P (c)	Adjusted FDI abroad (d)	Adjustment (e)	FDI of Japan in US, at historical cost (f)	Ratio market to book value BEA (g)	Ratio market to book value Nikkei 500 (h)	Adjusted FDI of Japan in US (i)	Adjustment (j)
2002	2 022 588	1 616 548	2.73	4 420 836	2 398 248	147 372	1.52	1.34	197 478	27 029
2003	2 718 203	1 791 891	3.03	5 426 477	2 708 274	157 176	1.76	1.73	271 914	4 647
2004	3 287 373	2 063 998	2.92	6 031 104	2 743 731	175 728	1.78	1.74	305 767	6 659

Sources:

(a) Line 18, Table 2, 'International Investment Position of the United States at Yearend, 1976–2005' available at http://www.bea.gov/international/xls/intinv05_t2.xls.
(b) BEA, data available at http://www.bea.gov/international/zip/9702.zip. From 2002–2004 data available at http://www.bea.gov/international/xls/FDI16_0205.xls.
(c) Ratio between S&P 500® Composite Price Index and S&P 500 Composite Book Value both available at www.globalfinancialdata.com.
(d) = (b) * (c)
(e) = (d) − (a)
(f) Data from BEA. From 1989–1999 data available at http://www.bea.gov/international/zip/extract.zip. From 2002–2004 data available at http://www.bea.gov/international/zip/9702.zip.
(g) Ratio between line 36 Table 2, 'International Investment Position of the United States at Yearend, 1976–2005' available at http://www.bea.gov/international/xls/intinv05_t2.xls and Bea's direct investment in the United States at historical cost from 1989–1999 available at http://www.bea.gov/international/zip/IID03-15.zip, from 1999–2002 data available at http://www.bea.gov/international/zip/9702.zip and from 2002–2004 available at http://www.bea.gov/international/xls/FDI16_0205.xls.
(h) Bloomberg.
(i) = (f) * (h)
(j) = [(f) * (g)] − (i)

To adjust the value of FDI at home we need to use foreign stock indices corresponding to the source country of each investment. Unfortunately only Japan publishes market to book value ratios for its main stock index. So we use this case as an example to estimate potential revaluations of foreign assets in the United States. The right-hand side of the table then looks at the market value of Japanese investment in the United States, estimated by assuming it is adjusted from book value at the typical market to book value used for all foreign FDI in the United States, and then compares it with an alternative adjustment based on the market to book value of the Nikkei. The table shows that in the early 1990s the investment of Japanese firms in the United States could have been undervalued, but that in recent years it has been overvalued. While it is unlikely that this number can be extrapolated due to the special circumstances of the Japanese stock market during this period, the example illustrates our point that FDI assets may be significantly mismeasured. In the specific case of the United States that we have discussed here, the analysis suggests a significant undervaluation of net foreign assets.

Another way of assessing the potential mismeasurement in the stock of FDI is by relying on micro evidence, that is, by following the evolution of stock prices in the aftermath of a takeover of a given corporation by a company from a different country. If this price goes up in an abnormal fashion, this increase in valuation will be lost by statistics that use the aggregate foreign stock market to value individual firms that do not trade in public markets. In a recent work based on micro data Chari et al. (2007) tackle this question specifically and show it could lead to a very substantial underestimation of the value of FDI. They analyse a sample of 370 takeovers of emerging market firms by developed countries' companies. For these transactions there were significant abnormal returns for the developed-market acquirers. These abnormal returns translated into a dollar value gain of 1.5 times the transaction price. More specifically their sample includes purchases for $111 billion, on which they estimate valuation gains of $142 billion. Furthermore, they show evidence that these abnormal returns are related to better governance in source countries or to the importance of R&D in the original company, providing some hints as to the sources of the valuation gain.

3.2. Testing for the sources of yield differentials

After discussing reasons why countries may earn different income on their net foreign assets (mismeasurement of assets and services, debt relief, liquidity and seignorage), we proceed to assess the empirical relevance of the different explanations.

Some of the underlying mechanisms reviewed above and studied in the literature may be fairly stable over time; others may depend on the circumstances of an economy at a specific time. Thus, we tackle the testing in two parts. First, we estimate a cross-section of yield privileges over a relatively long period to test for the effect of relatively stable variables. Then, we estimate an unbalanced panel with yearly data to discuss the effect of variables for which short-term volatility is key. Our dependent variable is always the return privileges obtained on net foreign assets. These are estimated in the two ways we discussed in Section 2, either through the fixed effects coefficients estimated in Equation (4) or by estimating the abnormal return of Equation (5), though only the second alternative can be used when we work with yearly data.

We use the cross-section mainly to test the mismeasurement hypothesis. To do so we include as independent variables the stock of FDI assets and liabilities as a percentage of the GDP (see Appendix B for descriptions and sources of all the variables used), and spending in R&D in each country. We expect FDI liabilities to come in with a negative sign, and FDI assets to be associated with larger than expected returns, though this result may be muted when including countries where FDI outflows may respond to unstable conditions in the home economy. Spending in R&D measures the ability of local firms to innovate and their higher earning potential in their targeted firms abroad and is expected to have a positive sign. So should a rule of law variable that is included to test whether it is the superior institutional framework of a particular country that allows it to earn extraordinary returns as in the Caballero–Wei hypothesis discussed above. Finally, to test for other sources of return privileges we include a variable for highly indebted poor countries (HIPC) which includes a group of poor countries that have been favoured by debt relief, a dummy for OPEC countries that appear to earn surprisingly low returns on their assets, as well as a measure of corporate taxes to test for the possibility of tax shifting.

Table 6 shows the cross-section results for 103 countries for which we could compile at least partial data up to 2004. Column (i) includes only the FDI variables measures. Columns (ii) and (iii) show the results when the sample is restricted to either industrial or non-industrial countries. Columns (iv) to (vi) include the other potential determinants of yield privileges: rule of law, the HIPC and OPEC dummies and corporate taxes. Finally, columns (vii) to (ix) focus on countries with complete current account data during the sample period.

The results in Table 6 provide some support for the mismeasurement hypothesis. In Table 6a where we use the abnormal return on net foreign assets as the dependent variable, we find that countries that are short on FDI typically have negative yield privileges. The effect seems to be large with a 1% increase in the FDI liabilities as a percentage of GDP inducing a decrease in net income payments of about 0.05% of GDP during the 23 years. The number is twice as high for industrial countries. For this group, for example a country with 20% of GDP, higher FDI liabilities would see a deterioration in its net income of about 2.28% of GDP (0.114 × 20). For industrial countries there is also a statistically significant effect on the asset side. The regression indicates that an increase equivalent to 20% of GDP in the FDI abroad increases net income by about 1.18% over the sample period. Of course these numbers are dwarfed by the effect of debt relief. The highly indebted poor countries (HIPC) have typically enjoyed debt relief equivalent to an improvement in the return

Table 6a. Return privileges (measured as abnormal returns over 1980–2004) and fundamentals

	Entire dataset						Only countries with full sample		
	All countries (i)	Industrial (ii)	Non-industrial (iii)	All countries (iv)	Industrial (v)	Non-industrial (vi)	All countries (vii)	Industrial (viii)	Non-industrial (ix)
FDI Assets / GDP	−0.005	0.059**	−0.178***	0.020	0.078**	−0.114**	0.039*	0.089***	−0.067
	(0.017)	(0.021)	(0.063)	(0.021)	(0.028)	(0.054)	(0.020)	(0.027)	(0.050)
FDI Liabilities / GDP	−0.051***	−0.114***	−0.010	−0.070***	−0.129***	−0.022	−0.083***	−0.127***	−0.035*
	(0.014)	(0.017)	(0.018)	(0.014)	(0.022)	(0.017)	(0.014)	(0.021)	(0.018)
Rule of law				−0.303	−1.118	0.026	0.107	−1.240	0.751
				(0.475)	(1.412)	(0.549)	(0.499)	(1.373)	(0.564)
Corporate tax rate				0.029	−0.041	0.019	0.028	−0.049	0.050
				(0.033)	(0.073)	(0.035)	(0.037)	(0.071)	(0.040)
Research & Development				−0.003	−0.611	−0.021	−0.346	−0.530	−0.048
				(0.491)	(0.642)	(1.372)	(0.491)	(0.671)	(1.326)
Dummy OPEC				−5.623***		−4.954***	−4.801***		−3.513**
				(1.154)		(1.060)	(1.571)		(1.353)
Dummy HIPC				3.432***		3.204***	4.032***		3.259**
				(1.041)		(0.961)	(1.405)		(1.198)
Constant	1.220**	1.354	0.528	0.708	5.277	0.150	0.709	5.039	−0.952
	(0.524)	(0.818)	(0.629)	(1.160)	(3.280)	(1.239)	(1.274)	(3.239)	(1.300)
Observations	103	25	78	77	23	54	59	22	37
R-squared	0.168	0.688	0.131	0.517	0.719	0.553	0.522	0.726	0.520

Notes: Standard errors in parentheses. See appendix for variable definition and sources.
* Significant at 10%; ** significant at 5%; *** significant at 1%.

Table 6b. Return privileges (measured as fixed effect in Equation 4) and fundamentals

	Entire dataset						Only countries with full sample		
	All countries (i)	Industrial (ii)	Non-industrial (iii)	All countries (iv)	Industrial (v)	Non-industrial (vi)	All countries (vii)	Industrial (viii)	Non-industrial (ix)
FDI Assets/GDP	−0.001 (0.002)	0.005** (0.002)	−0.016*** (0.006)	0.002 (0.002)	0.006* (0.003)	−0.007* (0.004)	0.002 (0.002)	0.006* (0.003)	−0.006 (0.005)
FDI Liabilities/GDP	−0.003** (0.001)	−0.008*** (0.002)	0.000 (0.002)	−0.004*** (0.001)	−0.009*** (0.002)	−0.001 (0.001)	−0.005*** (0.001)	−0.009*** (0.002)	0.000 (0.002)
Rule of law				−0.042 (0.039)	−0.082 (0.144)	−0.019 (0.041)	−0.022 (0.048)	−0.082 (0.148)	−0.004 (0.054)
Corporate tax rate				0.004 (0.003)	0.000 (0.007)	0.003 (0.003)	0.004 (0.004)	0.000 (0.008)	0.003 (0.004)
Research & Development				0.005 (0.040)	−0.034 (0.065)	0.007 (0.102)	−0.015 (0.047)	−0.040 (0.072)	0.020 (0.128)
Dummy OPEC				−0.291*** (0.094)		−0.243*** (0.079)	−0.414*** (0.152)		−0.332** (0.131)
Dummy HIPC				0.231*** (0.085)		0.216*** (0.071)	0.295** (0.136)		0.221* (0.116)
Constant	0.090* (0.049)	0.061 (0.080)	0.051 (0.060)	−0.039 (0.094)	0.225 (0.334)	−0.083 (0.092)	0.010 (0.123)	0.238 (0.349)	−0.097 (0.125)
Observations	103	25	78	77	23	54	59	22	37
R-squared	0.098	0.513	0.108	0.400	0.529	0.466	0.390	0.528	0.447

Notes: Standard errors in parentheses. See appendix for variable definition and sources.
* Significant at 10%; ** significant at 5%; *** significant at 1%.

Table 7. Yield privileges and short run variables

	All countries	Industrial	Non-industrial
Output volatility	−5.940** (2.525)	0.071 (5.608)	−6.337** (3.005)
Business cycle	0.828 (1.123)	−2.859 (2.362)	1.105 (1.359)
Percent change of nom. exchange rate	0.000 0.000	−0.003 (0.002)	0.000 0.000
Constant	−0.294 (0.225)	−0.004 (0.319)	−0.273 (0.298)
Observations	1267	426	841
R-squared	0.071	0.123	0.077

Notes: Time dummies added. Standard errors in parentheses. See appendix for variable definition and sources.
* Significant at 10%; ** significant at 5%; *** significant at 1%.

privilege of somewhat more the 3% of their GDP. OPEC countries, on the other hand, show a return that is lower than expected, of close to 5% of GDP.[12]

In summary, the results seem to provide some support to the mismeasurement hypothesis, in particular for industrial countries. However, the variables related to scientific innovation, rule of law and tax shifting variables do not appear significant in any specification. The results are virtually unchanged when using the fixed effect from Equation (4) as a measure of return privilege in Table 6b.[13]

The yearly panel estimation can provide a test of relevance of insurance services. To this end, we use a measure of output volatility estimated as a five-year centred standard deviation of output.[14] We also include a variable of business cycle under the presumption that insurance paid may respond to business cycle conditions. To test for the existence of valuation effects that come through the exchange rate we include a variable that measures the change in the nominal exchange rate.[15]

Table 7 shows the results from a fixed effects pooled panel that relates the abnormal returns in a specific year with fundamentals for that year. In these regressions we exclude the variables that do not change significantly within the sample for each country and restrict ourselves to the sample of countries with complete data. These regressions (except for the industrial subset where, as expected, no variable is significant) suggest that countries with higher volatility (defined as the standard deviation of real GDP × 100) appear to have lower returns on their net foreign assets as in the insurance hypothesis. The insurance channel also appears very strong: an increase in 1% in the volatility of the business cycle implies typically a loss in return privileges of about 0.05% of GDP for each year.

On the other hand a business cycle measure, obtained as deviations from a Hodrik–Prescott trend for real GDP, and changes in the nominal exchange rate appear unrelated to returns on net foreign assets, indicating that the main mechanism does

---

[12] This could be due to under-reporting of some of their investments abroad in order to avoid publicity.

[13] Again, to make these comparable the coefficients need to be multiplied by 23, the number of years on which the tests in Table 6a are conducted.

[14] We tried with a measure of correlation with world GDP but did not obtain significant results.

[15] In some specifications we interacted the change in the nominal exchange rate with a measure of the ability to issue debts in its own currency but we did not obtain any results.

not appear to be valuation changes through the exchange rate. Notice that in the specification of Table 7 we include time trends, a similar estimation without time trends delivers the same results.

4. INTRODUCING DARK MATTER

The previous section showed that some fundamentals may be important and stable drivers of yield differentials. If so, it may make sense to consider these return differentials as arising from an underlying asset that gives origin to the return differential.

Why is this interpretation useful and why does it help in the interpretation of global imbalances? First, because there has been a growing awareness that intangible capital is an important source of income. Corrado *et al.* (2006) argue that US national income accounts miss about $800 billion a year in intangible capital, and thus under-report the total capital stock of the economy in close to $3 trillion. Parente and Prescott (2002)[16] along the same lines, provide back of the envelope estimates of intangible investment that are even larger than those of Corrado and co-authors. The point is that to the extent that this capital is there, it will generate income on a steady basis. Second, because we have shown that abnormal returns build up over time and appear to be persistent. To the extent that they are persistent it is useful to factor them into the dynamics of payments on net foreign assets to get a more realistic picture of what these payments may be in the future, and ascribing them to an asset makes it unavoidable to consider them when analysing the sustainability of imbalances, something that has been missed in previous discussions that assumed that abnormal returns were the result of shocks that could/would easily be reverted or whose effect may suddenly disappear. Furthermore, if the return differentials arise from hidden assets, within firm transactions, risk or liquidity premia they correspond to embedded services that produce output that should be measured. This, in fact, is exactly what is done in standard GDP estimation, where many components of GDP are imputed by assimilating return differentials to the sale of specific services. A sector where net interest differentials are imputed as income is the banking sector.[17] In the case of the US, the System of National Accounts (SNA) recommended

> 'measuring implicit financial services to depositors, using the difference between a risk-free reference rate and the average interest rate paid to depositors, and it recommends measuring the implicit services to borrowers using the difference between the average interest rate paid by borrowers and the reference rate' ... 'depositors could dispense with the services of a bank entirely and keep their money in securities paying the reference rate of interest. Depositors who forego the opportunity to earn the reference rate in order to obtain the services of a bank choose to pay the implicit price for depositor services equal to the margin between the reference rate and the deposit rate' (Fixler *et al.*, 2003, pp. 33 and 34).

---

[16] See also McGrattan and Prescott (2006).
[17] We thank Joe Beaulieu for pointing this out to us.

In our context, the analogy would be that when a foreigner decides to invest, say in the US or in Switzerland at a lower rate, it is because she values the insurance services provided by this investment. In this case we would say the US and Switzerland are selling insurance abroad, in the same way banks sell financial services by paying a lower rate on their deposits. To the extent that the underlying risk properties of the economies remain relatively stable, then so will the return differential, and the return differentials will be a source of income. For example, Kugler and Weder (2004 and 2005) study these return differentials for Switzerland, a natural provider of insurance services, particularly after World War I. They find that the return differential arose when Switzerland remained neutral during World War I, and since then has remained very strong and persistent.

Thus we propose measuring the stock of net foreign assets (*NFA*) as the capitalized value of the net investment income (*NII*), discounted at a constant rate of interest (r):

$$NFA_t^{DM} = \frac{NII_t}{r} \tag{6}$$

The superscript *DM* corresponds to *dark matter*, a term that we have chosen to reflect the discrepancy between our measure of net foreign assets and the measure that can be obtained from official figures or from accumulating the current account imbalances. The name is taken from a term used in physics to account for the fact that the world is more stable than you would think if it were held together only by the gravity emanating from visible matter. In the same way that physicists infer matter in the world from its gravitational pull, and not from adding up the visible matter, we infer the assets from their returns, and not from adding the current account imbalances. As a result countries with net investment income larger than what is presumed on the basis of their asset base will have dark matter assets, while countries where the net investment income is too low will have dark matter liabilities.

In turn, we define the current account as the change in net foreign assets defined in (6):

$$CA_t = NFA_t^{DM} - NFA_{t-1}^{DM} = \frac{NII_t - NII_{t-1}}{r}. \tag{7}$$

This way of computing the current account has been suggested by Cline (2005) and previously by Ulan and Dewald (1989). It was discussed by US government officials, but the Bureau of Economic Analysis (BEA) eventually discarded it because it was difficult to choose a discount rate (see Landefeld and Lawson, 1991).

This estimation suffers from all the same problems that we confront when estimating the value of a firm using price-earnings ratio, such as making sure the earnings are relatively stable, that earnings show up as earnings and not as capital gains, that the earnings data be of good quality, and that the discount rate appropriately reflects expected growth and the opportunity cost of time. Even though the discounting interest rate can be taken from our estimation of specification (4), and is therefore not arbitrary, and even if in the estimation it appears to be relatively stable over the sample period, the relevant rate may change over time (with changes in expected growth or interest rates). We discuss income-data quality issues in Box 1 and Box 2.

Box 1. Is income data reliable?

Our measure does appear to hinge on the net income data, at least in comparison with official stock data. But how good is either of these data? Gros (2006a), for example, discussing the United States, points out that the stock data is wrong because US surveys systematically miss on assets that foreigners hold in the United States. Because it is known that the US income payments have remained relatively constant over time, the fact that its liabilities are larger than measured increases the inconsistency between the two series. Gros (2006b) tries to explain the puzzle by arguing that the income flow data is wrong as well, because foreign firms in the United States seem to understate retained earnings. Some evidence is provided by the fact that once investments are categorized as direct investment, reported retained earnings fall dramatically. Gros disregards transfer pricing as an explanation (so does Mataloni, 2000), and argues that retained earnings in the United States should be similar to those of US firms abroad, so that they could be pulled out altogether from balance of payments statistics. If one is willing to make this assumption, it would imply a $100 billion overestimation of the net income which in our methodology would be equivalent to a $2 trillion drop in net foreign assets (when a 5% discount rate is used). Because Gros (2006a) suggests that net foreign assets stocks are $1 trillion less than actually measured, in the Gros accounting system there is still a large inconsistency between official stock data and the income flow data. As of 2005 the puzzle in the US data was of the order of $5 trillion, representing the cumulative current accounts since 1980 that had not led to payments abroad. In the Gros account system the discrepancy is of the order of $4 trillion, because he claims net assets are $1 trillion less than reported (thus, around $6 trillion in debt) but that income payments are $100 billion less than what official figures register (which would be equivalent to a $2 trillion liability paying 5%).* Either way the purpose of our analysis it simply to point out the discrepancy between the two data sources and provide an attempt to understand why this is so. The Gros correction does not eliminate the discrepancy; it reduces it by a small amount.

---

* A point that has been made (Buiter, 2006) is that mistakes may arise because income data is computed on an accrual basis. Thus if a country is in default, for example, the interest accrued but not paid will still be imputed to the income flow. While this may lead to some distortions, these apply to a very small set of countries, and only until the default is resolved. Once this happens, it is true that the numbers are not revised backwards; however, our final estimation for the stock of assets, and therefore our cumulative current account numbers would still be correct.

Box 2. The tax shifting hypothesis

It has been pointed out that income data is unreliable as a result of tax avoiding strategies, whereby firms report income in low-tax locations (see, for example, Eichengreen, 2006, and Lawrence and Lara, 2006). Lawrence and Lara (2006), in the context of the Puerto Rican economy, argue that this advantage is highest for firms with large intangible assets, which explains why there is a disproportionate amount of R&D intensive industries such as pharmaceuticals, instruments and electronics located in the island: these firms allegedly 'allocate high-cost activities, such as R&D spending, to the parent company and highly profitable production activities (that benefit from the R&D) to the foreign (or Puerto Rican) subsidiary.' This argument has been used as an explanation for why the income account of the United States has remained stable in spite of growing cumulative imbalances. But does the tax shifting hypothesis stand up the test of the data? Our results in Tables 6a and 6b suggesting that the corporate tax rate is not a relevant driver of abnormal returns is consistent with earlier results by Mataloni (2000) who checks if reported profitability is sensible to firms with large intra-firm imports, but finds no relationship. But there is a more compelling reason why tax shifting cannot be a relevant factor. For the United States, for example, the BEA reports for 2005 $227 billion of income from foreign direct investments abroad. Most of this comes from Europe, Canada and Japan (that add up to $139 billion of the total), where it is unlikely that tax considerations are relevant. Among the low tax jurisdictions, Ireland stands out with $12 billion, Bermuda with $8 billion and UK Caribbean with $7.7 billion. What role can these jurisdictions play in explaining the stability of the US net income? It is easy to see that for tax shifting to explain the mismatch between asset and flow data on a sustained basis requires that profit shifting be increasing in a way that is not verified in the data. If the US runs a current account deficit of $600 billion in a particular year, this implies that there should be roughly $30 billion more in net payments the following year (using the panel average yield of 5%). So for this not to show up in the net income, tax diversion should have *increased* relative to previous years by that amount. For the about $4.3 trillion of cumulative deficits the US has run between 1994 and 2005, tax shifting should have increased about $214 billion if assets earn the typical yield. If the tax shifting hypothesis is correct, this would have been reflected by an equivalent increase in income originating in low tax jurisdictions. Going back to 1994, the earliest year when this data is available, firms had reported income from Bermuda of $3.2 billion, from Ireland of $1.5 billion and $0.35 billion from the UK Caribbean, so the change of approximately $15 billion is quantitatively small relative to the $214 billion that are necessary for tax shifting to be an important part of the story (this data can be retrieved from http://www.bea.gov/international/xls/usdiainc.xls).

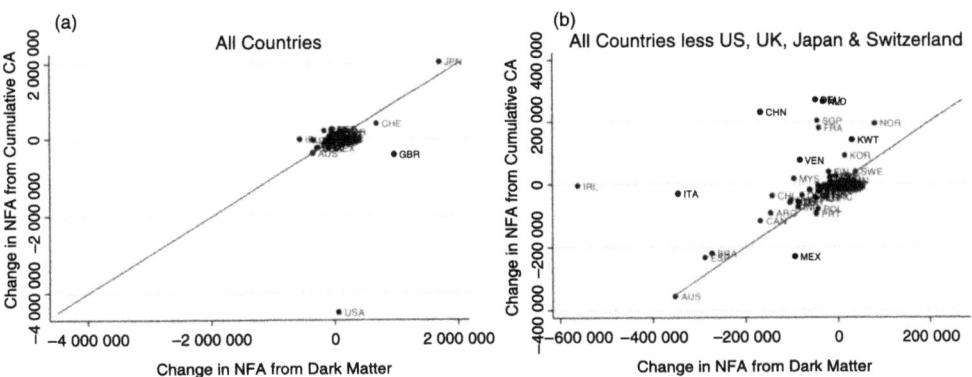

Figure 2. Official current account and change in net foreign assets, 1980–2004: (a) all countries; (b) all countries excluding the United States, United Kingdom, Japan and Switzerland

Table 8. Official and dark matter estimates of the current account

	Full sample	Excluding US	Excluding US and UK	Excluding US, UK and Japan
Change in dark matter NFA	0.648***	0.708***	0.963***	0.458***
	(0.204)	(0.068)	(0.049)	(0.067)
Constant	−22 957.46	19 265.42	33 722.684***	13 815.759*
	(44 569.766)	(14 985.336)	(9 770.491)	(7 691.446)
Observations	109	108	107	106
R-squared	0.086	0.504	0.787	0.309

Notes: Standard errors in parentheses.
* Significant at 10%; ** significant at 5%; *** significant at 1%.

One potential advantage of applying this methodology to the overall earnings on net foreign assets is that we average over a large number of firms and agents, so that the resulting earning flow may be relatively stable. Yet, if the earnings of any given year still give an unreliable measure of its true earning potential, if we average over an economy and look at trends over a couple of years, we should obtain reasonable results.[18]

To assess the coherence of the relationship between current account measures, Figure 2a plots the current account as measured from changes in the net stock of foreign assets computed from capitalizing the net investment income, against the official current account, for all the 109 countries for which we have complete data from 1980 through 2004.[19] Countries along the 45 degree line are countries where the two estimates of the current account match each other. Table 8 provides some OLS regressions to

---

[18] China provides a clear example of some of these problems. Its current account deficit surely dates much earlier than 1995 when it starts paying on its net foreign assets. We fully miss all these imbalances in previous years, thus showing that the multiyear perspective is critical for this methodology.

[19] In this exercise and in what follows we use net foreign investment income receipts, i.e. netting out net employee compensation which is not a form of capital income and we use the 5% typical yield to discount net income flows.

suggest that the correlation between the two measures is positive, strong and statistically robust. In fact, once the US and the UK are withdrawn from the sample the coefficient relating both measures is 0.96 and highly significant, though this result, as shown in the last column, is mostly driven by Japan.

Countries to the right of the 45 degree line have dark matter assets as their imputed net asset stocks appears larger than indicated by the official current account. Countries to the left of the 45 degree line have dark matter liabilities. While most countries lie close to the 45 degree line, the data shows some important outliers: the US, UK and Switzerland as owners of dark matter assets, and Japan, Ireland, Italy, Germany and China as owners of dark matter liabilities. Figure 2b zooms into the central cluster to verify that this positive relationship holds within that group as well.

To further understand the sources of the stock of dark matter (DM) it is useful to write it as:

$$DM = NFA_t^{DM} - NFA_t = \frac{NII_t}{r} - NFA_t = \frac{\tilde{r}(NFA_t + \mu_t)}{r} - NFA_t = \frac{\tilde{r}}{r}\mu_t + \frac{(\tilde{r}-r)}{r}NFA_t \qquad (8)$$

where NFA_t stands for the official measure of net foreign assets as estimated from the accumulation of the current account.[20] In this expression we allow for assets to be mismeasured, with μ indicating that error in measurement. In addition we assume assets to yield a rate of return $\tilde{r}$ different from the constant rate used for discounting. The two terms in the last expression of Equation (8) allow us to visualize that dark matter may have two origins: the capitalized return to unaccounted assets and to yield 'privileges'.[21] This makes sense to the extent that *ex post* returns reflect expected returns and the return premium is consistently paid, i.e. when the return privileges appear to be stable. In Section 2 we provided evidence that this was the case.

From the second term of the last equality in Equation (8) it should be clear that our difference with Gourinchas and Rey (2006) is that we capitalize the return differential, add it to the stock of net foreign assets, and then adjust the current account accordingly. It is the fact that we consider as an asset the capitalized value of the return differential that makes our description of the current account dynamics so different from the standard analysis.

---

[20] We choose to compare the dark matter assets to those that would result from accumulating the current account, not the measured stock of assets. The reason for this is that the measured stock already contains some of the drivers of dark matter, so that comparing its value to the adjusted measure would split the dark matter into two: the part that is accounted in the asset valuation (the more visible part of dark matter) and the part that is not. Because this could lead to erroneous interpretation of how dark matter assets evolve over time, we choose to group dark matter into a unique estimation.

[21] The second term in Equation (8) may change dramatically over time, making the stock of dark matter quite volatile. McKelvey (2005) refers to the very large volatility of dark matter, something that he found did not bear well with what he believed were stable underlying economic reasons for the existence of dark matter. Equation (8) clarifies the point by showing that dark matter will be affected by the capitalized value of changes in the actual return differentials. Thus small changes can lead to swings in our dark matter estimate. As much as in corporate finance, earnings in a particular year may provide a poor guide to the income of a particular corporation over the medium term. In our case the income flow is the average of many different individual returns, but it is still true that these returns may be affected by macro shocks, thus still exhibiting some volatility. Under this light, our estimates for any particular year should be taken with care, with averages over longer periods being more informative. Trends over 25 years, as we use in this paper, are relatively stable.

5. A NEW LOOK AT GLOBAL IMBALANCES

With a better understanding of what dark matter is, we apply our methodology to the understanding of global imbalances. In order to have a working benchmark Figure 3a presents the evolution of the net asset position of major global players as can be inferred from accumulating the current accounts over the last 30 years for Japan, the United States, the European Union and the rest of the world (ROW) (which is estimated as a residual so that all positions add up to zero) all expressed as a share of world GDP. It shows a world that is increasingly unbalanced with Japan and the rest of the world financing Europe and primarily the United States, which appears accumulating a growing external debt.

The work of Lane and Milesi-Ferretti (2001, 2006a, 2006b), resulting in the *External Wealth of Nations Database*, is an attempt to provide better estimates of net foreign positions. In the first of their three papers on the topic they correct official numbers by adjusting for a series of problems (capital account transfers, debt reductions, exchange rate changes, portfolio equity adjustments, etc.). However, to obtain comparability across countries, FDI was taken at book value. By the time of the 2006 version of their Wealth of Nations database, a large fraction of countries had started publishing reliable market value estimates of their net stock of FDI, so the latter version relies more heavily on this data. But, while this data improves on current statistics it is mostly based on official numbers so it does not provide a description that is very different from that of official statistics. Figure 3b therefore shows a similar picture to that of 3a with data taken from Lane and Milesi-Ferretti (2006a). As can be seen, the description provided

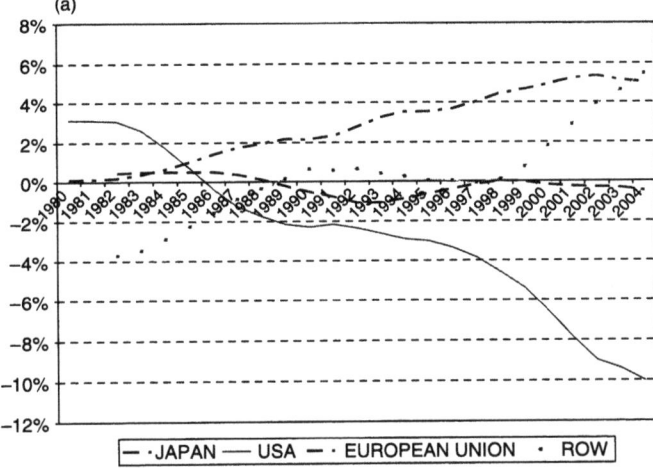

Figure 3a. Net asset positions from official data

Notes: European Union countries includes: Austria, Belgium, Finland, Germany, Italy, the Netherlands, Spain, Sweden, the United Kingdom. Official net foreign assets: accumulated current account from IFS, code: ALDZF divided by world GDP, WEO, Subject Code: NGDPD. Initial stock of assets corresponds to the net investment position from the following source.

Source: IFS lines 79AADZF-79LADZF, see appendix for details.

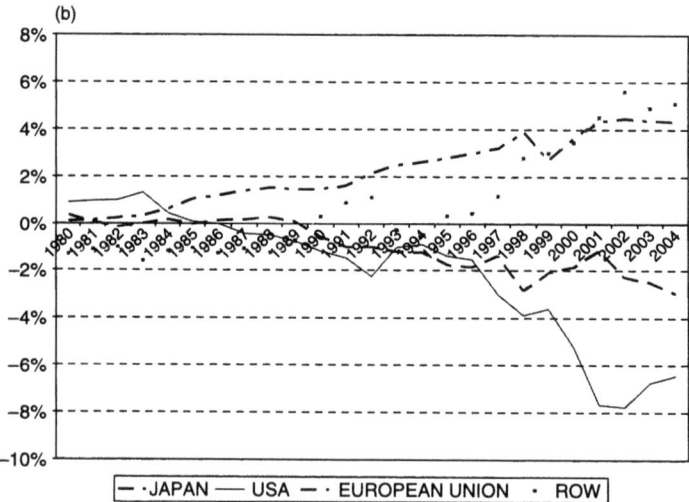

Figure 3b. Net foreign assets from Wealth of Nations database

Notes: European Union countries includes: Austria, Denmark, Finland, France, Germany, Greece, Ireland, Italy, the Netherlands, Portugal, Spain, Sweden, the United Kingdom.

Source: Lane and Milesi-Ferretti (2006a), divided by world nominal dollar GDP from WEO, see appendix for details.

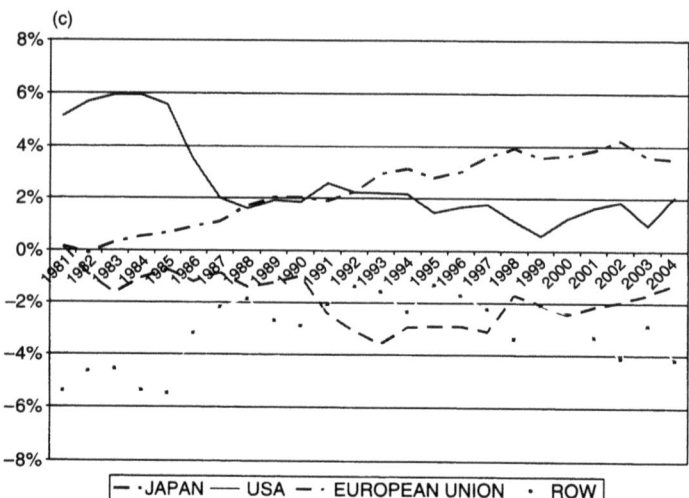

Figure 3c. Net foreign assets with dark matter

Notes: European Union countries includes: Austria, Denmark, Finland, France, Germany, Greece, Ireland, Italy, the Netherlands, Portugal, Spain, Sweden, the United Kingdom.

Source: IFS, lines (AGDZF-AHDZF) / 0.05, divided by world nominal dollar GDP from WEO (see Appendix B).

by Lane and Milesi-Ferretti is similar to that depicted in official statistics. In both databases the net asset positions seem to trend for most of country groups.

Figure 3c presents an alternative view, using the net asset positions that we construct by capitalizing the net investment income for each country. As can be seen, the world

Box 3. Is China a net creditor?

It has been argued that China is accumulating a large amount of foreign assets. Its official reserves, topping $1 trillion, are indeed the largest in the world. But what does dark matter have to say about China's net asset position? Figure 4 shows the evolution of the net foreign asset position of China including dark matter. It unveils that in spite of its large official reserves, China is still a net debtor, not a creditor. The graph also shows that China has reduced its net foreign debt considerably in recent years and that reduction has been very quick, yet China remains an important importer of dark matter and that is why it still pays out on its net asset position.

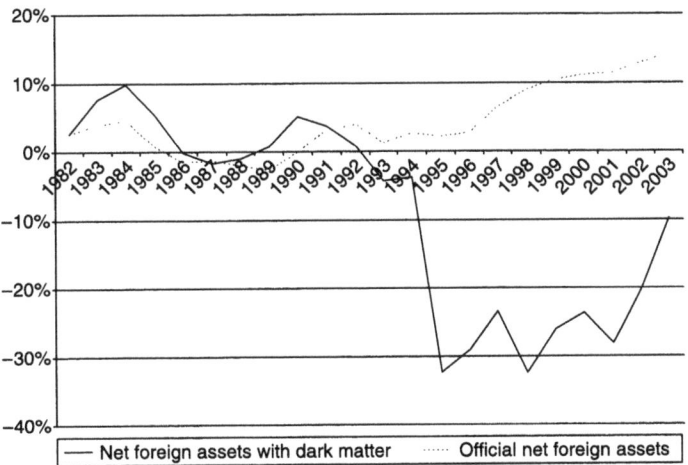

Figure 4. Net foreign assets position with dark matter, China (as % of China's GDP)

Notes: In the first year the two series start at the value of net foreign assets with dark matter.

Sources: Net foreign assets with dark matter: IFS, lines (AGDZF-AHDZF) / 0.05, divided by world GDP, WEO, Subject Code: NGDPD, see appendix for details.
Official net foreign assets: accumulated current account from IFS, code: ALDZF divided by world GDP, WEO, Subject Code: NGDPD see appendix for details.

looks quite different, at least relative to the previous two graphs. First and foremost, the United States does not appear as a net debtor but as a net creditor and its net foreign asset position remains stable over the last 20 years. Japan shows a pattern that is similar to that in official data, i.e. a growing creditor, while the European Union and the rest of world are net debtors. (Box 3 discusses the case of China.) Perhaps the most striking feature of Figure 3c is that it shows a world that is surprisingly balanced with relatively little trend in the net asset position for most groups.

5.1. An analysis of the United States

The centre of the discussion on the sustainability of recent global imbalances has focused squarely on the persistent and large US current account deficits.[22] In spite of this, over the recent years net investment income has been stable, indicating that accumulation of dark matter assets is compensating the large current account deficits leaving its net asset position unchanged. Typically the answer to the question of why the net investment position of the US appears more stable than implied by its current account, particularly when thinking about the 2001–2005 period, was that the US enjoyed capital gains associated with exchange rate fluctuations. But these were viewed as unreliable, as exchange rates can move the other way without notice (Lane and Milesi-Ferretti, 2006a). Were the US dollar to appreciate, the US would be left not only with a large current account deficit but also with a large capital loss in its net stock of foreign assets, compounding the downfall. The exchange rate channel has been discussed by Gros (2006a) and Kitchen (2006), who conclude it is not an important part of the story. In addition the story runs into problems when applied to the 2004/5 period, when the dollar did not further depreciate relative to the euro, while net income remained stable.

So, while it is a fact that the United States has been able to maintain a stable income flow in spite of large and increasing current account deficits, can dark matter (or return differentials) explain the discrepancy? There are two ways of answering the puzzle. Given the close to zero net investment income, and the approximately $5.2 trillion in accumulated debt (as measured through the cumulative current account deficits observed between 1980 and 2005) it seems we are missing this much of US assets. Alternatively, we could try to account for missing income payments from abroad of about $250 billion, that would compensate the payments that measured debt should be generating.

The first piece of the puzzle is provided by FDI mismeasurement. Table 5 computed the potential mismeasurement of the FDI data. While we did not provide an estimate for the potential underestimation of foreign assets in the United States we did compute an upper bound for the underestimation of US assets abroad. Our exercise suggested a potential adjustment in the stock of FDI assets of close to $3 trillion. Because we provide an upper bound to the required adjustment in FDI assets the number is likely to be somewhat smaller, but it has the potential to go a long way in explaining the missing gap and, in fact, could justify up to $150 billion of the $250 billion of missing income payments. One feature that suggests that our proposed adjustment may not be too far from reality is that it does not differ significantly from the 1.5 adjustment coefficient found by Chari *et al.* (2007) using micro level data.

How could we estimate the risk premia payments to the United States? One alternative is to multiply the amount of US debt held by foreigners by the return privilege of

---

[22] Some authors such as Engel and Rogers (2006), Mendoza *et al.* (2006) or Caballero *et al.* (2005) as well as two papers by us (Hausmann and Sturzenegger, 2006, 2007), suggest the current state of affairs is sustainable and not a source of concern. On the other hand Cline (2005), Obstfeld and Rogoff (2005a, 2005b), Roubini and Setser (2004), Lane and Milesi-Ferretti (2005) and Higgins *et al.* (2005), among others, consider the situation to be unsustainable.

Table 9. Portfolio assets for the US economy in 2005 (in millions of dollars)

	Official assets in the United States	
(a)	US Treasury securities	1 288 881
(b)	Other private assets in the United States	360 516
(c)	US Treasury securities	704 875
(d)	US securities other US Treasury securities	4 390 682
(a) + (b) + (c) + (d)	Total portfolio assets	6 744 954
	Income privilege (@ 0.68%)	45 866

Sources: Lines 28, 29, 37 and 38 of Table 2, 'International Investment Position of the United States at Yearend, 1976–2005' available at http://www.bea.gov/international/xls/intinv05_t2.xls.

Table 10. Dark matter assets and income (in millions of dollars)

		Dark matter sources	Income equivalent
(a)	FDI asset	2 743 731	137 187
(b)	FDI liabilities	na	Na
(c)	Insurance	917 314	45 866
(d)	Seigniorage	325 000	16 250
(e)	Liquidity	63 800	3 190
	Total	4 049 845	202 493

Sources:
(a) Table 5, income estimated at 5%.
(c) Table 9, income privilege estimated at 0.68%.
(d) Line 38 of Table 2, 'International Investment Position of the United States at Yearend, 1976–2005' available at http://www.bea.gov/international/xls/intinv05_t2.xls. Income estimated at 5%.
(e) Income estimated by adding lines 1 + 3 of Table 9 at 0.16%. Stock is income divided by 0.05.

US portfolio assets estimated, for example, by Gourinchas and Rey (2006). These authors estimate for the post-Bretton Woods period a total return advantage of 0.68% for US portfolio debt. Table 9 shows the amount of US debt held by foreigners, which can be divided into official and corporate instruments (all data is for 2005). The total holding of US debt by foreigners adds up to about $6.75 trillion, which implies a yield privilege of $45 billion, or alternatively, almost $1 trillion in additional wealth.

On the other hand, the evidence does not seem to assign an important role to seignorage. Buiter (2006) estimates dark matter assets from seignorage (holdings of US dollar bills abroad) of between $210 billion and $525 billion, a small share of the total. The BEA reports a holding of foreigners in 2005 of $325 billion, at a 5% typical return this implies an extra income of $16 billion. Even less important is the liquidity premia channel. Longstaff (2004) finds the average liquidity premia for US treasuries to run between 10 and 16 basis points. Applied to the stock of US treasuries held abroad which currently adds to about $2 trillion (see Table 9), gives an upper bound estimate for net income of $3 billion, equivalent to an additional stock of assets of $64 billion.

Table 10 adds up dark matter sources for the United States. Our back of the envelope calculations, using the work of other scholars, allows us to estimate that the sources of dark matter discussed may add up to close to $4 trillion, mostly compensating the accumulated current account over the recent years. It is these assets that have allowed the United States to maintain its current income stable in spite of measured current account imbalances.

There are basically three ways of assessing whether dark matter assets will continue to play a role in the future. One is to analyse the underlying reasons for the existence of dark matter, and seek to understand whether they will continue to play a role in coming years. In our analysis, the reasons for why the return differential exists may be identified in the health of innovation and creativity of the US corporate sector, the underlying stability of the US economy, the role of the dollar as a leading global store of value. To the extent that these fundamental features remain stable, so will the return differential. As global markets continue to grow, these return privileges may act on a larger base, and thus potentially lead to increases in dark matter assets.

A second way to assess persistence of the mechanisms we focus on, and their contribution to sustainability of the US current account, is to look at historical evidence. Did other countries enjoy similar return differentials in the past? Were these stable? Meissner and Taylor (2006) address this issue by analysing the United Kingdom at the end of the 19th century, as well as the United States in the postwar period. They argue that the evidence points to the fact that yield differentials declined over time, which they use as a cautionary note on the possibility of the United States sustaining large differentials in the future, though – we may add – they conclude this from extrapolating a linear trend. In addition, they also find that these differentials for the United States, and for the United Kingdom, were fairly stable as a share of GDP, due to an increase in leverage. In the case of the United Kingdom the process continued up until an abrupt collapse at the outbreak of World War I, leaving open the question as to what would have happened if such event had not occurred. A similar but more flexible estimation than that of Meissner and Taylor (2006) would allow for a quadratic trend. If the specification of Equation (4) was augmented with a quadratic trend we would be able to see how the return privilege changes over time. To see this we re-estimate the fixed effect model using the specification

$$\frac{\Delta NII_{it}}{GDP_{it}} = r\left[\frac{CA_{it}}{GDP_{it}}\right] + \alpha_i + \gamma_{1i}t + \gamma_{2i}t^2 + \varepsilon_{it} \qquad (9)$$

In Figure 5 we plot the estimated return for the US economy as estimated from Equation (9). As can be seen it declined in the late 1980s (which explains why the trend in Meissner and Taylor turned out negative) but has been increasing in recent years. In fact the estimation since 1990 shows an almost linear and positively sloped trend.

Finally, a third alternative is to look at the time series properties of dark matter stock over recent years. This is an alternative way of presenting our results on the cumulative abnormal returns. We already argued that these were persistent, and this should translate in a relatively persistent stock of dark matter. We show this here with

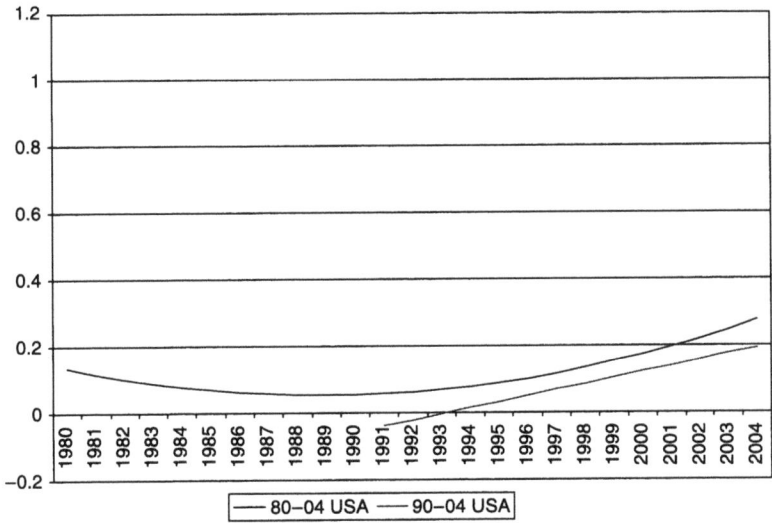

Figure 5. An estimate of the US return privilege

Notes: Predictions from the following specifications:

$80 - 04\,USA = Fixed\_effect_{US} + Trend\_effect^*_{US}(year - 1980) + Square\_trend\_effect^*_{US}(year - 1980)^2.$

$90 - 04\,USA = Fixed\_effect_{US} + Trend\_effect^*_{US}(year - 1990) + Square\_trend\_effect^*(year - 1990)^2.$

the aid of Figure 6, which benefits from the recent release of 2006 data that we have included in the figure. The stock stands now at over 40% of GDP. Since 1982 it has fallen only in 5 years and the largest drop, which took place in 1985, was barely of 1.6% of GDP. In short it would take an unprecedented deterioration of the value of dark matter to even approximate the net asset position that today worries analysts.[23] In recent years the accumulation has been very large, including 2006, during which the US economy added half a trillion in dark matter assets.

6. CONCLUSIONS AND FUTURE RESEARCH

In a nutshell our story is very simple. The net income paid by countries on their net foreign assets is affected by significant return differentials that originate in fundamental differences of these economies. In addition, payments on net foreign assets appear substantially more stable than what could be inferred from current account dynamics. Therefore when assets are valued using actual payments, net asset positions for Japan, Europe, the United States and the rest of the world seem fairly stable over time. In the specific case of the United States, which has drawn substantial attention due to its growing measured current account imbalances, we find that this return differential

---

[23] Econometrically one can show that the trend is positive standing at about 2.4% of GDP for the period 1982–2005, and strongly statistically significant (p-value = 0.00019).

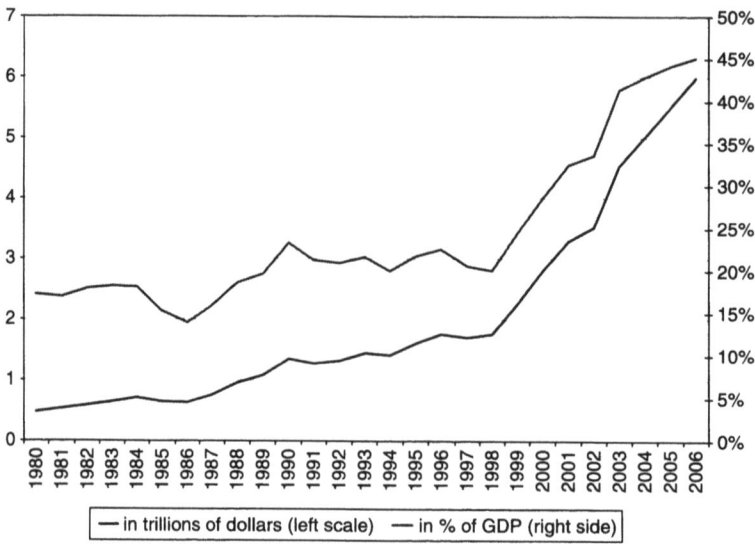

Figure 6. US stock of dark matter

Sources: Net foreign assets with dark matter: We take the yearly change in net income lines 13 + 30 of http://www.bea.gov/international/xls/table1.xls and divide it by 0.05. The result is subtracted from the current account (lines 1 + 18 + 35) of the same table. The resulting variable is accumulated over time. For net foreign assets with dark matter as percentage of GDP we divide by GDP from IFS, line 11199B.CZF. The last observation of the GDP (year 2006) is from WEO, subject code: NGDPD.

has grown in recent years allowing the United States to have a fairly stable net income on its foreign asset position. We think that this return differential should not be viewed as the result of US investors outsmarting investors in the rest of the world, or due to a stream of unprecedented good luck. Rather, it may well reflect some underlying fundamentals such as unaccounted export of know-how carried out by US corporations through their investments abroad, as well as the sale of insurance and liquidity services. The latter factors relate explicitly to characteristics of the United States that cannot be easily replicated elsewhere, and explains why the United States looks like a consistently smarter investor, making more money on its assets than it pays on its liabilities. For the United States as well as for other countries, it is these and other characteristics that explain the return differential. The discussion on the instability of global imbalance should focus on the sources of these return differentials: the stability of a given economy, its role as a cradle for ideas, or its ability to offer superior financial instruments. These issues have only recently taken centre stage in the discussion on global imbalances, whereas previously the debate had focused mostly on domestic savings or on speculating about the willingness of official creditors to finance the measured imbalances.

Dark matter also sheds a different light on the often discussed US savings puzzle. According to the official statistics, the United States appears as a profligate consumer with dismal savings. However, our numbers suggest that the US savings rate may be understated by the amount of dark matter it exports and the savings of the rest of the world overstated by the amount of dark matter it imports. To the extent that there are unreported capital gains, these could be included in the current account and in national accounts, increasing the savings rate and national income.[24] If we did so it could be argued that the United States may have been saving significantly more than accounted by official statistics. The accumulation of dark matter assets is perceived by households as a source of income, and the US consumer is appropriating these benefits and spending accordingly. The result is a consumption level that seems inconsistent with measured statistics but that is normal and sustainable given actual wealth.

Our computation of dark matter leaves open several interesting areas of research. As a starter, we believe it signals the importance to improve the estimates of asset stocks in the balance of payments. Alternatively, it would be interesting to look at dark matter by sector and region, to get a better sense of where it is being created and deployed. While we have worked with the statistical properties of aggregate dark matter, it could certainly be split into different components such as distinguishing the piece that comes from the yield gap from the rest or distinguishing the piece that is captured in official net foreign assets (the 'visible' part of dark matter) from the piece that is not. Our approach has also put the focus on net investment income which can also be analysed in other ways; for example splitting its changes in those arising from current account results, capital gains, increases in leverage and changes in interest rates. These alternative decompositions may lead to new insights. Likewise, while we have somewhat looked into the evolution of dark matter for the United States, and briefly for other countries, individual country cases, in particular if the different decompositions can be made, are likely to be different and equally interesting.

Globalization and financial integration have made asset positions all the more relevant. As the gross stock of assets and liabilities increases, valuation adjustments on these assets may overshadow the traditional measure of the current account as drivers of the net asset position. If return privileges permanently tend to stabilize net income across countries, they make current imbalances less worrisome than what could be inferred from a simple analysis of current account dynamics.

---

[24] According to Perozek and Reinsdorf (2002), national income is defined as originating from current production of goods and services, so it excludes capital gains. This is because with capital gains excluded from income, national saving becomes conceptually equal to domestic investment plus net foreign investment. According to these authors when making consumption decisions, households appear to treat capital gains differently from ordinary income, so a measure of income that includes capital gains would not relate as well to consumption as the National Income and Product Accounts (NIPA) concept of income. Also because capital gains tend to be volatile, if included, measures of income or saving would exhibit large fluctuations that would limit their usefulness. Alternatives to the definition of income that is used in the NIPAs are, of course, possible. Haig (1921) and Simons (1938), for example, define income as consumption plus change in wealth, which has the effect of including capital gains. At the opposite pole is Fisher (1906), who identifies income with consumption and treats it as a flow of services rendered by capital. If capital gains were to be included then measures of savings would have been under-reported in the case of the United States.

Discussion

Anne Sibert
Birkbeck College, London and CEPR

The profession is indebted to the authors: with their provocative first draft of this paper, with its snazzy title, they made balance of payments accounting trendy. They detail the splash that they made in their first footnote. The current version of the paper is far more sedate, but will still cause controversy.

The authors begin with a simple regression. A country's within-period budget constraint says that the country's net exports of goods and services minus net transfers made plus net investment income (including capital gains) equals the change in net asset holdings. Thus, multiplying the change in net asset holdings by the interest rate, which is assumed to be constant over time and across countries, and using the budget constraint, the authors write that the change in net investment income is equal to the sum of the interest rate multiplied by the current account, a 'privileges' term and a statistical error term (errors and omissions in the balance of payments multiplied by the interest rate). The privileges term comprises long-term transfers and unmeasured capital gains, both multiplied by the interest rate. Regressing the change in measured net investment on the current account and a fixed country term then yields an estimate of each country's 'privilege' and the interest rate.

What emerges from this exercise is that 'privileges' – both positive and negative – are relatively rare and that positive privileges are enjoyed by such countries as the United States, the United Kingdom and Malawi. Upon seeing this result, one must wonder about the specification. It is unlikely that the factors that ensure privilege for the United States and the United Kingdom are at work in Malawi. Indeed, one might surmise that Malawi – one of the poorest countries on earth – only looks as if it has 'privilege' because it is receiving sizeable debt relief. The authors could have avoided this confusion by removing the long-term transfers (which can be measured by the capital account) from the privilege term and putting them in with the current account term where they belong conceptually. This would also have eliminated the authors' need to include dummy terms for highly indebted poor countries later on in the paper when testing for the source of extraordinary returns.

Even if the apples and oranges problem were eliminated, one must have some qualms. First, errors and omissions are an unlikely statistical error term as they may well be unrecorded capital flows, say, the capital outflows associated with unrecorded investment income. Second, investment income in the balance of payments data is probably a rather noisy measure of actual investment income.

The authors go on to explain privilege as resulting from *dark matter*. It is typical to explain yield privileges as arising from two factors: valuation changes that are not measured as investment income in the balance of payments and differential rates of return. The authors' empirical measure of privilege appears to ignore the second factor. This is because their concept of dark matter enables them to explain what appear to be differential rates of return as actually resulting from valuation changes. Dark matter is an unrecorded service that is bundled with a financial asset and, when exported with the asset, generates a favourable valuation change.

As an example, suppose that the world rate of interest on risk-free consols is 5% and that a large country with an active secondary market for its consols finances its conventionally measured current account deficit of 100 units by issuing 100 units of consols that pay 4%. Using the dark matter concept the country is viewed as having exported dark matter in the form of liquidity services worth 20 units. Its corrected current account deficit is thus 80 units and the decrease in its net foreign assets is only 80 units – the present discounted value of its net interest payments at the world rate of interest of 5%. It is not viewed as getting a preferential interest rate; instead, the export of dark matter resulted in a reduction in the value of the outstanding asset.

The authors then return to their initial equation to measure black matter. Recall that this equation said that the change in net investment income equals the interest rate times the sum of the measured current account, unmeasured valuation changes, long-term transfers and errors and omissions. If it is then assumed that there are no errors and omissions and either that there are no long-term transfers or that long-term transfers are somehow conceptually the same as unmeasured valuation changes, it can then be stated that the change in net investment income is equal to the interest rate times the sum of the measured current account and the unmeasured valuation changes. If black matter is then identified as unmeasured valuation changes, we have the paper's Equation (7): black matter is the change in net investment income divided by the interest rate minus the current account. Measured this way, the United States, the United Kingdom and Switzerland are all exporters of dark matter. This is a bit heroic, however, as errors and omissions are large; long-term transfers are important for many countries and are not conceptually the same as black matter; net investment income is notoriously poorly measured; the choice of a 'world' interest rate is controversial.

This paper was probably motivated by the recent and puzzling experience of the United States. At the start of the 1980s the United States was a small net creditor. Between 1980 and today the United States has run cumulative measured current account deficits that dwarf its 1980s measured foreign net asset position. As a result one would expect that the United States would now be sizeably in debt and making large interest payments. Surprisingly, however, the United States still has measured positive net investment income. This puzzle has recently attracted much attention. Many researchers argue that the United States is 'privileged' in that it receives a higher return on its foreign assets than it pays on its liabilities. This is because – it is claimed – US liabilities are mostly low-return debt and US assets are mostly high return equity. More strikingly, Gourinchas and Rey (2006) argue that US investors earn higher returns on their cross-border returns than do foreigners within each asset class as well: US investors' returns on foreign equities and bonds were higher than foreigners' returns on US equities and bonds by 6.21% and 3.72% *per year*, respectively. The authors' claim that the US is an exporter of dark matter is consistent with this evidence.

Another view is provided in an interesting and careful new paper by Curcuru *et al.* (2007). They use data from actual bond and equity portfolios to argue that there has been – in fact – *no* return differential. This is because US equity markets have performed relatively well over the past 12 years and bond returns have been more or less equalized across the developed world.

Cédric Tille
Federal Reserve Bank of New York[25]

Introduction

A striking feature of the world economy is the ability of some countries, including the United States, to borrow large amounts from foreign investors without any corresponding increase in their net factor payments to the rest of the world. Understanding the drivers of this disconnect is relevant for assessing the sustainability of current imbalances, as the ability of some countries to borrow on favourable terms can reduce the need for a prompt re-balancing of current accounts.

The authors review the evidence on such return privileges across a broad range of countries, and assess the implications for the sustainability of current imbalances. The next section of my comments briefly reviews the main claims of the paper. The third section focuses on potential mismeasurements of FDI holdings highlighted by the authors. The fourth section presents a breakdown of the dark matter measure across various components, with different implications in terms of sustainability, and the final section concludes.

Return privileges and their determinants

The central point of the paper is reflected in Equation (4). In a context where all assets and liabilities earn a yield r we would expect the dynamics of the net investment income to parallel the current account. This is not the case in general, and Equation (4) includes a country-specific term α (a privilege) that captures the component of overall returns which does not take the form of income streams, i.e. are not reflected in yields. This privilege can consist of capital gains, insurance or liquidity premia, or exports that are not captured in the data.

The authors find that such privileges are relatively uncommon, and significant only for a handful of countries. Many of these are poor countries for which the privilege

---

[25] I thank Matthew Higgins and Tom Klitgaard for useful comments. The views expressed here are those of the author and are not necessarily reflective of views at the Federal Reserve Bank of New York or the Federal Reserve System.

reflects debt forgiveness. More importantly for global imbalances, several large countries show significant privileges. In particular, the net income payments by the United States and the United Kingdom are more favourable than what one would infer from their net foreign assets. In addition to documenting the presence of return privileges, the authors find that they are quite persistent and should be taken into account when assessing the sustainability of external imbalances.

The determinant of return privileges are assessed through an econometric exercise which shows three main points. First, HIPC countries benefit from favourable returns, reflecting the write-off of some of their debts. Second, OPEC countries face unfavourable returns, possibly reflecting a concentration of their external assets in low-yield securities. Third, industrialized countries with large FDI liabilities face unfavourable returns. This last point is somewhat puzzling. If FDI holdings entail a component that is not captured in the data, such as managerial skills from the foreign parent company, one would expect FDI recipients to face unfavourable returns. One would, however, expect this effect to be relatively more pronounced for non-industrialized countries, while the econometric analysis shows the opposite pattern, with the effect being insignificant among these countries.

Are FDI holdings substantially mismeasured?

In Section 3.1 the authors argue that US FDI assets and liabilities are not evaluated correctly by the Bureau of Economic Analysis. Specifically, they stress that FDI assets of US multinationals abroad should be valued using US equity prices instead of local prices, as the BEA does. Combining the ratio between book and market value of the S&P and the FDI asset at historical costs, the authors argue that the market value of US FDI assets abroad is nearly twice that reported by the BEA ($6.0 trillion at the end of 2004, compared to $3.3 trillion from the BEA, Table 5). The difference between the two measures accounts for the bulk of the overall 'dark matter' assets estimates presented in Table 10.

This large gap mostly reflects the particular method chosen by the authors, which can lead to a large overestimation. The BEA presents three measures of FDI assets and liabilities: historical cost, current cost and market value, with the difference between historical cost and market value reflecting the revaluation of the equity component of the investment. As pointed out by the authors, the BEA uses foreign stock prices to estimate the market value of US FDI assets, and using US stock prices could lead to different results. One can, however, assess this point in a simple way directly from the BEA data. Taking the ratio between market value and historical cost for FDI liabilities gives the adjustment by the BEA that reflects US stock prices. One can then apply this ratio from the liability side to the historical value of FDI assets in order to compute an alternative market value.

The resulting estimates of FDI assets are shown in Figure 7. The BEA data at historical cost and market value are represented by the dotted and solid lines respectively

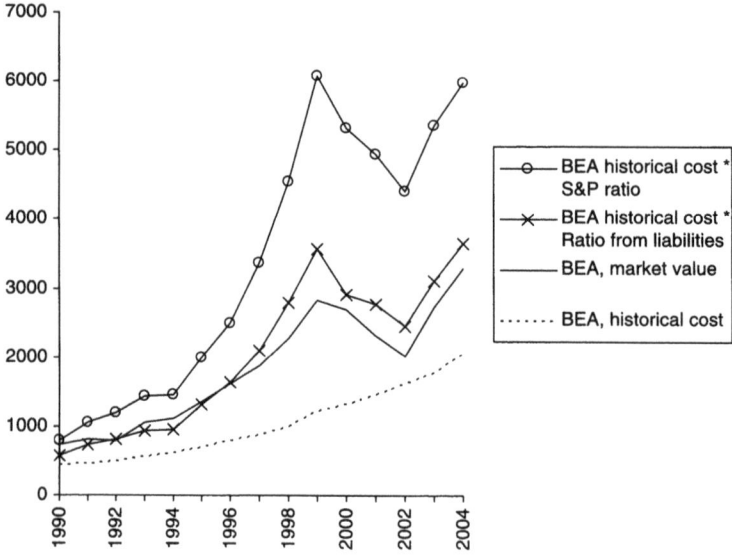

Figure 7. FDI assets ($ billion)

(columns a and b in Table 5). The crossed line shows the estimates computed by multiplying the assets at historical costs by the ratio of market value to historical costs from the liability side. The rounded line shows the authors' estimates multiplying the assets at historical costs by the S&P ratio of market to book value (column d in Table 5). Using the S&P ratio clearly leads to estimates that are much larger than the ones obtained from using the ratio from FDI liabilities, with the latter raising the estimate of FDI assets at market value by only 10% in 2004. The large adjustment computed by the authors in Table 5 should therefore be taken with caution, as it does not merely reflect the use of stock prices in different countries.

In addition to computing an alternative estimate of FDI assets at market value, we can derive the corresponding estimate for FDI liabilities by multiplying liabilities at historical costs by the ratio of market value to historical costs from the asset side. Doing so leads to a net FDI position that is somewhat larger than from the BEA data at market value, although the difference is moderate, averaging 3% of GDP since 1990. While measuring FDI holdings is a delicate exercise due to the lack of market prices, the claim by the authors that the BEA measures are substantially off the mark due to the particular equity prices used is questionable.

How sustainable is dark matter?

In Section 4, the authors present a capitalized measure of the return privileges, and refer to the difference between this measure and the cumulated current accounts as 'dark matter'. Specifically, a country with positive dark matter has a capitalized value of net income payments that is more favourable than what one would infer from its past current account deficits. The authors then use this measure to argue that current imbalances are less worrisome than suggested by the current account themselves. In particular, they argue that the large current account deficits run by the United States have been offset by exports of dark matter.

A closer look at the evidence, however, suggests that sustainability is more of a concern than the authors argue. The capitalized measure of net income payments, NFA^{DM}, is computed as:[26]

$$NFA_{t-1}^{DM} = \frac{1}{r} NII_t$$

Contrasting this measure with the official net international investment position, we write:

$$NFA_{t-1}^{DM} - (A_{t-1} - L_{t-1}) = \frac{r_t^{AVG} - r}{r}(A_{t-1} - L_{t-1}) + \frac{1}{2}\frac{r_t^D}{r}(A_{t-1} + L_{t-1})$$

$$r_t^{AVG} = \frac{1}{2}(r_t^A + r_t^L) \quad r_t^D = r_t^A - r_t^L$$

where A_{t-1} and L_{t-1} are gross external assets and liabilities at the end of period $t-1$, r_t^A and r_t^L are the yields on assets and liabilities in period t. The above relation shows that the gap between the capitalized measure and the net international position reflects two terms. The first is a cyclical component which captures the difference between the average yield on assets and liabilities and the constant discount factor (5%). Consider the case of a country that is a net debtor $(A_{t-1} - L_{t-1} < 0)$ and faces a low interest rate $(r_t^{AVG} - r < 0)$. The low rate reduces its stream of payments to foreign investors, as well as the capitalized value of these payments, which translates into positive dark matter $(NFA_{t-1}^{DM} > A_{t-1} - L_{t-1})$. The second term reflects the yield differential between assets and liabilities. If a country earns a larger yield on its assets, its net interest payment is more favourable than if the yield was the same on both assets and liabilities.

In addition to these two factors, the dark matter measure computed by the authors also reflects the gap between the net international investment position and the cumulated current account. This gap stems from valuation effects that have received a growing attention in the literature[27] and capture the impact of fluctuations in exchange rates and asset prices on the value of assets and liabilities. Such effects are sizeable as can be seen from Figures 3a and 3b in the paper. In particular, the US net international investment position has been stable in recent years (Figure 3b) despite the large current account deficits (Figure 3a).

Breaking the dark matter between the cyclical component, the yield differential component, and the valuation gain component, is relevant in assessing sustainability.

---

[26] I use a different timing convention than the author, with yields in year t combining income streams in year t and positions at the end of year $t-1$.
[27] See for instance Gourinchas and Rey (2005), Higgins et al. (2007), Lane and Milesi-Ferretti (2006b).

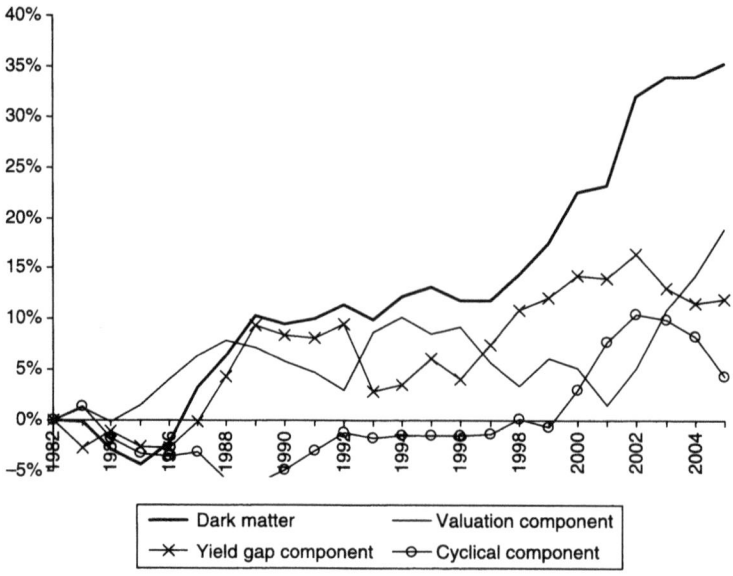

Figure 8. Decomposition of US dark matter (% GDP)

The first component is by definition temporary. The second component is likely to be more durable given the persistence of yield differentials. The final component falls in between: while valuation effects have favoured the US in recent years, the underlying movements in exchange rates and asset prices could prove short-lived.

Figure 8 shows the results for the United States. The decomposition across the three components is computed separately for FDI and other holdings, as the yield gap is concentrated in the former (Higgins et al., 2007).[28] The thick line shows the stock of dark matter, corresponding to Figure 6 in the paper. The valuation component is represented by the thin line, while the cyclical and yield gap components are given by the rounded and crossed lines, respectively. Figure 8 shows that the increase in dark matter since 2000 has been driven by valuation gains, reflecting the depreciation of the dollar, and the cyclical component, reflecting the low level of interest rates. By contrast the yield gap component, which is likely to be the most sustainable, has been steady. While the United States has been able to export dark matter over the last 5 years, this reflects factors which could well prove temporary, hence the sustainability of the current situation is more fragile than the authors argue. A similar analysis can be conducted for the United Kingdom (Figure 9) which also benefits from a return privilege, again showing a sizeable role for temporary factors.[29]

---

[28] The estimates of the cyclical and yield differential components are sensitive to the extent of disaggregation. Computing them directly on total holdings shows a larger role for the yield differential.

[29] As for the United States the computations are done separately for FDI and other holdings, as the yield gap is concentrated in FDI (Whitaker, 2006).

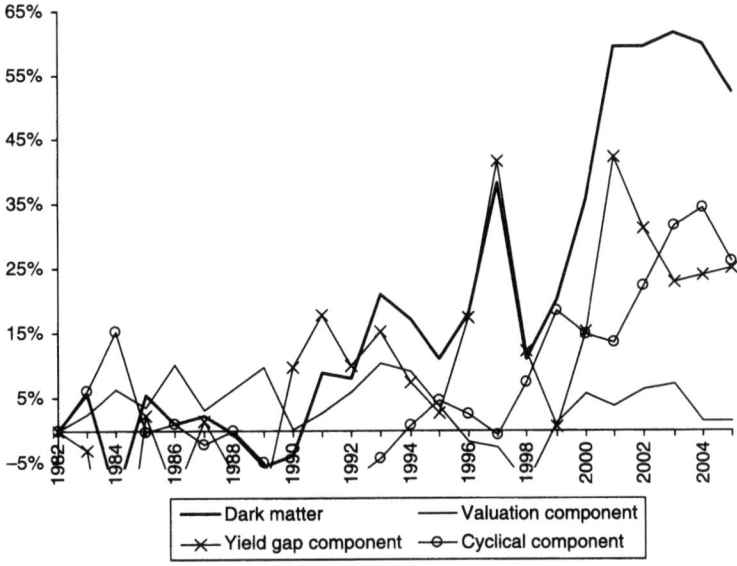

Figure 9. Decomposition of UK dark matter (% GDP)

Conclusion

The paper presents a broad review of the discrepancy between current accounts and net factor payments in many countries, and documents the existence of a privilege in several countries. This privilege suggests that the concerns about the sustainability of current imbalances could be tempered, as these imbalances have not fed into large payments burdens for the debtor countries. While ignoring return privileges could lead to an overtly pessimistic view of the current situation, as the paper argues, one should be careful not to draw an overtly optimistic view, as several factors that played a role in recent years could prove temporary.

Panel discussion

All meeting participants were intrigued by the paper's approach and results, but most Panel members felt that the version presented and discussed in New York drew excessively strong conclusions from insufficient data and unclear computations. The extensively revised version published in this issue heeds many of their critical comments and suggestions.

Gian Maria Milesi-Ferretti focused his comments on data definitions and statistical procedures. In particular he questioned whether and how one should value FDI assets of foreigners in the United States using indicators from the country of ownership's stock market, and thought different sources of data of different quality should all be analysed in order to obtain a complete picture of foreign positions. While FDI data can be highly unreliable, statistics computed from portfolio surveys are generally very accurate. He pointed out that net foreign asset and net foreign income dynamics are readily explained by valuation effects over the last few years, and that past evidence is difficult to extrapolate in an environment of increasingly efficient financial integration. Philip Lane felt that a new 'dark matter' concept may or may not be needed to understand the data. Rate of return differentials and measurement problems are well understood to exist, and can be analysed without resorting to dark matter. Among measurement problems, tax-related reasons why some investment income may be reported as service income may be particularly important. He also pointed out that the BEA valuation of greenfield FDI investment is not really based on local stock market values.

Paul Krugman agreed that it would be important to understand very clearly how BEA actually computes the relevant statistics. At a more substantive level, he felt that the resilience of US net foreign investment income need not be relevant to sustainability concerns. In the last few years, positive net investment income has resulted from the decline of the dollar exchange rate and the relative strong performance of non-US stock markets. Neither of these are reasons to be cheerful as regards the strength of the US economy and the sustainability of its external position. From this perspective, 'dark matter' – while potentially useful as a conceptual measure – may give a false sense of comfort. Matthew Higgins noted that in recent cosmological theories 'dark energy' plays a role, and jokingly wondered whether that concept may also be applied to international financial issues. He pointed out that to ensure sustainability of a persistent trade deficit in the order of 6% of GDP, flows of FDI would have to amount to perhaps 4% of GDP, an unrealistic and never observed order of magnitude for the United States.

Richard Portes listed five reasons why he thought the concept of dark matter misleading and potentially dangerous. First, the authors' story rests on highly implausible assumptions. Second, the computations' results give a dangerous sense of comfort. Third, the BEA income flow data are faulty in many respects. Fourth, the source of excess net returns on US investment is unclear. Finally, and most importantly, the computations assume a constant rate of return, but returns on the US dollar are very likely to be falling. As once happened to the pound sterling, the US dollar is losing international currency status. Its increasing substitutability by other currencies, such as the euro, has to erode rate of return differentials: any 'dark matter' should be disappearing, and this is an important reason to be worried about the sustainability of US deficits. Federico Sturzenegger replied that the pound sterling's yield advantage declined only slightly over a protracted period of time, until World War I. The US yield differential has been remarkably stable for decades. It may well persist if the underlying factors do, and the data indicate that it does persist.

APPENDIX A

All countries

Albania, Angola, Argentina, Australia, Austria, Bahrain, Bangladesh, Benin, Bolivia, Botswana, Brazil, Bulgaria, Burkina Faso, Cambodia, Cameroon, Canada, Chile, China, P.R.: Mainland, Colombia, Congo, Republic of, Costa Rica, Côte d'Ivoire, Cyprus, Denmark, Dominican Republic, Ecuador, Egypt, El Salvador, Estonia, Ethiopia, Fiji, Finland, France, Gabon, Germany, Ghana, Greece, Guatemala, Haiti, Honduras, Hungary, Iceland, India, Indonesia, Iran, Islamic Republic of, Ireland, Israel, Italy, Jamaica, Japan, Jordan, Kenya, Korea, Kuwait, Lao People's Dem. Rep, Libya, Madagascar, Malawi, Malaysia, Mali, Malta, Mauritius, Mexico, Morocco, Mozambique, Myanmar, Namibia, Nepal, the Netherlands, New Zealand, Nicaragua, Niger, Nigeria, Norway, Oman, Pakistan, Panama, Papua New Guinea, Paraguay, Peru, Philippines, Poland, Portugal, Romania, Rwanda, Saudi Arabia, Senegal, Singapore, South Africa, Spain, Sri Lanka, Sudan, Swaziland, Sweden, Switzerland, Syrian Arab Republic, Tanzania, Thailand, Togo, Trinidad and Tobago, Tunisia, Turkey, Uganda, United Kingdom, United States, Uruguay, Venezuela, Rep. Bol., Yemen, Republic of, Zimbabwe.

Industrial countries

Australia, Austria, Canada, Cyprus, Denmark, Finland, France, Germany, Greece, Iceland, Ireland, Israel, Italy, Japan, Korea, the Netherlands, New Zealand, Norway, Portugal, Singapore, Spain, Sweden, Switzerland, United Kingdom, United States.

Emerging countries

Argentina, Brazil, Bulgaria, Chile, China, P.R.: Mainland, Colombia, Côte d'Ivoire, Dominican Republic, Ecuador, Egypt, El Salvador, Greece, Hungary, Korea, Malaysia, Mexico, Morocco, Nigeria, Pakistan, Panama, Peru, Philippines, Poland, South Africa, Thailand, Tunisia, Turkey, Uruguay, Venezuela, Rep. Bol.

OPEC countries

Ecuador, Gabon, Indonesia, Iran, Islamic Republic of, Kuwait, Libya, Nigeria, Saudi Arabia, Venezuela, Rep. Bol.

HIPC countries

Benin, Bolivia, Burkina Faso, Cameroon, Ethiopia, Ghana, Honduras, Madagascar, Malawi, Mali, Mozambique, Nicaragua, Niger, Rwanda, Senegal, Tanzania, Uganda.

APPENDIX B

Variable name	Description	Source
Business Cycle	Deviation from a HP trend of gdpusd	Uses gdpusd.
CA	Current account	IFS, code: 78ALDZF available at http://ifs.apdi.net/imf/ImfBrowser.aspx
Research & Development	Research and development expenditure as a percentage of GDP	WDI, average of available data for each country
Corporate Tax Rate	Corporate income tax rate	KPMG
Dummy HIPC	Dummy for HIPC members	See Appendix A for list of countries
Dummy OPEC	Dummy for OPEC members	See Appendix A for list of countries
emerging	Dummy for emerging countries	See Appendix A for list of countries
FDI assets	FDI assets in millions of current dollars	Lane and Milesi-Ferretti database available at http://www.imf.org/external/pubs/cat/longres.cfm?sk=18942.0
FDI liabilities	FDI liabilities in millions of current dollars	Lane and Milesi-Ferretti database available at http://www.imf.org/external/pubs/cat/longres.cfm?sk=18942.0
gdpusd	Gross domestic product of each country in current dollars	WEO, Subject Code: NGDPD, available at http://www.imf.org/external/pubs/ft/weo/2006/02/data/download.aspx.
gdpwrd	World gross domestic product in current dollars	WEO, Subject Code: NGDPD, available at http://www.imf.org/external/pubs/ft/weo/2006/02/data/download.aspx.
indust	Dummy for industrial countries	
ner	Nominal exchange rate month in December	IFS, market rates available at http://ifs.apdi.net/imf/ImfBrowser.aspx.
Δ% of nominal exchange rate	Change in nominal exchange rate December–December	Percentage change in NER
Net_Income	Net income = Income credit − Income debit	IFS: code of income credit: 78AGDZF, code of income debit: 78AHDZF, available http://ifs.apdi.net/imf/ImfBrowser.aspx
Output volatility	5 year centred standard deviation of gdpusd.	Uses gdpusd.
rgdp	Real GDP	IFS, code: 99BVPZF available at http://ifs.apdi.net/imf/ImfBrowser.aspx
Rule of Law	Rule of law	Rule of law, includes several indicators that measure the extent to which agents have confidence in and abide by the rules of society. (Source: Kaufmann et al. (2002)).

REFERENCES

Blanchard, O., F. Giavazzi and F. Sa (2005). 'The US current account and the dollar', NBER Working Paper No. 11137, 1–65.
Buiter, W. (2006). 'Dark matter or cold fusion?' Goldman Sachs, Global Economics Paper No. 136.
Caballero, R., E. Farhi and P.O. Gourinchas (2005). 'An equilibrium model of "global imbalances" and low interest rates', mimeo, MIT, September.
Chari, A., P. Ouimet and L. Tesar (2007). 'Observable dark matter? The net present value of FDI flows to emerging markets', mimeo, University of Michigan.
Cline, W. (2005). *The United States as a Debtor Nation*, Institute for International Economics, Washington DC.
Cooper, R. (2005). 'Living with global imbalances', *IIE Policy Brief*, 28(6), 615–27.
Corrado, C., C. Hulten and D. Sichel (2006). 'Intangible capital and economic growth', No. 24, Federal Reserve Board, Washington.
Curcuru, S.E., T. Dvorak and F.E. Warnock (2007). 'The stability of large external imbalances: The roles of returns differentials', NBER Working Paper 13074.
Dooley, M., D. Folkerts-Landau and P. Garber (2004). 'The revised Bretton Woods system', *International Journal of Finance and Economics*, 9(4), 307–13.
Economist, The (2006). 'America's dark materials', January.
Eichengreen, B. (2006). 'Global imbalances: The new economy, the dark matter, the savvy investor, and the standard analysis', *Journal of Policy Modeling*, 28(6), 645–52.
Engel, C. and J. Rogers (2006). 'The US current account deficit and the expected share of world output', NBER Working Paper, No. 11921.
Fisher, I. (1906). *The Nature of Capital and Income*, Macmillan, New York.
Fixler, D., M. Reinsdorf and G. Smith (2003). 'Measuring the services of commercial banks in the NIPAs', *Survey of Current Business*, 83(9), 33–44.
Frankel, J. (1982). 'In search of the exchange risk premium: A six-currency test assuming mean variance optimization', *Journal of International Money and Finance*, 1, 255–74.
Gongloff, M. (2006). 'Is dark matter in the deficit?', *The Wall Street Journal*, February.
Gourinchas, P.O. and H. Rey (2005). 'International Financial Adjustment', NBER Working Paper, No. 11155.
— (2006). 'From world banker to world venture capitalist: US external adjustment and the exorbitant privilege', in R. Clarida (ed.), *G7 Current Account Imbalances: Sustainability and Adjustment*, University of Chicago Press, Chicago.
Gros, D. (2006a). 'Foreign investment in the US (I): Disappearing in a black hole?', CEPS Working Document No. 242.
— (2006b). 'Foreign investment in the US (II): Being taken to the cleaners?', CEPS Working Document No. 243.
Haig, R.M. (1921). *The Federal Income Tax*, Columbia University Press, New York.
Hausmann, R. and F. Sturzenegger (2006). 'Why the US current account is sustainable', *International Finance*, 9(2), 223–40.
— (2007). 'The valuation of hidden assets in foreign transactions: Why "dark matter" matters', *Business Economics*, 42(1), 29–35.
Higgins, M., T. Klitgaard and C. Tille (2005). 'The income implications of rising US international liabilities', *Current Issues in Economics and Finance*, 11(12), 1–9, Federal Reserve Bank of New York.
— (2007). 'Borrowing without debt? Understanding the US international investment position', *Business Economics*, 42(1), 17–27.
Ju, J. and S.J. Wei (2006). 'A solution to two paradoxes of international capital flow', IMF Working Paper No. 06/178.
Kaufmann, D., K. Aart and P. Zoido-Lobaton (2002). 'Governance matters II: Updated indicators for 2000–01', Working Papers – Governance, Corruption, Legal Reform 2772, World Bank.
Kitchen, J. (2006). 'Sharecroppers or shrewd capitalists? Projections of the US current account, international income flows and net international debt', mimeo, Office of Management and Budget.
Kozlow, R. (2002). 'Valuing the direct investment position in US economic accounts', available at http://www.bea.gov/bea/papers/Kozlow-Val.pdf

Kugler, P. and B. Weder (2004). 'International portfolio holdings and Swiss franc returns', mimeo, University of Mainz.
— (2005). 'Why are returns on Swiss franc assets so low? Rare events may solve the puzzle', *Applied Economics Quarterly*, 51(3), 231–46.
Krugman, P. (2006). 'Trade deficit', *The New York Times*, April.
Landefeld, S. and A. Lawson (1991). 'Valuation of the US net international investment position', *Survey of Current Business*, 71, 40–49.
Lane, P. and G.M. Milesi-Ferretti (2001). 'The external wealth of nations: Measures of foreign assets and liabilities for industrial and developing countries', *Journal of International Economics*, 55, 263–94.
— (2006a). 'The external wealth of nations Mark II: Revised and extended estimates of foreign assets and liabilities, 1970–2004', IMF Working Paper, No. 06/69.
— (2006b). 'A global perspective on external positions', in R.H. Clarida (ed.), *G-7 Current Account Imbalances: Sustainability and Adjustment*, University of Chicago Press, Chicago.
Lawrence, R. and J. Lara (2006). 'Trade performance and industrial policy', mimeo, Kennedy School of Government.
Longstaff, F.A. (2004). 'The flight-to-liquidity premium in U.S. Treasury bond prices', *The Journal of Business (University of Chicago Press)*, 77(3), 511–26.
Mandel, M. (2006). 'Why the US economy is stronger than you think', *Business Week*, May.
Mataloni, R. (2000). 'An examination of the low rates of return of foreign-owned US companies', *Survey of Current Business*, 80(3), 55–73.
McGrattan, E.R. and E.C. Prescott (2006). 'Unmeasured investment and the 1990s US hours boom', *Federal Reserve Bank of Minneapolis Staff Report*, No. 369, June.
McKelvey, E. (2005). 'Dark matter in US international transactions?', Goldman Sachs Economics Research, US Economic Analysis, No. 05/50, December.
Meissner, C. and A.M. Taylor (2006). 'Losing our marbles in the new century? The great rebalancing in historical perspective', NBER Working Paper, No. 12580.
Mendoza, E., V. Quadrini and V. Rios Rull (2006). 'Financial integration, financial deepness and global imbalances', mimeo, University of Maryland.
Milesi-Ferretti, G.M. (2006). 'How much progress has been made in addressing global imbalances?', *World Economic Outlook*, April, 28–31.
Obstfeld, M. and K. Rogoff (2005a). 'The unsustainable US current account revisited', NBER Working Paper No. 10864, Cambridge, MA.
— (2005b). 'Global current account imbalances and exchange rate adjustments', *Brookings Papers on Economic Activity*, 1, 67–123.
Parente, S. and E. Prescott (2002). *Barriers to Riches*, MIT Press, Cambridge, MA.
Perozek, M. and M. Reinsdorf (2002). 'Alternative measures of personal saving', *Survey of Current Business*, 82(4), 13–24.
Roubini, N. and B. Setser (2004). 'The US as a net debtor: The sustainability of the US external imbalances' (http://pages.stern.nyu.edu/~nroubini/papers/Roubini-Setser-US-External-Imbalances.pdf)
Simard, E. and E. Boulay (2006). 'Market valuation of equity in the international investment position: Canada's experience', BOPCOM-06/12 Nineteenth Meeting of the IMF Committee on Balance of Payments Statistics.
Simons, H.C. (1938). *Personal Income Taxation: The Definition of Income as a Problem of Fiscal Policy*, University of Chicago Press, Chicago.
Ulan, M. and W. Dewald (1989). 'The US net international investment position: Misstated and misunderstood', in J. Dorn and W. Niskanen (eds.), *Dollars, Deficits and Trade*, Kluwer Academic, Norwell, MA.
Wall Street Journal, The (2006). Editorial, 'Trade deficit disorder', March.
Whitaker, S. (2006). 'The UK international investment position', *Bank of England Quarterly Bulletin*, Q3, 290–96.

Europe and global imbalances

SUMMARY

Although Europe in the aggregate is not a major contributor to global current account imbalances, its trade and financial linkages with the rest of the world mean that it will still be affected by a shift in the current configuration of external deficits and surpluses. We assess the macroeconomic impact on Europe of global current account adjustment under alternative scenarios, emphasizing both trade and financial channels. Finally, we consider heterogeneous exposure across individual European economies to external adjustment shocks.

— *Philip R. Lane and Gian Maria Milesi-Ferretti*

Europe and global imbalances

Philip R. Lane and Gian Maria Milesi-Ferretti
Institute for International Integration Studies, Trinity College Dublin and CEPR; International Monetary Fund and CEPR

1. INTRODUCTION

Economic globalization has been one of the major trends shaping the world economy in recent years. On the real side, international trade has expanded substantially, with the emerging Asian countries in general, and China in particular, taking a prominent role. On the financial side, international capital flows have increased even more rapidly than product trade, leading to a remarkable rise in cross-border holdings of assets and liabilities. These developments imply tighter real and financial linkages across countries and regions, with attendant implications for the transmission of shocks and co-movements in macroeconomic variables.

Increased international trade and capital mobility have the potential to provide economic benefits through a more efficient international allocation of production and capital and greater cross-border risk diversification. They may also have facilitated the financing of larger and more persistent current account imbalances – more

---

We have benefited from the comments of the referees and the editors and participants in seminars at the ECB, European University Institute, Banca d'Italia and the University of Vigo, plus conversations with Steve Kamin and Frank Warnock. We thank Vahagn Galstyan and Agustin Benetrix for excellent research assistance, and Sonali Jain-Chandra and Ivanna Vladkova-Hollar for their help in undertaking the simulations on valuation effects. Lane also gratefully acknowledges the financial support of the Irish Research Council on Humanities and Social Sciences (IRCHSS) and the HEA-PRTLI grant to the Institute for International Integration Studies. The views expressed here are the authors' only and do not represent those of the IMF. The Managing Editor in charge of this paper was Philippe Martin.

specifically, unprecedented US trade and current account deficits and sizeable surpluses in emerging Asia and oil exporters. While there is a lively debate on how long trade and current account imbalances of this size can persist, it is clear that a potential sharp correction of such imbalances is a source of risk that, in an era of financial globalization, stretches beyond those countries that must reduce external gaps and also extend to those countries that are linked through trade and finance to the adjusting economies. Accordingly, our goal in this paper is to assess the potential impact on Europe of a reduction in external imbalances across the world's major economic regions.

Although the euro area – and Europe, taken in the aggregate – are in approximate external balance, a reduction in global current account imbalances could still have a major impact on the European economy. A contraction in the US deficit and the surpluses run by Asia and oil exporters would involve a shift in the global distribution of expenditure, with attendant implications for exchange rates and the level and composition of production in the major economic regions. European economies will be affected by these external developments through an array of trade and financial linkages, with potential implications for macroeconomic policy, especially in the event of a sudden movement in the external environment.

To focus our analysis, we examine a range of alternative scenarios by which global current account adjustment may take place. We consider three alternatives: a 'soft landing' scenario in which trade and current account imbalances are reduced gradually, and no major policy change occurs; a 'disruptive' scenario in which the United States ceases to attract large-scale capital inflows at a low interest rate; and a 'policy action' scenario in which adjustment is facilitated by policy changes in the major economic regions. We explore these scenarios using the Global Economic Model (GEM), a micro-founded dynamic general equilibrium model of the world economy developed at the International Monetary Fund.

A particular innovation in our contribution is to analyse the role of both trade and financial linkages in the adjustment process. The acceleration of financial globalization in recent years means that gross holdings of external assets and liabilities are now much larger than in previous adjustment episodes, such as the turnaround in the US current account deficit in the late 1980s. In turn, as pointed out in a number of recent contributions, this implies that changes in exchange rates and asset prices will have significant repercussions on the value of countries' external assets and liabilities (the so-called 'valuation effects'), in addition to the effects operating through the trade balance and current account.

From a European perspective, the increase in holdings of foreign assets and liabilities in recent years means that the transmission mechanism by which external adjustment in the United States affects Europe has changed. In particular, in addition to trade linkages and net capital flows, the balance sheets of European firms, governments and households will be affected by the changes in exchange rates and asset prices that are likely to accompany the adjustment process. In light of the fact that scenarios involving a narrowing in the US trade deficit are characterized by a depreciation of the US dollar in real effective terms, we quantify the net dollar exposure of the major economic regions and provide estimates of the implications of dollar adjustment for the value of their external holdings.

After considering the implications of external adjustment for Europe as a whole, and the euro area in particular, we turn our focus to individual European national economies. In particular, we seek to ascertain which economies may be most affected by changes in international trade patterns and in international financial markets that may accompany current account adjustment. To do so, we examine differences across the individual national economies in their trade and financial linkages vis-à-vis the United States, as well as in their external positions: while aggregate Europe is in broad balance, some national economies are running deficits that are proportionally bigger than the US deficit, while others are major surplus countries.

The main findings of our analysis are as follows. First, there has been a shift in the pattern of co-movement between the US and European external positions. While European and US current account balances have historically been negatively correlated, the correlation has been positive over the last decade – with the US deficit largely financed by Asia and, in recent years, the oil-exporting nations. On the other hand, the negative co-movement between the net foreign asset positions of Europe and the United States has become stronger over the last decade, reflecting the increased importance of the valuation channel and the financial impact of currency movements.

Second, the weakening of the US dollar likely to accompany a reduction in the US trade deficit would have a non-negligible negative wealth effect on European investors, by reducing the value of their dollar-denominated claims. However, this effect would likely be smaller than in China and Japan, that hold larger net dollar positions. Third, there is considerable heterogeneity across Europe (and within the euro area) both in terms of net positions and bilateral financial holdings in the United States. Accordingly, to the extent that a contraction in global imbalances accompanied by a shift in the global financial environment (e.g. an increase in global interest rates) and in US-specific asset and currency values, this may have differential wealth and cyclical effects across Europe.

This work relates to several recent contributions on the international adjustment process.[1] On the empirical side, Lane and Milesi-Ferretti (2001, 2005, 2006, 2007b) have shown the importance of valuation effects in explaining the evolution of net foreign asset positions for a large number of countries. In relation to the United States, Gourinchas and Rey (2005) have highlighted the role played by the valuation channel in stabilizing the external position, while Tille (2003) and Gourinchas and Rey (2007) have developed a detailed sectoral decomposition of the sources of valuation effects. A particularly valuable contribution for our purposes is Tille (2005), who constructs estimates of the currency composition of the international balance sheet of the United States.

---

[1] The 2006 report by the European Economic Advisory Group provides an excellent overview.

In terms of theoretical contributions, our model simulations closely follow Faruqee *et al.* (2007). Obstfeld and Rogoff (2000, 2005, 2007) have developed a simple analytical framework that allows them to quantify the scale of exchange rate adjustment associated with a closing of current account balances. Of these, Obstfeld and Rogoff (2005) is the closest to our own work in specifying a three-region model of the world economy and allowing for the operation of the valuation channel. Cavallo and Tille (2006) have extended this contribution by allowing for gradual adjustment in the external account, with the pace of current account adjustment influenced by valuation dynamics. Blanchard *et al.* (2005) also incorporate the valuation channel in a portfolio-balance model that allows for imperfect substitutability of assets across countries.

The structure of the rest of the paper is as follows. Section 2 describes the evolution of global current account balances and net foreign asset positions in recent years, with special attention paid to the co-movements between the European and US external positions. In addition, it documents the scale and pattern of international trade and financial integration, highlighting in particular the bilateral linkages between Europe and the United States. Section 3 reports results from a number of adjustment scenarios produced by the GEM, which include a correction for the role played by the valuation channel. The impact of heterogeneity across individual European economies is discussed in Section 4. Finally, we discuss the options available to policymakers in minimizing the risk of a hard-landing scenario and offer some conclusions in Section 5.

2. EUROPE'S EXTERNAL POSITION IN A GLOBAL CONTEXT

In this section we consider the evolution of the current account balance of European countries taken as a group, as they relate to global trends, as well as the degree of trade and financial integration of Europe with the rest of the world in general, and the United States in particular.

2.1. Current account balances: stylized facts

The much-debated topic of global current account imbalances is usefully summarized by Figure 1, which plots the current account balances of Europe and the United States together with those of countries/regions that are running significant current account surpluses. Current account balances are expressed in relation to world GDP, so as to provide a perspective on their global relevance. The figure shows that surpluses in emerging Asia, Japan, and more recently oil exporters have been the main counterpart to the widening US current account deficit. In contrast, there has been broad balance in the current account of Europe (and the euro area) throughout the period.

In order to understand the likelihood that these trends will continue and the possible consequences of their reversal, it is useful to relate them to the evolution of current account balances over a longer time period, focusing more specifically on

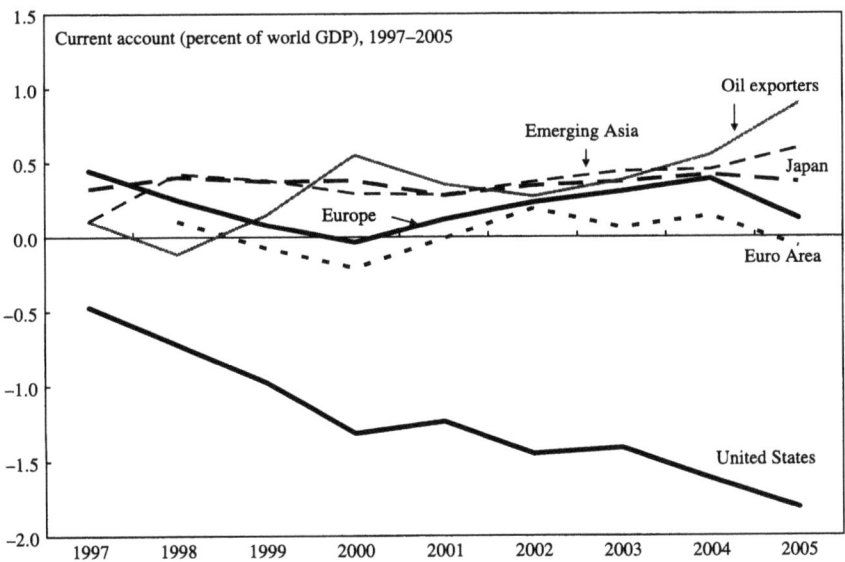

Figure 1. Current account balances, major regions, 1997–2005 (percentage of world GDP)

Notes: Emerging Asia group includes: Hong Kong S.A.R., India, Indonesia, Korea, Malaysia, Philippines, Singapore, Taiwan province of China, and Thailand. The Europe group includes the 12 euro area countries plus Denmark, Iceland, Norway, Sweden, Switzerland, and the United Kingdom. The oil exporters' group includes: Algeria, Angola, Azerbaijan, Bahrain, Republic of Congo, Ecuador, Equatorial Guinea, Gabon, Iran, Kuwait, Libya, Nigeria, Oman, Qatar, Russia, Saudi Arabia, Syrian Arab Republic, Turkmenistan, United Arab Emirates, Venezuela, and Yemen.

Source: IMF, Balance of Payments Statistics.

Europe and the United States. Accordingly, Figure 2 plots the current account and net foreign asset positions over 1970–2006 for aggregate Europe (with the euro area also shown) and the United States, scaled by their respective GDP levels. Over the entire period, there is clearly a negative co-movement between the current accounts of the two regions; this is especially clear during the mid-1980s, when the European current account surplus grew in mirror image to the deterioration of the US external balance, reflecting in particular the sizeable current account surplus in Germany. However, the last decade has seen a noticeable shift – the late 1990s saw the United States and Europe simultaneously undergo a deterioration in the current account balance, with positive co-movement also seen during the 2001 growth slowdown and again in 2005–2006. While the correlation in current account balances was –0.68 during 1970–95, it has been positive at 0.40 during 1996–2006 – a striking reversal.

Figure 3 provides an additional perspective by charting the current account balance of the aggregate of the United States and Europe. It shows that the collective deficit has never been as large as the current value – around 3 percent of GDP in 2006, twice as much as in the mid-1980s – reflecting the large deficit in the United States. Adding Japan to the picture does not change the main message, despite the strong negative co-movement between its current account balance and the one of the

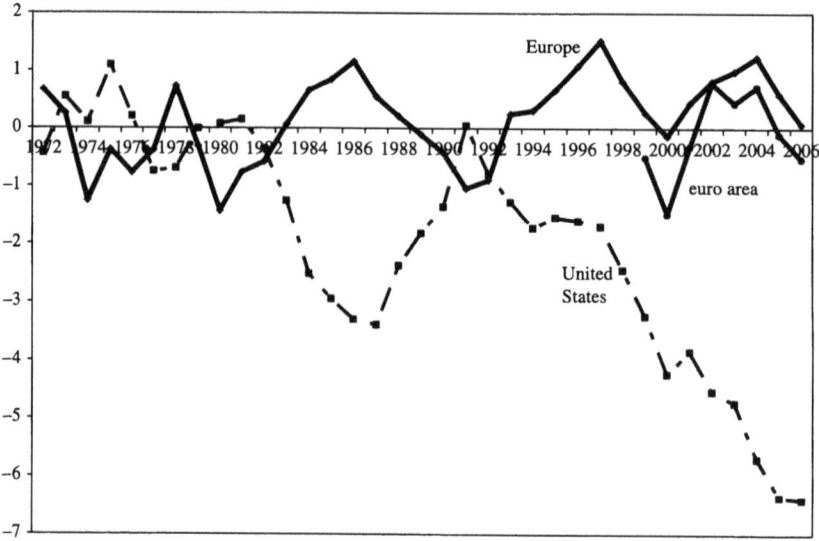

Figure 2. Current account balances: Europe versus the United States (percentage of GDP)

Notes: The chart depicts current account balances in percent of each region's GDP. Aggregate Europe includes the 12 euro area countries plus Denmark, Iceland, Norway, Sweden, Switzerland, and the United Kingdom.
Source: IMF, Balance of Payments Statistics.

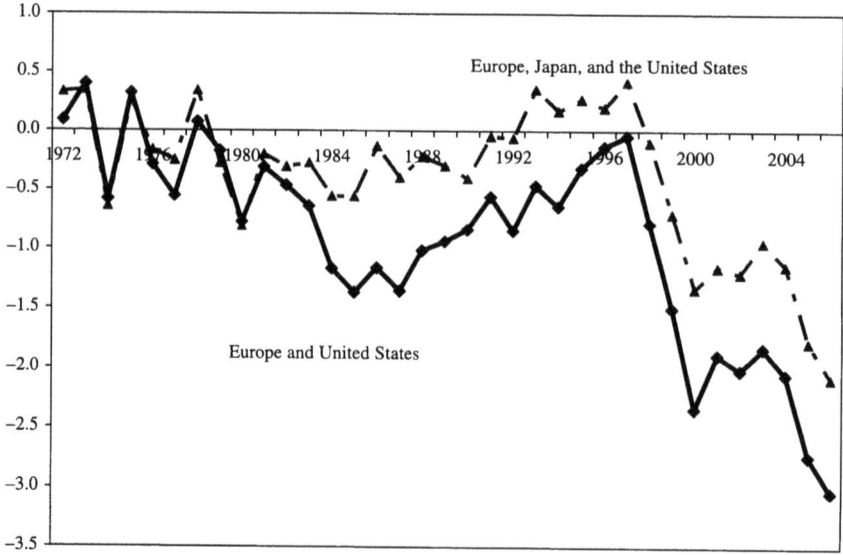

Figure 3. Current account: aggregate balance of Europe, Japan, and United States (percentage of GDP)

Notes: The chart depicts the aggregate current account balance of the two country groups, scaled by their combined GDP.
Source: IMF, Balance of Payments Statistics.

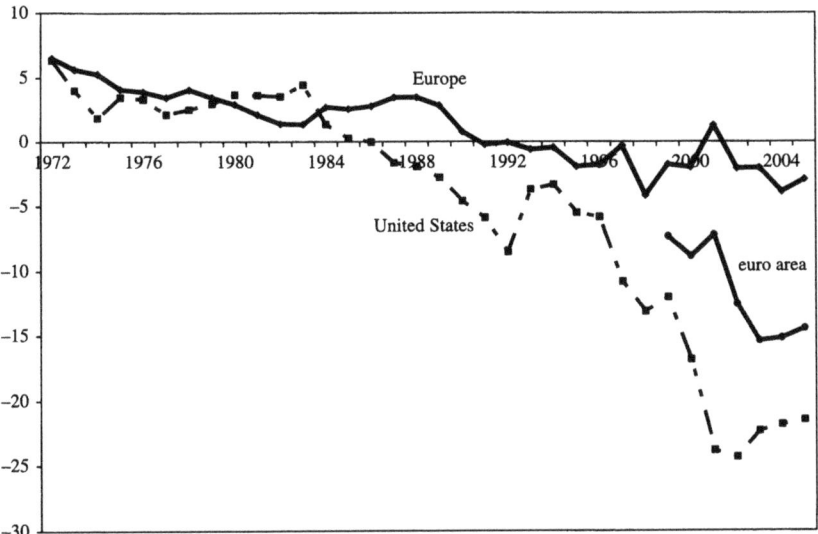

Figure 4. Net foreign asset positions: Europe and the United States (percentage of GDP)

Source: authors' calculations based on Lane and Milesi-Ferretti (2006) and national data.

United States. Namely, the combined current account balance of Europe, Japan, and the United States was close to balance in the mid-1980s and shows a significant deficit today.[2]

We turn now to the implications of these trends in current account balances for the creditor and debtor position of Europe and the United States. Current account surpluses imply net capital outflows – purchases of foreign assets by domestic residents, including the Central Bank, exceed foreign residents' purchases of domestic assets. Hence countries running surpluses should see an improvement in their net external position and countries running deficits should see a worsening. Figure 4 plots the net external asset positions of Europe and the United States. In light of the current account developments depicted in Figures 1 and 2, one feature is particularly striking – namely, during 2002–2005 the net foreign asset position of Europe deteriorated and the position of the United States improved slightly, despite the fact that Europe ran current account surpluses and the United States ran deficits. It is well known that exchange rate and asset price changes cause fluctuations in the value of external assets and liabilities – the so-called valuation effects – which are unrelated to the underlying current account developments.[3] Hence Figures 1 and 4, taken together,

---

[2] See Faruqee (2004) for a related discussion. The current account balance in Japan has historically shown a strong positive co-movement with the European current account balance, which has disappeared over the past decade, while the negative co-movement with the US current account balance has persisted.

[3] The current account balance includes investment income earned on assets and paid out on liabilities, but not changes in the value of assets and liabilities due to asset price fluctuations. See, for example, Lane and Milesi-Ferretti (2005, 2007b) and Gourinchas and Rey (2005).

Table 1. Direction of trade in goods, 1984 and 2004

Trading partner→ Country/Region ↓	Europe[a]	United States	Japan	Emerging Asia[b]	Other	Total
1984						
Euro area	8	4	1.1	1.6	12.4	26.9
United States	3.3		2.1	2.2	6.6	14.2
Japan	2.9	6.9		6.1	8.3	24.2
Emerging Asia	5.7	9.3	8.5		8.6	32.5
2004						
Euro area	8.6	3.9	1.2	4.2	11.8	29.8
United States	4.1		1.6	4.8	9.6	20
Japan	3.2	4.1		10	4.5	21.8
Emerging Asia	12	12	11.4		14.8	51.1

Notes: Bilateral exports and imports as a ratio of country/region's domestic GDP. For the euro area, the Europe category excludes intra-euro area trade. Sum of regions does not add to total, due to unallocated trade.

[a] Includes Denmark, Norway, Sweden, Switzerland, and the United Kingdom as euro area partner countries, and these five countries plus the euro area as trading partners for other countries and regions.

[b] Emerging Asia includes China, Hong Kong S.A.R., India, Indonesia, Korea, Malaysia, Philippines, Singapore, Taiwan province of China, and Thailand.

Source: authors' calculations based on IMF, Direction of Trade Statistics.

suggest that these valuation effects have been moving in opposite directions for Europe and the United States. Indeed, the change in the bilateral euro/dollar exchange rate since early 2002 has been very significant. In Section 2.3, we look more closely at the factors underlying these valuation effects by documenting the evolution of Europe's degree of international financial integration with the world economy in general, and the United States in particular, and reviewing the role of the valuation channel in driving the dynamics of net foreign asset positions in recent years.

2.2. Trade linkages

The volume of trade between countries is an important indicator of their international interdependence: all else equal, a country is more exposed to a shock in some partner country, the stronger the trade linkages between the countries. Table 1 shows the size of bilateral trade in goods (as a ratio of GDP of the 'home' country or region) in 1984 and 2004 (comparable data on services is unfortunately not available). Trade volumes have generally increased in the last two decades, and particularly so vis-à-vis emerging Asia. For the euro area, trade with the United States is relatively small and – scaled by GDP – has not increased much over the past 20 years. Indeed, emerging Asia is now as important a trading partner as the United States for the euro area, despite being only one-third the size of the United States. (Similarly, Europe and emerging Asia are broadly similar in importance as trading partners for the United States.) This suggests that the direct macroeconomic impact on Europe of a slowdown in the United States (or a switch in expenditures away from imports towards domestically produced goods) through the trade channel is necessarily limited in magnitude, even if this would certainly be a significant shock for the European traded goods' sector.

However, bilateral trade volumes understate the full impact of the trade channel – US and European firms compete in third markets and an expansion in US exports triggered by a dollar depreciation would pose a competitive threat to European exporters.[4] In addition, the impact on trade flows of a strengthening of the euro vis-à-vis the dollar would depend on what happens to the euro's real effective exchange rate. In particular, the impact of dollar depreciation on Europe will depend on whether the currencies of China and other countries in emerging Asia (as well as oil exporters) strengthen against the dollar. We will return to this issue in the next section when we describe the model scenarios.

The table also highlights how important trade links with the United States (as well as with Japan and Europe) are for the emerging Asia region, in relation to its GDP. Therefore, as discussed in Eichengreen and Park (2006), the direct effect of a decline in US demand for imports would, *ceteris paribus*, be felt much more strongly in emerging Asia than for Europe.

2.3. Financial linkages

Financial linkages represent a second key form of macroeconomic interdependence. Along one dimension, an important form of financial interdependence is provided by co-movements in asset pricing, where shifts in financial returns in one region influence financial returns in other regions. Here, we focus on the extent of cross-border holdings of assets and liabilities – if domestic investors are net holders of an asset or currency issued by another country, they will be directly affected by shifts in the value of that asset or currency.[5] Accordingly, as shown in the accounting framework presented in Appendix 1, the volume of cross-border holdings is an important indicator of the importance of exchange rate and asset price changes for the value of countries' net external position.

Figure 5 plots the level of cross-border assets and liabilities (expressed as a ratio to GDP) for the aggregate European economy over 1984–2004 (which includes intra-European cross-holdings) on the left scale; in addition, it shows the evolution of the level of bilateral assets and liabilities between Europe and the United States on the right scale. The figure confirms that financial globalization has grown rapidly – the ratio of foreign assets and liabilities to GDP has grown by a factor of 3.5 over 1984–2004 (from 130% to over 450%). The figure also shows that the bilateral financial position vis-à-vis the United States has grown at only a marginally slower pace. This

---

[4] The weight of the United States in the IMF's real effective exchange rate index of the euro area, which takes into account third-market effects, is around 20%, equal to the aggregate weight of Switzerland and the United Kingdom. See Bayoumi *et al.* (2005).

[5] See Lane and Milesi-Ferretti (2003) on the rationale for using this ratio as a volume-based indicator of international financial integration.

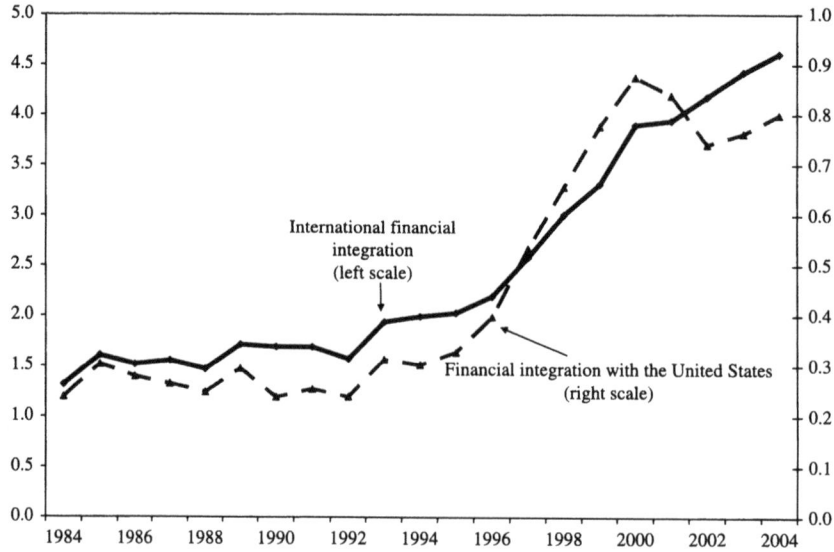

Figure 5. The international financial integration of Europe (percentage of GDP)

Notes: International financial integration is defined as the sum of foreign assets and liabilities (as a ratio to GDP) for a group of European countries, including intra-European cross-holdings. Financial integration with the United States is the sum of US-located foreign assets and liabilities (as a ratio to GDP) for this group of countries.
Source: Lane and Milesi-Ferretti (2006) and other sources described in Section 2.

suggests that the importance for the wealth of European investors of movements in the value of US assets and the dollar against European currencies has grown sharply over this period.[6]

In terms of the overall international investment position, the United States accounted for only 17% of the aggregate cross-border holdings of Europe in 2004, reflecting the predominance of intra-European cross-holdings in the total. However, the United States is by far the most important extra-European destination for European investors: for instance, according to ECB data, it accounted in 2005 for 36% of the foreign equity holdings of euro area investors and 32% of the foreign bond holdings (the shares for FDI and other investment are lower at 21% and 14% respectively).

In summary, then, the United States is the major extra-European destination for outward investment from Europe, with the scale of the engagement growing rapidly over the last two decades. These financial linkages provide a potentially important transmission mechanism by which fluctuations in financial returns in the United States affect the wealth of European investors – we probe the role of such valuation shocks in the international adjustment process in the next subsection and in Section 3.4 below.

---

[6] The data underlying this figure are based on the geographical distribution of foreign assets and liabilities. As we will emphasize in the next section, there is an important distinction between the geography of international investment and its currency composition – in particular, the importance of the dollar is not co-terminus with the scale of investment in the United States. Martin and Rey (2000, 2004) provide a theoretical framework to understand the geographical allocation of portfolio investment.

2.4. The dynamics of net foreign asset positions: a decomposition

In the preceding discussion, we have highlighted that the evolution of net external positions depends not only on whether the country is accumulating net external assets or liabilities through current account surpluses or deficits, but also on changes in the value of its external portfolio driven by valuation effects. As is shown in the accounting framework laid out in Appendix 1, the change in the ratio of net foreign assets to GDP can be decomposed into several factors: the trade balance, net investment income, net capital gains (valuation effects), the effects of growth (since GDP is in the denominator of the ratio) and, finally, capital account transfers and errors and omissions. Table 2 provides such a decomposition of the changes in net foreign asset positions between the end of 2001 and the end of 2005 for the United States, Japan, and the euro area.

Despite running a large cumulative trade deficit, the US ratio of net foreign assets to GDP improved slightly during this period. This can be mainly attributed to large capital gains but positive net investment income (despite being a net debtor) and good economic growth were also positive contributory factors.[7] In contrast, the euro area ran a cumulative trade surplus but capital losses and negative net investment income flows meant that its net liability position doubled in size during this period. Other European countries, such as Switzerland and the United Kingdom, also experienced valuation losses during this period. Finally, the Japanese net foreign asset position relative to GDP was little changed, with the sizeable current account surplus (consisting of surpluses in both the trade balance and net investment income) offset by capital losses.

Table 3 provides some clues as to the sources of these capital gains and losses for the euro area and the United States by showing the local-currency rates of capital gain (that is, capital gains divided by the initial stock of assets) in selected investment categories.[8] For the euro area, capital gains on portfolio debt liabilities exceeded capital gains on portfolio debt assets – since the euro area has a negative net position in portfolio debt, this contributed to aggregate capital losses. Capital gains on FDI liabilities also exceeded capital gains on FDI assets, although the impact of this differential was attenuated by the small positive net FDI position of the euro area. Finally, capital gains on portfolio equity assets exceeded capital gains on portfolio equity liabilities. However, the euro area has a substantial negative net position in the portfolio equity category (about 7% of GDP), so that the net impact was negative on the overall position. In contrast, the United States enjoyed a superior capital gains differential in all investment categories. Furthermore, its long position in FDI and

---

[7] For a net debtor country, like the United States, faster economic growth will reduce the size of net external liabilities relative to GDP. Conversely, for creditor countries faster growth will reduce the size of their net external assets relative to GDP.

[8] A limitation is that the data on FDI for the euro area is calculated at book value, rather than market value. During periods of significant changes in stock market prices, this will underestimate the size of capital gains and losses in this category.

Table 2. Evolution of net foreign assets, 2002–2005: underlying factors 2002–2005

Factor →	NFA at end-2001	Change in NFA 2001–2005	Cumulative trade balance	Cumulative investment income	Valuation changes	Effects of growth	Other factors[a]
Term in eq (2) →	b_{01}	$b_{05} - b_{01}$	$\sum_{t=2002}^{2005} bgst_t$	$\sum_{t=2002}^{2005}\left(\dfrac{i_t^A A_{t-1} - i_t^L L_{t-1}}{Y_t}\right)$	$\sum_{t=2002}^{2005} \dfrac{KG_t}{Y_t}$	$\sum_{t=2002}^{2005}\left(-\dfrac{g_t + \pi_t}{(1+g_t)(1+\pi_t)} b_{t-1}\right)$	$\sum_{t=2002}^{2005} \varepsilon_t$
Euro area	−7.2	−7.2	3.3	−2.0	−9.2	2.7	−1.9
Japan	32.5	0.8	5.7	7.1	−7.4	−2.9	−1.7
United States	−23.8	2.3	−20.6	0.9	17.2	4.5	0.4

Notes: The decomposition of the dynamics of net foreign assets is according to Equation (2) in Appendix 1: $b_{05} - b_{01} \equiv \sum_{t=2002}^{2005}\left(bgst_t + \dfrac{i_t^A A_{t-1} - i_t^L L_{t-1}}{Y_t} + \dfrac{KG_t}{Y_t} - \dfrac{g_t + \pi_t}{(1+g_t)(1+\pi_t)} b_{t-1} + \varepsilon_t\right)$

[a] Cumulative capital account transfers and errors and omissions.

Source: authors' calculations based on IMF, Balance of Payments Statistics, national data, and Lane and Milesi-Ferretti (2006).

Table 3. Capital gains on external portfolios in the euro area and the United States, 2002–2005

	Euro area			Exchange rate €/$ (% change)	United States		
	Portfolio debt	Portfolio equity	FDI		Portfolio debt	Portfolio equity	FDI
Assets							
2002	−7.5	−26.5	−11.5	−16	20.9	−15.8	−19.3
2003	0.1	18.8	1.1	−17	18.0	43.0	28.0
2004	1.3	8.9	−1.4	−7.3	11.4	19.1	11.2
2005	8.3	21.3	3.5	15.5	−2.4	15.2	6.5
Liabilities							
2002	3.9	−21.3	−0.1		1.4	−18.3	−24.2
2003	−1.9	6.0	8.7		−1.6	35.3	18.1
2004	4.5	7.3	2.5		−0.6	12.7	5.8
2005	6.0	20.7	1.1		−7.6	4.7	1.3

Notes: Rate of capital gains in euro on foreign assets and liabilities of the euro area; rates of capital gains in dollars on foreign assets and liabilities of the United States.
Source: authors' calculations based on Lane and Milesi-Ferretti (2006).

portfolio equity meant that high average returns in these categories fed strongly into the aggregate position.

Finally, Table 3 shows that the euro-dollar exchange rate plays an important role in determining the returns the euro area earns on its foreign assets. For instance, there is a close correspondence between the euro-denominated capital gains earned on foreign portfolio equity assets and the sum of the dollar-denominated capital gains on US portfolio equity liabilities and the rate of dollar-euro appreciation, reflecting the importance of portfolio equity investment by the euro area in the United States. Although the bulk of the euro area's external holdings are in other European countries, the currencies of these countries are much more stable vis-à-vis the euro – the dollar is the dominant foreign-currency exposure faced by the euro area.

3. INTERNATIONAL ADJUSTMENT

In the previous section we have highlighted a number of stylized facts concerning the evolution of global current account imbalances and international financial integration. In particular, we have highlighted that Europe in the aggregate has a broadly balanced current account position, and – relative to its GDP – trades less with the United States than other regions of the world (particularly emerging Asia). We have also highlighted that financial linkages between Europe and the United States have grown substantially over the past two decades, and may therefore amplify the transmission of shocks from one region to the other. In this section, we take a general equilibrium perspective and discuss how a change in the pattern of global current account imbalances – and its attendant implications for macroeconomic variables, including exchange rates – may affect the European economy.

While there is considerable debate on the extent to which the current pattern of global trade and current account imbalances in general, and the United States current account deficit in particular, should be cause for concern, there is little doubt that the United States cannot run a trade deficit of 6% of GDP forever, and that the adjustment process is likely to entail a realignment in international relative prices. However, views differ on many other aspects of the adjustment process, including the likelihood that the current pattern of international borrowing and lending could continue for a while, the risks of a costly adjustment, the magnitude of the needed adjustment in exchange rates, and the 'trigger' for the adjustment.

For example, it is possible to envisage a 'soft-landing' scenario where the United States continues to experience substantial net capital inflows, trade and current account imbalances are slowly reduced, factors are gradually reallocated from the non-traded to the traded sector in a smooth fashion, and exchange rates adjust gradually. Such a scenario need not involve any persistent deviation from potential output, with the gradual shift in the composition of demand mirrored by the required inter-sectoral reallocation of capital and labor. At the other extreme, a 'hard-landing' scenario – possibly triggered by a shift in investors' preferences away from US assets – could involve a more rapid unwinding of current imbalances, accompanied by significant swings in exchange rates with possible disruptive effects on financial markets and economic activity.

At a qualitative level, the implications for Europe of these scenarios are well understood. An appreciation of the euro against the dollar would reduce the competitiveness of European exporters vis-à-vis US firms in global markets, while a growth slowdown in the United States would lower external demand for European exports. As for financial market variables, a decline in US asset values and the dollar would reduce the value of European investment positions in the United States. In the short run, the ensuing contractionary impact on domestic output of these developments could be offset by a compensatory increase in domestic demand and/or by an increase in external demand from other parts of the world. In this regard, measures to support domestic demand and raise the level of potential output are heavily debated in policy circles, with a weakening of the euro vis-à-vis Asian currencies in real terms also perceived as an important part of the adjustment process.

3.1. Unwinding of global imbalances – a model-based perspective

To provide a quantitative perspective on an unwinding of global imbalances, we present adjustment scenarios based on the IMF's Global Economic Model (GEM), a state-of-the-art multi-country dynamic stochastic general equilibrium model. We then integrate this analysis, which does not explicitly allow for valuation effects, with simulations capturing the extent to which the exchange rate adjustments predicted by the model affect the external position of countries. In particular, we focus on three possible scenarios featuring a reduction in the US current account deficit, which span some of the views discussed in the literature and alluded to in the previous subsection.

- The first is a 'benign' scenario in which an increase in the US private saving rate gradually reduces the US trade and current account deficits. The mirror image of the slow adjustment in the US current account is the willingness of other countries to continue to purchase US assets.
- The second is a disruptive scenario, characterized by a decline in the level of competition worldwide and a sudden decline in foreigners' willingness to hold US assets, with large changes in exchange rates and a significant output decline in the short run.
- The third scenario features instead joint policy action by the major 'players', designed to facilitate the reduction in global imbalances and supporting growth.

The interested reader will find a detailed technical description of model and scenarios in Faruqee *et al.* (2007).

3.2. A brief description of the model

The model has four regions: the United States; the euro area and Japan; emerging Asian economies; and the rest of the world. While not ideal, the choice of aggregating the euro area and Japan reflects a number of common elements: both regions have experienced slow productivity and output growth relative to their historical averages in recent years, are characterized by relatively high markups, face similar demographic pressures, and have floating exchange rates. Also, as mentioned in Section 2, the dynamics of the current account balances of Europe and Japan have historically been strongly positively correlated. A full disaggregation would of course be a desirable but computationally very complex extension – for this exercise, its salient features are captured in the analysis of valuation effects that follows.[9]

Each region produces both tradable and non-tradable goods using capital, labour, and intermediate inputs, with constant elasticity of substitution production functions. Bilateral trade flows take place between the blocks – relevant share parameters are calibrated so as to ensure that the model broadly replicates actual trade flows among the major areas. Goods and labor markets are imperfectly competitive and subject to nominal rigidities. There are two types of consumers: liquidity-constrained ones that consume their disposable income, and forward-looking consumers that are non-Ricardian – that is, they treat a portion of government debt as net wealth. The model also includes an array of adjustment costs in consumption and labour supply (habit persistence), investment, and the composition of trade so as to ensure that it reasonably matches data properties at business-cycle frequencies.

---

[9] Faruqee (2004) discusses scenarios of global current account adjustment using an earlier three-region version of GEM calibrated on the United States, the euro area, and the rest of the world.

Monetary policy in the United States, the Japan-euro area block, and the rest of the world is characterized by an interest rate feedback rule *à la* Taylor that gradually moves inflation toward a constant desired rate. In the first scenario, monetary policy in emerging Asia is geared towards maintaining a fixed exchange rate vis-à-vis the dollar. In the other scenarios emerging Asia is assumed to abandon the exchange rate peg and adopt a monetary policy rule similar to the one in the other regions. In all countries, fiscal policy is aimed at stabilizing the debt-to-GDP ratio over the medium term.

There is free capital mobility between regions, with one international bond being traded internationally. The interest rate parity condition is augmented by a country-specific risk premium, whose size depends on the difference between actual and desired net foreign assets. Therefore, desired holdings of net foreign assets (or foreign liabilities) in each region over the medium term play a key role in determining the equilibrium level of current account balances and exchange rates. In the long run, motivated by assumptions about demography and productivity differences, the United States is assumed to be the only debtor region, with the remaining regions holding positive net foreign assets. The model features a decline in the medium-term rate of productivity growth in emerging Asia, as its income level approaches the one in more advanced economies, and a decline in output growth in Japan and the euro area, reflecting demographic trends.

In the model, the current set of imbalances are assumed to reflect primarily saving behaviour by both the private and public sector, rather than investment dynamics fuelled by (excessively) optimistic productivity and growth expectations as in the second half of the 1990s. More specifically, the two main driving forces behind the current account dynamics are temporarily low private and public savings in the United States, together with a portfolio preference shock generating strong demand for US assets abroad, particularly in emerging Asia. Both contribute to the US current account deficit, the latter by reducing the rate of return required by foreigners in order to hold US assets.[10]

Clearly parameter values play an important role in shaping the response of the world economy to the various shocks. While we refer the reader to Faruqee *et al.* (2007) for details on model parametrization, we highlight here two parameter values that help interpret the quantitative features of the model.

- The first key parameter is the elasticity of substitution between domestically produced and foreign-produced traded goods, which influences the extent of relative price adjustment necessary to induce a change in the relative consumption of these goods. In line with the calibration of most large macroeconomic models, this elasticity is chosen to be 2.5 – a value which is higher than the one that would be consistent with macroeconomic evidence on the response of imports and exports

---

[10] Hunt and Rebucci (2005) discuss the role of this channel in explaining the emergence of the US current account deficit. This 'risk premium' in other smaller and less-developed countries typically rises as net external liabilities accumulate, acting as a brake on the size and persistence of current account deficits.

to real exchange rate fluctuations (albeit lower than the one that microeconomic estimates of responses of trade to relative prices suggest).[11] As a result, the adjustment in real effective exchange rates associated with reduced external current account imbalances is generally smaller relative to other model-generated estimates in the literature (such as, for example, Blanchard *et al.*, 2005; Obstfeld and Rogoff, 2005, 2007; and Krugman, 2007).[12]

- The second parameter captures the extent of 'non-Ricardian' behavior – that is, the extent to which consumers that are forward-looking treat their holdings of public debt as net wealth. In line with results obtained from a calibration of a finite-horizon Dynamic Stochastic General Equilibrium (DSGE) model (Kumhof *et al.*, 2005) the long-run relation between public debt and the net external position (and hence between the current account and the fiscal balance) is such that a permanent one percentage point increase in public debt reduces desired net foreign assets by half a percentage point in the long run. Other open-economy DSGE models (see, for example, Erceg *et al.*, 2005) do not incorporate any long-run relation between public debt and the external position, and imply a smaller 'offset' (0.1 to 0.2) over the medium term.

It is important to stress a few other limitations of the model. First, the model has a rich 'real' structure and a realistic role for monetary policy, but a very stylized structure of international financial flows, with only one internationally traded bond and hence no room for capturing the effects of exchange rate and asset price changes on gross external positions. We address this issue later in the section. Second, the limited financial linkages between countries, together with the relatively small scale of cross-regional trade and the stabilizing role of monetary policy, imply that international spillovers are relatively small. For instance, international linkages would be strengthened if equity holdings were endogenously included in the model and if the value of these holdings were affected by shifts in 'global sentiment', in addition to domestic fundamentals.

Forward-looking agents are fully rational in the model, and interest differentials reflect risk premia (associated *inter alia* with deviations of net foreign assets from their desired level). In the baseline scenario, the unwinding of the imbalances is predictable since it reflects the dissipation of past shocks, and risk premia are such that investors hold the (possibly changing) desired amount of net foreign assets at market interest rates. In the other scenarios, a 'surprise' set of unanticipated events occurs – but expectations adjust to these shocks, such that subsequent dynamics are again predictable. Exchange rate dynamics that might be induced by an autonomous revision of panglossian expectations (as in Krugman, 2007) could be proxied in our model by a sudden asset preference shock away from US assets (as, for example, in the disruptive scenario). It is also worth noting that investors in the model would respond to news about anticipated shifts in future fundamentals (as in Devereux and Engel, 2006).

---

[11] Obstfeld and Rogoff (2007) discuss alternative parametrizations of this elasticity of substitution.

[12] An exception is the study by Engel and Rogers (2006).

Finally, for the purpose of interpreting the results for Europe, the model aggregation is not ideal in that the euro area is considered together with Japan, while the rest of Europe constitutes part of the very heterogeneous rest of the world block. A 'de facto' disaggregation is undertaken in the exercise on valuation effects that follow.

3.3. Model-based adjustment scenarios

As mentioned earlier, the US trade deficit – currently 6% of GDP – has to eventually decline to ensure that US net external liabilities do not grow without bound. Analogously, the large trade surpluses of Asian economies and oil exporters have to shrink to ensure that their external assets eventually stabilize as a ratio of GDP. We focus on three possible adjustment scenarios (also described in IMF 2005b, 2006).

- The first, baseline scenario sees little change in economic policy across regions. Monetary policy is anchored by a Taylor rule aimed at stabilizing inflation except – as mentioned earlier – in emerging Asia, where the exchange rate is pegged to the US dollar. Fiscal policy stabilizes the debt to GDP ratio. The dynamics are primarily driven by the gradual rebound in the temporarily low private savings rate in the United States, which entails a slow reduction in the US current account deficit.
- The second, 'disruptive' scenario features instead a sharp decline in other countries' willingness to hold US assets and an abandonment of emerging Asia's peg to the dollar, with the resulting abrupt exchange rate realignments temporarily reducing global competition pressures (higher price and wage mark-ups). Monetary policy responds to these inflationary pressures, and the combined effect of shocks and policy responses causes a generalized decline in output relative to trend in all regions of the world.
- Finally, the third scenario is characterized by the implementation of a set of policies designed to reduce imbalances and stave off the risks of a disorderly adjustment. In emerging Asia, there is a shift towards a flexible exchange rate regime, with monetary policy following a Taylor rule similar to the one in other regions. The ensuing decline in the accumulation of reserves is assumed to reflect a decline in the desired stock of long-run net foreign assets, and hence entails an increase in private consumption. Finally, there is a modest increase in productivity assumed to be driven by financial sector reform. In the United States, there is a reduction in the US budget deficit from 4% of GDP in the baseline to broad balance by 2011.[13] In the euro area and Japan, structural reforms are assumed to raise productivity and growth by lowering mark-ups in both labour and product markets, thereby reducing precautionary savings. Finally, a boost to consumption and investment is assumed to take place in oil exporters, as their infrastructure is

---

[13] The budget deficit is assumed to subsequently widen to some extent, driven by demographic trends.

upgraded and consumption reflects the improvement in the terms of trade. While the model does not specifically include an oil shock as one cause of global imbalances, it is reasonable to assume a gradual positive response of consumption and investment in oil exporters, should oil prices remain high as currently projected by futures markets.

Figure 6 summarizes the main features of the three scenarios, focusing on the United States, emerging Asia, and the Japan/euro area block. It displays the behaviour of output growth, the current account, net foreign assets, and the real effective exchange rate, defined as the ratio of trading partners' price levels to the domestic price level (so that an increase implies a real depreciation).[14]

3.3.1. Baseline scenario.
In this scenario (represented by the solid line in Figure 6), the negative shock to US private savings that emerged in the early 2000s unwinds slowly, leading to a gradual reduction in the US trade and current account deficits. The slow current account adjustment implies a substantial accumulation of external liabilities by the United States, which reach 50% of GDP by 2015 and over 80% in the very long run, matched by the accumulation of external assets elsewhere, particularly in emerging Asia and in the euro area–Japan bloc. The slow trade balance adjustment is accompanied by a gradual depreciation of the dollar vis-à-vis all trading partners, of over 15% in real effective terms over the long run. In emerging Asia, because of the exchange rate peg, real effective appreciation occurs through a positive inflation differential vis-à-vis other countries.[15]

3.3.2. Disruptive scenario.
This scenario, depicted by the dark dashed line in Figure 6, is characterized by a sharp reversal of the portfolio preference for US assets, an abandonment of emerging Asia's peg to the dollar that results in an abrupt exchange rate realignment, and reduced global competitive pressures. The latter effect, akin to the worldwide adoption of protectionist measures, is proxied in the model by an increase in margins (a decline in product market competition) in all regions of the world.[16] As a result of these shocks, the dollar falls very sharply vis-à-vis all currencies, but particularly so vis-à-vis the currencies in emerging Asia.[17] The dollar depreciation is driven by the decline in demand for US assets, and the adjustment of the US current

---

[14] Although the GEM is a micro-founded model, calculations about the welfare impact of the scenarios are complicated by preference shocks (such as shifts in discount rates that affect savings behaviour).

[15] The model has no room for effective sterilized exchange rate intervention, which would delay real exchange rate adjustment. Consequently, this adjustment in emerging Asia is relatively rapid, despite the exchange rate peg. See also Faruqee et al. (2006) on the macroeconomic impact of a protectionist response to global imbalances.

[16] For example, the abandonment of the dollar peg by emerging Asia may imply the disappearance of a factor which has increased competition in the traded goods' sector and thus helped keep inflation low.

[17] Using a portfolio balance model, Blanchard et al. (2005) highlight that if China abandons a dollar peg, the yen and the euro would appreciate vis-à-vis the dollar, because the market loses an investor with 'extreme' dollar preference. Of course, the bilateral euro appreciation need not imply a real effective appreciation. Obstfeld and Rogoff (2005) consider a disruptive scenario in which Asia maintains its dollar peg, which implies a much larger bilateral appreciation of the euro against the dollar.

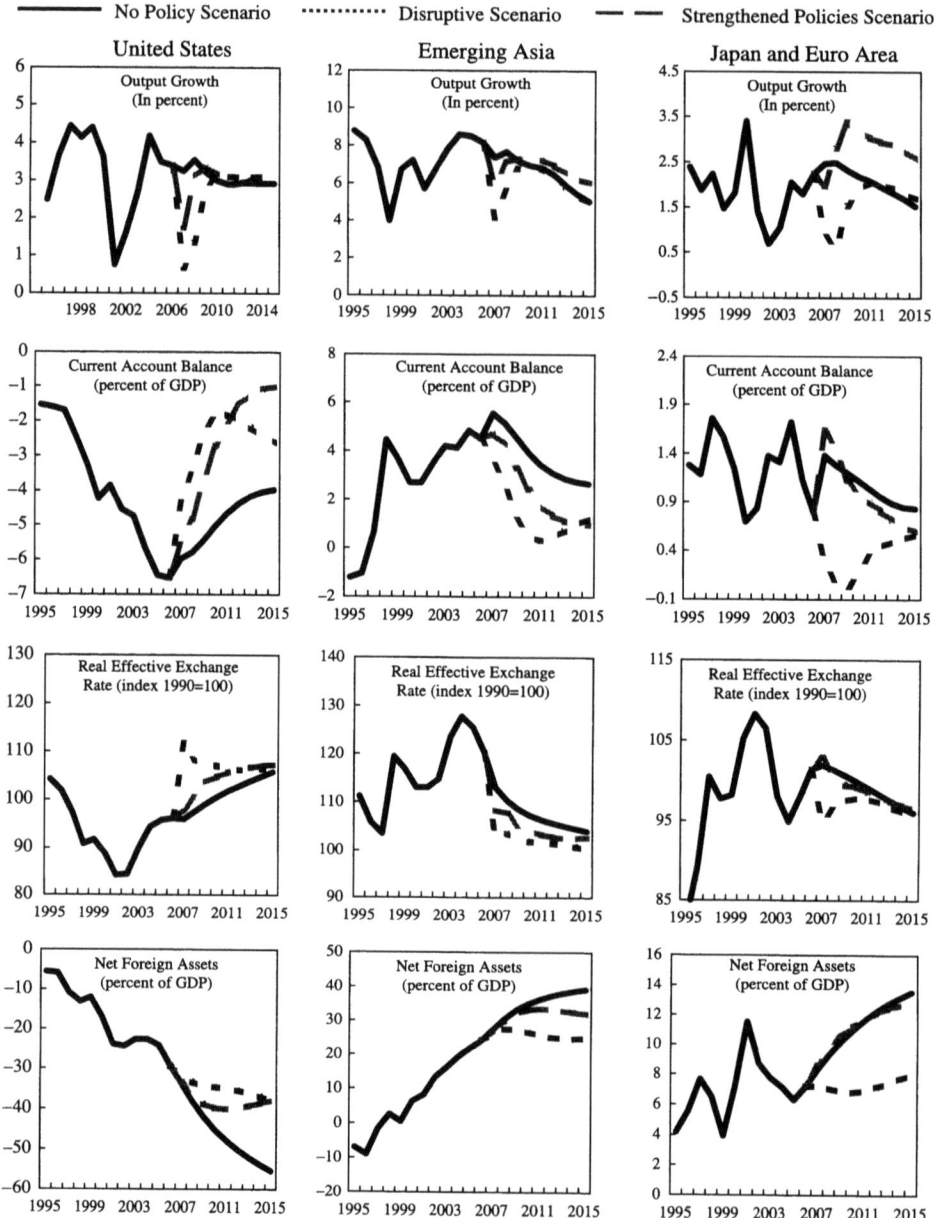

Figure 6. Adjustment of global imbalance

Source: authors' estimates.

account is very abrupt. Correspondingly, the current accounts in other regions of the world worsen. *De facto*, the adjustment process is 'collapsed' in a very short period, and hence more disruptive. In terms of output performance, the disruptive effects are enhanced by reduced competition, which generates inflationary pressures, and the monetary policy responses to such pressures, which lead to higher interest rates and a generalized decline in activity in all regions.[18]

While the characterization of the disruptive scenario – by construction a 'low-probability event' – is necessarily stylized and policy responses do play a relevant role in determining the size of output decline, it is worth noting that the model does not capture the possible financial market disarray and negative effects on confidence that a sharp and unexpected currency realignment may plausibly trigger. These effects could well induce significant declines in output.

3.3.3. 'Policies' scenario.
In addition to the gradual 'baseline' unwinding of imbalances generated by rising US private saving, this scenario envisages the implementation of a series of policy measures which broadly reflect those outlined in several G-7 and IMFC Communiqués. These policies include: (i) a substantial reduction in the US budget deficit, from 4% of GDP (the baseline level) to broad balance excluding social security by early in the next decade; (ii) increased exchange rate flexibility and measures raising private consumption in emerging Asia; (iii) growth-enhancing structural reforms in the euro area and Japan; and (iv) a boost to investment in oil exporters.[19] The intended objective of these policies is to sustain global growth while helping the reduction of global imbalances.

In this scenario, depicted by the grey dashed line in Figure 6, the US current account adjusts more rapidly, since all policy actions go in the direction of reducing US net external borrowing. The corresponding exchange rate adjustment is more rapid in emerging Asia, where the abandonment of the peg implies a more rapid real appreciation, occurring through a shift in the nominal exchange rate rather than through inflation as in the baseline. While world growth declines in the short run, reflecting the initially contractionary effects of fiscal adjustment in the United States, it is higher over the medium term, thanks to higher growth in Japan and the euro area and the lower interest rates associated with a declining US public debt.

Clearly, not all policies have the same impact on the US current account deficit. The most significant impact comes from US fiscal policy – a 1% of GDP reduction in the budget deficit improves the current account balance by 0.5% of GDP over the medium term, and hence accounts for almost half of the total US current account

---

[18] The assumption that central banks follow Taylor Rules in setting monetary policy implies that interest rates are raised sharply in response to a temporary burst in inflation. As shown by our discussant Paolo Pesenti, a more 'doveish' monetary policy would lead to a smaller growth decline in the United States (a fall of 1% of GDP, rather than 2% under the assumed Taylor rule). However, this would be at the price of a peak inflation rate of 6% (rather than 4% under our scenario) and a sharper dollar depreciation.

[19] Increased exchange rate flexibility in Asia is captured by assuming that the region shifts to a monetary policy rule similar to the one in other parts of the world, while the increase in private consumption is generated by an increase in consumers' 'impatience'. In addition, the shift in the exchange rate regime is associated with a decline in desired net foreign assets, which can be interpreted as resulting from a decline in the accumulation of reserves. Structural reforms in the euro area and Japan are assumed to lead to an increase in goods' and labor market competition, with the decline in mark-ups eliminating about two-thirds of the gap with US levels over a ten-year period. Also, increased productivity growth is assumed to be reflected in lower precautionary savings. Finally, increased domestic demand in oil exporters is generated by an investment shock (triggered by higher productivity) as well as higher consumption.

adjustment relative to the baseline. Policies in emerging Asia contribute about one-quarter of the total US current account adjustment. In this context, one should note that the baseline already includes substantial real appreciation in emerging Asia through inflation differentials, and hence the net contribution of the change in the exchange rate regime is not very large. A somewhat smaller contribution to US current account adjustment comes from the increase in spending in oil exporters. Finally, the quantitative impact of structural reforms in Japan and the euro area on the US current account is relatively modest, but plays an important role in sustaining world growth as US domestic demand declines.

3.3.4. Implications for the euro area.
The euro area represents over two-thirds of the 'Japan–euro area' bloc. In terms of the small list of key variables shown in Figure 6, there are substantial differences between the Japan and the euro area in regard to current account balances (where Japan has a hefty surplus, while the euro area is in broad balance), net foreign assets (that in Japan are around 40% of GDP, while the euro area is a net external debtor), and recent trends in real effective exchange rates (where the euro has appreciated by around 20% in real effective terms between February 2002 and February 2007, while the yen has depreciated by around 17% during the same period).

Together, these trends would suggest that, in the scenarios depicted in Figure 6, current account adjustment and real effective exchange rate appreciation would be more substantial in Japan than in the euro area. Assumptions along those lines underpin our next exercise, which attempts to quantify the valuation effects on the external position that would be implied by the three scenarios just described.

3.4. Valuation changes

While the scenarios presented in the previous section provide a useful perspective on some possible features of global external adjustment, they do not include the impact of currency realignments on net external positions. The main reason why the model cannot properly capture valuation effects is that it only allows for one internationally traded bond and hence only net exposures between countries – in other words, a debtor country has only external liabilities and no external assets, while a creditor country has only external assets and no external liabilities. This limits the impact of exchange rate changes on the value of a country's assets and liabilities. For example, at end-2005 the United States' net external position (excluding gold) was negative for about $2.7 trillion. However, its net US dollar position was around minus $9 trillion, because the United States holds substantial external assets denominated in foreign currency.

We are not the first in considering how valuation effects affect external adjustment in models where the US current account deficit shrinks. Blanchard *et al.* (2005), Obstfeld and Rogoff (2005, 2007), and Cavallo and Tille (2006) have also considered these issues, albeit with a simpler underlying macroeconomic structure and a more stylized calibration of portfolio structure.

In order to infer the potential implications of exchange rate adjustment for the value of the external holdings in the model, we start from the currency and asset composition of the international balance sheet for the main country blocs in 2005. We then consider a set of projections for capital inflows and outflows (and their currency composition) for all scenarios, such that the net flows are equal to the model's projected current account balances. The projected flows, together with the model-based path for exchange rates, allow us to calculate the evolution of gross external assets and liabilities, and more specifically the impact of valuation changes on the net external position. In undertaking this exercise, we separate out projections for the euro area and Japan, both in terms of external current account adjustment and in terms of external portfolios. As mentioned earlier, we assume that the real exchange rate and current account adjustment is larger in Japan than in the euro area. We also consider China separately from the rest of emerging Asia, assuming that real exchange rate and current account adjustment in China are broadly of a similar order of magnitude as for the region as a whole.

The exposure of a country to movements in exchange rates clearly depends on the currency composition of its international balance sheet. Estimating such currency composition is a difficult exercise. This is especially true for currencies such as the dollar and the euro that are heavily employed in international financial trade, since even information about the geographical distribution of external portfolios is only of limited value when many countries issue debt denominated in these currencies. For instance, the net dollar position of the euro area is the sum of dollar assets located in the United States (which is not equal to the sum of total euro area assets in the United States, since the United States also issues euro-denominated liabilities), plus dollar assets located elsewhere, minus the dollar liabilities issued by euro area residents to non-residents.

Appendix 2 discusses how we estimated the currency composition of the external portfolio for the United States, the euro area, Japan and China. The data are summarized in Table 4. It shows that all countries are short in their domestic currencies and that the euro area, Japan and China are each long in dollars (although the figures for China are subject to significant uncertainty, given the lack of data on the currency composition of its portfolio). However, Japan and China are much larger 'dollar creditors' than the euro area relative to their GDP levels. This reflects their aggregate net creditor status and a portfolio composition that is more heavily weighted towards the dollar than is the case for the euro area. Finally, as already highlighted by Tille (2005), the US net dollar liability position is very substantial.

An important caveat to our analysis is the lack of systematic data on cross-border hedging. Note that hedging vis-à-vis other domestic residents would only shift the risk within an economy, but would not affect its overall exposure to the rest of the world. Hau and Rey (2006) indicate that the level of hedging for portfolio equity positions

Table 4. Currency composition of net external position, 2005 (% of GDP)

	Net external position	Net domestic currency position	Net US dollar position	Net other currencies position
China	12.5	−28.3	29.2	11.6
Euro area	−15.0	−65.5	16.8	34.5
Japan	35.9	−26.9	38.5	21.9
United States	−21.5	(−74.8)	−74.8	53.4

Source: authors' calculations (see Appendix 2).

is limited, and the BIS foreign exchange survey suggests that most hedging is undertaken with domestic counterparties. In addition, hedging long-term exposures is very costly. Nevertheless, to the extent that at least some of the net positions we estimate are indeed hedged, our estimation would only provide an upper bound on the valuation effects of cross-currency fluctuations.[20]

Projections of capital flows and of their currency composition are necessary to keep track of valuation changes in the years following the initial shock. Recent years have seen a major increase in cross-border flows, so that external assets and liabilities have been increasing sharply in relation to GDP. We assume that this trend will continue in the future, albeit at a slower pace. Inflows and outflows of specific types – direct investment, portfolio equity, portfolio debt, other investment flows, and reserves – are assumed in most cases to remain constant as a share of GDP, broadly reflecting recent trends (Appendix, Table A1). In order to ensure that net capital flows equal the model's path for the current account, we assume that for each country/bloc there is one residual category of flows that acts as 'adjustor' – foreign exchange reserves for emerging Asia, portfolio debt assets for the euro area and Japan, and portfolio debt liabilities for the United States.

With regard to the currency composition of countries' external portfolios, we make a stark simplifying assumption – namely, that the share of each asset and liability category denominated in dollars and other currencies remains constant over time. This implies that countries fully offset the impact of valuation changes on the currency composition of their portfolio: as the dollar depreciates, for example, the currency composition of flows ensures that the dollar share of each asset and liability category remains constant. This assumption turns out to be less restrictive than it appears at first sight: in the two scenarios involving 'large' currency movements in the short run, the initial currency exposure is key in determining the valuation effects, and that exposure is predetermined.

---

[20] Campbell et al. (2006) find that the dollar is almost uncorrelated with the US equity market and negatively correlated with the world equity market, suggesting that international investors may wish to hold long dollar positions as a risk-minimization strategy.

Valuation changes in the model are captured as follows. For dollar-denominated assets and liabilities, their domestic-currency value is adjusted to reflect changes in the exchange rate between the dollar and the domestic currency. In addition, for portfolio equity assets in the United States we assume that their capital value increases in line with the US GDP growth rate. For the remaining foreign-currency assets, we make the following assumptions:

- for foreign direct investment and portfolio equity assets by non-US countries outside the United States, we assume that their dollar value increases in proportion to the effective depreciation of the US dollar;
- for portfolio equity assets (and liabilities) we also assume capital gains in proportion to output growth in the rest of the world (for assets), and domestic output growth (for liabilities). We do not make a corresponding valuation adjustment for FDI flows in light of the fact that for FDI reinvested earnings are counted investment income (and correspondingly as new FDI) while for portfolio equity holdings retained company profits are reflected in the firm valuation, but not in investment income.

Table 5 shows the main results in terms of capital gains and losses for the various scenarios, showing both capital gains and losses induced by changes in real exchange rates as well as overall capital gains and losses (including those arising from the assumed capital gains on portfolio equity holdings). Capital gains as of 2008 and 2015 are calculated as the present value of the difference between the net foreign asset position and the cumulative value of the current account at that date (measured in US dollars), as a ratio of 2005 GDP. The applied discount rate is 6%, about 1% higher than the current interest rate on long-term US bonds.

- Clearly, the United States stands to gain from valuation effects in all scenarios. While exchange-rate related valuation gains are larger in the baseline, in light of the larger stock of US dollar liabilities, higher growth in the policies scenario drives higher growth-induced capital gains on US equity holdings overseas, and hence larger overall gains in that scenario.
- For all remaining country groups, the disruptive scenario generates the largest capital losses. These are particularly high in China and Japan, because of the scale of exchange rate appreciation as well as of net dollar exposure – in the euro area, capital losses are only about one-third as high as in Asia. The assumption that capital gains made by foreigners on portfolio equity liabilities are related to the country's growth rate magnify China's total net capital losses on the external position, as can be seen by comparing total with exchange-rate-induced capital losses.[21]
- With regard to the euro area, exchange-rate-induced capital losses are significant but much smaller than for China and Japan. Faster growth of the euro area

---

[21] This result is crucially driven by the assumption concerning capital gains on portfolio equity as well as by the additional assumption that China accumulates portfolio equity liabilities (worth over 10% of GDP by 2015, compared to around 3% now).

Table 5. Net foreign assets and capital gains, adjustment scenarios: effects of exchange rates and asset prices

	China	Euro area	Japan	United States
Net foreign assets, 2005 (% of GDP)	12.5	−15.0	35.9	−21.5
Financial openness, 2005 (% of GDP)[a]	95.9	269.7	163.8	196.8
Baseline				
Net foreign assets, 2008 (% of GDP)	24.0	−16.3	34.3	−33.5
PV of capital gains/losses by 2008 (% of 2005 GDP)	−4.0	−3.5	−8.6	2.1
of which: exchange rate-related capital gains	−3.0	−4.3	−8.1	0.4
Net foreign assets, 2015 (% of GDP)	26.1	−14.4	38.0	−43.4
PV of capital gains/losses by 2015 (% of 2005 GDP)	−18.4	−5.5	−16.3	8.4
of which: exchange rate-related capital gains	−12.4	−7.6	−16.0	3.9
Policies scenario				
Net foreign assets, 2008 (% of GDP)	21.9	−15.8	33.9	−30.9
PV of capital gains/losses by 2008 (% of 2005 GDP)	−5.2	−3.6	−9.3	3.7
of which: exchange rate-related capital gains	−4.2	−3.9	−8.4	1.8
Net foreign assets, 2015 (% of GDP)	15.3	−14.4	32.4	−24.5
PV of capital gains/losses by 2015 (% of 2005 GDP)	−17.1	−6.7	−17.5	10.0
of which: exchange rate-related capital gains	−10.7	−6.5	−15.0	4.0
Disruptive scenario				
Net foreign assets, 2008 (% of GDP)	15.5	−18.0	23.6	−24.7
PV of capital gains/losses by 2008 (% of 2005 GDP)	−16.0	−4.1	−17.2	6.9
of which: exchange rate-related capital gains	−15.1	−5.0	−16.1	5.1

Notes: Exchange-rate-related capital gains are calculated by excluding the effects of economic growth on the value of portfolio equity assets and liabilities.

[a] Sum of external assets and liabilities (in percentage of GDP).

economy in the 'policies' scenario imply larger capital gains for non-residents on euro area's equity assets, and therefore total net capital losses on the external position are larger in the policies scenario than in the baseline, although the exchange-rate-related losses are somewhat smaller.

How would these gains and losses affect the external adjustment path depicted in Figure 6? For given long-run values of net external assets and liabilities across regions, valuation gains and losses would allow regions experiencing capital gains to sustain – other things being equal – higher consumption equivalent to the annuity value of such gains, and correspondingly require higher surpluses (and hence lower consumption) to achieve desired long-run asset holdings in regions experiencing capital losses. However, the size of long-run real exchange rate adjustment would be unchanged relative to the situation without valuation effects.[22] Of course, looking forward, it would be desirable to fully embed portfolio choices in a general equilibrium model.

---

[22] In contrast, in the exercise undertaken in Obstfeld and Rogoff (2005), valuation effects reduce the need for exchange rate adjustment. This occurs because the authors focus on the exchange rate adjustment needed to reduce the US current account deficit by a given percentage of GDP. A dollar depreciation reduces the stock of US net external liabilities, and therefore its debt service burden relative to GDP. This implies that the trade balance adjustment necessary to achieve the needed reduction in the current account deficit is smaller, and hence the needed dollar depreciation is smaller.

While this line of research is currently receiving much attention (see, for example, Devereux and Sutherland, 2006; Engel and Matsumoto, 2006; Ghironi et al., 2006), it is still in its early days.

A final important point concerns the possibility that exchange rate adjustment will not take place as the model scenarios suggest. In particular, in all model scenarios, the real effective appreciation in emerging Asia – occurring through inflation in the baseline, and nominal appreciation in the other scenarios – is relatively rapid.[23] Obstfeld and Rogoff (2005) present a scenario where Asian countries maintain a dollar peg even as the US current account shrinks and the dollar weakens. In the three-region world they consider the third region – Europe – bears the brunt of the adjustment, with a sharp appreciation of the euro as the US deficit shrinks and Asia's surplus increases.

4. HETEROGENEITY

An additional factor in considering the European impact of a global correction is the heterogeneity across Europe in terms of initial conditions and exposure to a correction in the US external imbalance. We consider three dimensions of heterogeneity: first, differences in trade patterns; second, different financial exposures to movements in the dollar and US asset prices; and, third, differences in external positions.

4.1. The trade channel

Table 6a shows that intra-European trade constitutes the lion's share of total international transactions for European countries. The level of direct trade with the United States and East Asia is relatively low in most cases, the main exception being the high level of trade between Ireland and the United States. In addition, the data show that the United States and East Asia are broadly similar in importance as trading partners for most European countries (although, of course, the sectoral composition of trade is likely to be very different across these two regions). Accordingly, the direct impact of a slowdown (or a switch in expenditures away from imports towards domestically produced goods) in the United States on individual European countries through the trade channel is limited in magnitude. Moreover, a redistribution in spending from the United States to East Asia (as in benign adjustment scenarios) would have a roughly neutral aggregate impact, with rising trade with East Asia compensating for a decline in trade with the United States.

However, the scale of direct trade is an incomplete measure, since European firms may compete with American firms for market share in common third markets. For this reason, it is also informative to take into account such third-country effects in quantifying the importance of the trade channel. Accordingly, Table 6b shows the

---

[23] Technically, this occurs in the baseline because the model does not have scope for sterilized intervention.

Table 6a. European countries: bilateral trade patterns, 2004

	Europe	United States	Japan	Emerging Asia	Rest of the world	Total
Austria	69.0	3.2	1.0	2.8	6.3	82.2
Belgium	125.9	10.1	3.3	5.8	23.7	168.7
Finland	40.0	3.0	1.3	4.3	12.1	60.7
France	32.1	2.6	0.7	2.5	7.1	45.1
Germany	40.6	4.8	1.5	5.3	7.3	59.4
Greece	20.3	1.5	0.8	2.7	7.8	33.1
Ireland	60.6	15.9	2.6	6.6	5.4	91.1
Italy	28.1	2.4	0.7	2.8	8.1	42.2
Netherlands	81.8	7.0	2.5	12.0	13.8	117.2
Portugal	43.3	2.1	0.6	1.5	6.8	54.2
Spain	32.0	1.5	0.7	2.3	7.8	44.3
Denmark	45.4	2.7	1.2	4.0	5.6	58.9
Norway	39.8	3.7	1.1	2.8	4.8	52.2
Sweden	48.0	4.8	1.3	3.8	6.5	64.4
Switzerland	48.2	5.3	2.0	4.9	6.4	66.9
United Kingdom	21.4	4.4	1.0	4.1	6.4	37.4
Central and Eastern Europe	59.0	2.3	1.2	4.2	12.8	79.6

Note: (Exports + Imports)/GDP.
Source: IMF, Direction of Trade Statistics.

Table 6b. Trade weights in multilateral real exchange rates

	Europe	United States	Asia	Rest of the world
Austria	0.78	0.08	0.07	0.07
Belgium-Luxembourg	0.78	0.09	0.08	0.06
Finland	0.64	0.09	0.12	0.14
France	0.72	0.1	0.1	0.08
Germany	0.68	0.11	0.11	0.09
Greece	0.72	0.08	0.07	0.14
Ireland	0.64	0.21	0.10	0.05
Italy	0.69	0.11	0.10	0.10
Netherlands	0.81	0.07	0.07	0.05
Portugal	0.82	0.08	0.05	0.04
Spain	0.78	0.07	0.07	0.08
Denmark	0.76	0.08	0.1	0.06
Sweden	0.69	0.13	0.1	0.08
United Kingdom	0.61	0.18	0.12	0.09
CEEC	0.80	0.05	0.05	0.10
Japan	0.28	0.29	0.32	0.11
United States	0.32	0	0.26	0.42

Note: 'Double export' weights from European Commission's basket of 41 major trading partners for 2004.

weight of the United States in the multilateral real exchange rates for various European countries. The trade weights used are so-called double export weights, in order to capture not only competition in the domestic markets of the various competitors but also competition in export markets elsewhere. The bilateral exchange rates between the currency of a given country and the currencies of its competitor countries are weighted according to the competitors' share in the total supply of competing goods (including the supply by domestic producers) in each market separately and the relative share of each market in the total exports of the given country.

The results in Table 6b largely back up the data on trade volumes in Table 6a: while the United States has a high trade weight for Ireland and the United Kingdom, its weight is typically less than 10% for most European countries. Similarly, it is again the case that East Asia is comparable in importance to the United States in relation to trade weights.

Overall, the message from Tables 6a and 6b is that the trade channel is only of limited importance for most European countries – however, it poses a particular vulnerability for Ireland and, to a lesser extent, the United Kingdom. Moreover, scenarios in which contraction and/or depreciation in the United States is offset by expansion and/or appreciation in Asia represents a broadly neutral aggregate trade environment for most European countries.

4.2. The valuation channel

In Figure 6 we showed that European countries now hold much higher levels of cross-border assets and liabilities than was the case 10 or 20 years ago. As is demonstrated in the accounting framework in Appendix 1, this means that shifts in the rates of return earned on foreign assets and paid out on foreign liabilities are an increasingly important source of movements in net foreign asset positions and generate cross-border wealth effects. In this subsection, we examine the impact on European wealth of a decline in US asset markets and a depreciation in the dollar against European currencies.

Table 7 shows the estimated net dollar positions for individual European economies in the various investment categories. Our method of calculating these positions largely follows the procedures employed in Section 3 to measure the net dollar positions of the aggregate euro area, the United States, Japan and China. In particular, the net dollar position in the FDI category is the sum of a country's FDI stock in the United States plus 50% of its FDI stock in offshore financial centres. Similarly, for most countries, the net dollar position in the portfolio equity category is the sum of a country's portfolio equity stock in the US plus 50% of its portfolio equity stock in offshore financial centres. However, for five members of the euro area – Austria, Greece, France, Italy and Portugal – we are able to use their directly reported dollar positions in the portfolio asset category. In order to calculate net dollar exposures in the portfolio debt category for the other countries, we follow the pattern we observed

Table 7. Net dollar exposures (in percentage of GDP), 2004

	FDI assets	Portfolio equity	Portfolio debt	Bank	FDI liabilities
Austria	1.6	5.6	3.1	−3.0	2.2
Belgium	5.0	3.9	17.1	−2.2	7.9
Finland	4.1	3.7	4.7	−3.0	0.8
France	8.9	5.7	0.1	−4.4	3.9
Germany	7.7	2.5	4.4	4.3	4.2
Greece	0.6	0.9	0.4		0.8
Ireland	10.4			−9.6	68.8
Italy	1.6	4.1	0.2	−2.4	1.4
Luxembourg	1.1			97.2	27.0
Netherlands	22.6	30.9	31.0	2.5	16.0
Portugal	1.1	1.2	1.1	−3.1	1.3
Spain	4.5	1.2	10.3	−5.4	6.8
Denmark	7.7	8.0	21.9		9.8
Sweden	6.3	7.7	20.3	−12.9	10.3
United Kingdom	10.8	16.0	9.7	−21.6	22.9
Norway	16.1	11.7	29.9	−8.0	2.3
Switzerland	2.0	13.1	32.2	9.4	11.0

Notes: Methodology to calculate dollar exposures is described in Section 4. Net dollar positions of banks (excluding securities, where possible) are calculated from data reported by national central banks (Austria, Finland, France, Germany, Ireland, Italy, Luxembourg, the Netherlands, Portugal, Sweden, United Kingdom, Switzerland) (awaiting responses from the other central banks).

for the aggregate euro area in the previous section by assuming that total portfolio dollar assets are 3.5 times as large as direct portfolio debt assets in the United States and that total portfolio dollar liabilities are 1.67 times as large as portfolio debt liabilities vis-à-vis the United States.

We also report the estimated net dollar position of the banking sectors in each European country. For most countries, we obtained these data from the websites of national central banks; otherwise, we calculated the net dollar position of the banking sector as the sum of net foreign-currency claims on the United States plus 75% of net foreign-currency claims on other countries.[24]

Finally, we add as a memo item the level of FDI liabilities vis-à-vis the United States. This is included, since one transmission mechanism that is periodically discussed is the impact of exchange rate movements on direct investment decisions, with dollar depreciation assumed to have an adverse impact on the level of American direct investment into Europe.

---

[24] We assume that the 'foreign currency' assets and liabilities of European banks in the United States are denominated in dollars. The 75% ratio for foreign currency assets and liabilities vis-à-vis other countries is based on aggregate BIS data on the currency composition of foreign-currency assets and liabilities of its reporting banks. While the assets and liabilities of banks primarily take the form of loans and deposits (part of the 'other' category in the international investment position), the banking sector is also a holder of securities, so there is some overlap with the portfolio debt and equity categories for those countries that do not provide a breakdown between loans/deposits and other instruments.

An important message from Table 7 is that the level of dollar exposure is relatively small for most European countries. Among the members of the euro area, three groups can be distinguished, with the group of Austria, Finland, Greece, Italy, and Portugal having a low level of dollar exposure, a second group comprising Belgium, France, and Germany having an intermediate level of exposure, while the financial centres of Ireland, Luxembourg and the Netherlands have a much higher level of exposure.[25] We also highlight that the group of euro 'outs' (Denmark, Sweden and the United Kingdom) have a higher average level of dollar exposure, as do Norway and especially Switzerland. In regard to the banking sector, net dollar positions are negative for most European countries (the UK banking sector has an especially large short dollar position – see Elliott and Min, 2004), with the main exceptions being the long net dollar positions in Germany, Luxembourg and Switzerland. Finally, turning to FDI liabilities vis-à-vis the United States, Ireland has by far the largest exposure – US FDI in Ireland amounts to 69% of Ireland's GDP. Among the other countries, US FDI is substantial only for the euro 'outs' and the financial centres of Luxembourg and the Netherlands.[26]

Clearly, the information in Table 7 could be used to examine alternative shocks to the dollar and to US asset prices.[27] For a 20% dollar depreciation, in line with the disruptive scenario laid out in Section 3, all European countries would experience capital losses. The loss on FDI, portfolio equity, and bond positions for most countries would be about 1.5–3% of GDP, partially offset by a capital gain from the short dollar position in the banking sector. While the overall effect is the same order of magnitude as current account imbalances for these countries, the wealth effect from such a loss is minor. A group of countries would register noticeably higher capital losses: these include the Netherlands, Denmark, Sweden, Norway, the United Kingdom and Switzerland, even if capital gains in the banking sector provide a partial offset for the United Kingdom and Sweden. Once again, the same caveat about the lack of information on cross-border hedging applies here.[28]

Under a disruptive adjustment scenario, slower economic growth and an increase in interest rates would have a negative impact on world asset prices – and particularly US asset prices, since the shock involves a shift in portfolio preferences away from

---

[25] We do not report the portfolio equity and debt positions for Ireland and Luxembourg, since these categories are heavily influenced by the presence of large mutual fund sectors that mostly cater to offshore investors. Since shares in mutual funds are classified as portfolio equity liabilities, regardless of the investment profile of the mutual fund, these countries have large negative net equity positions and large positive net debt positions.

[26] The level of US FDI in Luxembourg and the Netherlands is over-stated due to the role of these countries as a home for holding companies that are employed by US parents to conduct direct investment in other destinations. The table does not show the level of US FDI in Central and Eastern Europe – but this stock is only a small fraction of the GDP levels of these countries.

[27] Warnock (2006) considers the impact of a simultaneous 10% decline in the dollar and 10% fall in US equity and bond markets on counterpart countries.

[28] However, the capital gains to the banking sector in the United Kingdom (and other international financial centres) will largely accrue to the foreign-owned banks that are most heavily involved in international banking transactions – that is, it may be associated with an increase in the value of the FDI liabilities of the United Kingdom and/or a larger profit outflow to the parent entities. See also Elliot and Min (2004).

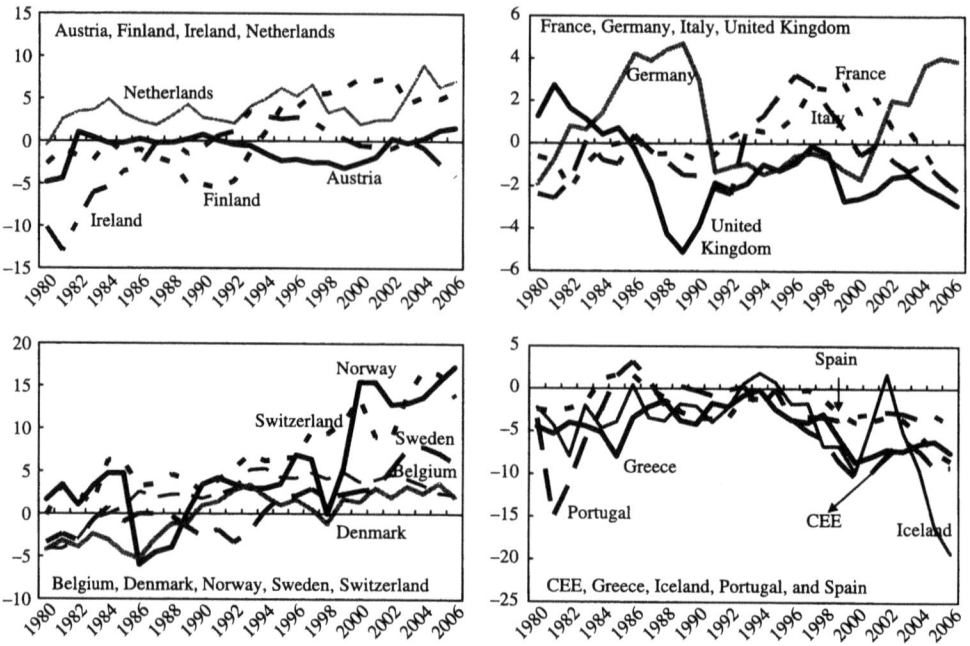

Figure 7. Europe's current account balances (percentage of GDP)

Source: IMF, Balance of Payments Statistics.

US assets.[29] This would amplify the capital losses suffered by countries with large investment positions in the United States. While asset price changes would have an additional impact on net external positions, they would have a more pronounced effect on domestic financial wealth, in light of the still strong home bias in asset holdings. From this perspective, the effects on economic activity would likely be strongest in the countries suffering the largest decline in asset prices. Indeed, the disruptive scenario described in Section 3 features a sharper decline in activity in the United States than elsewhere.

4.3. Net external positions

Figures 7 and 8 show that the broad external balance of the European economy obscures significant differences in external positions across individual European countries. These differences are highlighted in Table 8, which shows the distribution of current account balances and net foreign asset positions, plus the decomposition of the latter between net equity and net debt. There is a bi-modal distribution of current account balances, with one group running sizeable surpluses (Belgium, Germany,

---

[29] In terms of historical co-movements between asset prices and exchange rates, it is noteworthy that Campbell *et al.* (2006) find little correlation between the dollar-euro exchange rate and the US stock market.

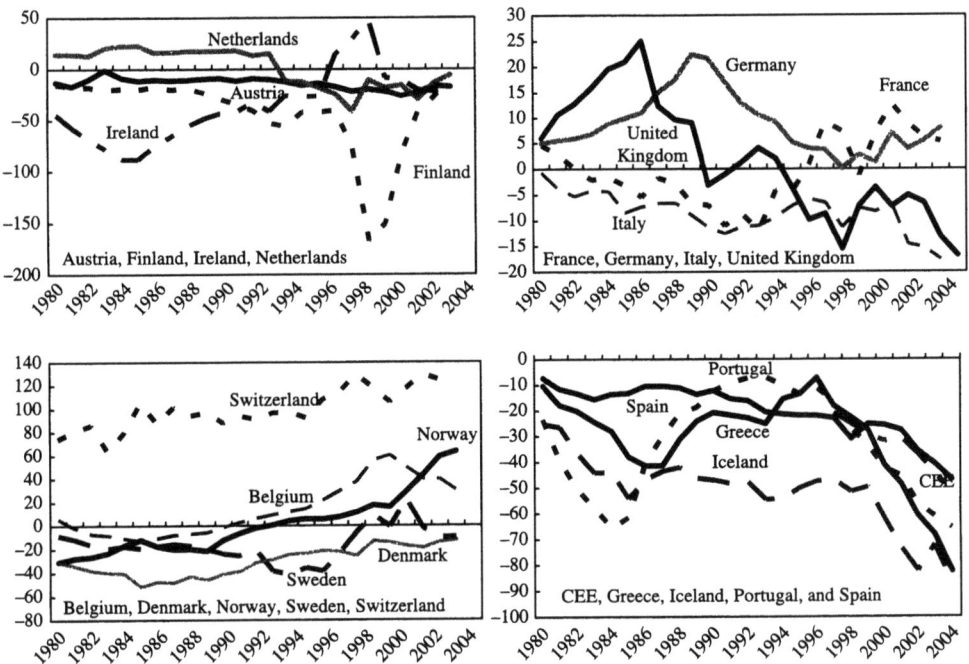

Figure 8. Europe's net foreign assets (percentage of GDP)

Source: Lane and Milesi-Ferretti (2006).

Table 8. Current account and net foreign assets, 2005 (percentage of GDP)

	Current account	Net foreign assets	Net equity	Net debt
Austria	1.4	−16.4	2.9	−19.4
Belgium	2.5	31.1	16.1	15.0
Finland	4.9	−13.3	−12.6	−0.7
France	−1.8	7.0	17.4	−10.4
Germany	4.1	16.9	16.3	0.6
Greece	−8.0	−79.8	−20.3	−59.5
Ireland	−2.7	−26.3	−197.3	170.9
Italy	−1.6	−14.9	14.0	−28.9
Luxembourg	12.5	118.7	−2698.1	2816.7
Netherlands	7.8	2.3	26.8	−24.4
Portugal	−9.3	−64.6	−29.5	−35.1
Spain	−7.4	−43.7	−7.4	−36.3
Denmark	3.3	1.1	21.8	−20.7
Norway	15.7	62.8	35.3	27.5
Sweden	6.6	−10.6	37.4	−48.0
Switzerland	16.6	93.1	6.7	86.3
United Kingdom	−2.2	−11.2	20.7	−31.9
Central and Eastern Europe	−4.7	−44.4	−38.0	−6.5

Notes: Data for 2005. Central and Eastern Europe comprises Bulgaria, Croatia, Czech Republic, Estonia, Latvia, Lithuania, Hungary, Poland, Romania, Slovak Republic and Slovenia.

Sources: Authors' calculations based on Lane and Milesi-Ferretti (2006) and *World Economic Outlook* database.

Luxembourg, the Netherlands, Norway, Sweden, and Switzerland) and another group running deficits of similar magnitude to the US deficit (Greece, Portugal, Spain and the Central and Eastern European countries). This distribution is broadly replicated for net foreign asset positions (the correlation is 0.85), highlighting the persistence of these imbalances.

In terms of exposures, these differences in external positions matter for several reasons. First, to the extent that the correction of global imbalances involves an increase in global interest rates (for instance due to an increase in domestic investment in Asia and the oil producers, as in the 'policies' scenario in Section 3), this will have a positive impact on the financial terms of trade of countries with a positive net debt position and a corresponding negative impact on countries with a negative net debt position. Table 8 shows that there are considerable differences between aggregate net positions and net debt positions. In particular, the external liabilities of some countries primarily take the form of equity – the CEEC group provides a good illustration, with FDI the predominant form of liabilities (Lane and Milesi-Ferretti, 2007a).[30] Conversely, most of the advanced European countries (whether aggregate creditors or debtors) have negative net debt positions – with the typical creditor nation in effect employing leverage to build a positive net external equity position. For these countries, an increase in world interest rates raises the cost of leveraging. Aside from the financial centres of Ireland and Luxembourg, the only European countries that have positive net debt positions and would thereby enjoy a positive terms of trade effect from an increase in world interest rates are Belgium, Norway, and Switzerland.

A second possibility – related to the 'disruptive' scenario in Section 3 – is that international investors will show increased risk aversion in relation to the currencies of those countries running significant current account deficits. In this case, it is important to differentiate between those countries that are members of the euro area (where the broad external balance of the aggregate euro area suggests that the euro would not be weakened under this scenario) and those outside the euro area (that is, the CEEC group). In particular, an increase in international risk aversion may reduce capital flows to these countries, with the countries most at risk being those with large recourse to external financing and significant net external debt denominated in foreign currency.[31]

Third, a disruptive adjustment scenario would have a negative impact on global equity values, through its negative impact on global economic growth.[32] As discussed earlier, the negative wealth effect of a decline in domestic equity values would be quantitatively the most important. In addition, the advanced European economies

---

[30] However, some CEEC countries do have significant net external foreign-currency debt (e.g. Hungary).

[31] See Lane and Milesi-Ferretti (2007a) for a discussion of capital flows to CEE countries.

[32] In addition to the direct valuation effects from holding US assets, European wealth may be affected indirectly via the transmission of financial shocks in the United States to asset prices in Europe and other regions. At one level, European asset prices may be negatively affected through the decline in wealth of investors taking losses in the United States. Coeurdacier (2006) provides a recent theoretical model of this mechanism.

with large net external equity positions would suffer a negative valuation effect, even for those countries with a limited net dollar exposure.

4.4. Policy discussion

Although it is important not to over-state the scale of heterogeneous exposures across Europe, this section has indicated that differences in trade patterns, financial exposures, and net external positions mean that a disruptive adjustment in global imbalances would constitute an asymmetric shock. Adjustment to this shock may in principle require non-trivial bilateral real exchange rate movements between European countries.[33] Real exchange rate adjustment between creditor and debtor members of the euro area would need to be accomplished through differential inflation rates – this would plausibly be a slow process in light of the low inflation rate in creditor countries, and may therefore be associated with more pronounced cyclical slowdowns in debtor countries, especially so if structural rigidities hinder the intersectoral reallocation of resources (see Blanchard, 2006). Outside the euro area, the other advanced European economies all have strong domestic anchors for monetary policy and can achieve bilateral adjustment vis-à-vis the euro area through nominal exchange rate movements.

Countries of Central and Eastern Europe that are running large current account deficits and do not have similarly robust domestic monetary anchors would instead face a tension between external adjustment and a desire to maintain a stable nominal exchange rate against the euro, as a precursor to eventual euro adoption. A key policy issue in these countries is ensuring that the economies are flexible enough to cope with a potentially large shift in international relative prices and external demand.

5. CONCLUSIONS

This paper has attempted to assess the potential impact on Europe of an unwinding of global imbalances. We have emphasized that the growth in trade and financial linkages between Europe and the rest of the world means that the spillover impact on Europe of a contraction in the US deficit and Asian surpluses is now larger than 20 years ago. That said, we have also shown that the scale of global integration in trade and finance remains limited, and the exposure of Europe to external shocks should not be overstated.

In terms of overall adjustment, the model simulations show possible paths for current accounts, real exchange rates, and growth under alternative adjustment scenarios. In particular, they highlight how a reduction in the US trade deficit is likely

---

[33] The vulnerability of high current account deficit countries to a decline in global liquidity is well exemplified by the sharp decline in the Icelandic krona during the first half of 2006.

to be associated with substantial real dollar depreciation, but – if exchange rates in Asia are allowed to adjust – need not imply large real exchange rate changes for the euro area.

The scenarios also suggest that 'structural reforms' in the euro area – broadly interpreted to encompass measures that increase competition in goods and labour markets and stimulate productivity growth – can help the adjustment process from a global perspective by modestly helping US current account adjustment, but especially by helping sustain world growth. Of course, the most important dimension of these policies is their domestic impact on European economic performance. However, with increasing levels of global economic integration, even the determination of domestically orientated policies must take into account international factors. Indeed, a major motivation for structural reforms is to boost the flexibility of European economies so as to improve their capacity to cope with globalization and swings in the external environment.

A particular contribution of our paper has been to quantify the importance of the valuation channel in these alternative adjustment scenarios. In particular, we have shown that the exposure of Europe to the dollar, while non-negligible, is much smaller than the exposure of emerging Asia and Japan. To the extent that a real effective depreciation of the dollar occurs primarily vis-à-vis the largest creditor countries and regions – emerging Asia, Japan, and oil exporters – the consequences for Europe in general, and the euro area in particular, would not be large.

Clearly, the risks for Europe are much more significant if creditor country currencies, many of which closely track the US dollar, fail to adjust, so that at least in the short term a weakening of the dollar would imply a substantial real effective appreciation for Europe and the euro area. In turn, this could have strong negative repercussions on activity, underscoring the importance of policy measures that help sustain output and demand.

Looking forward, a shift in international portfolio preferences may well be associated with an increase in the role of the euro as a reserve currency (see, for example, Chinn and Frankel, 2007). While we have not addressed this issue in the paper, one could envisage scenarios where net exports are negatively affected by the appreciation of the euro, but economic activity benefits from a decline in required returns on euro area assets.

Finally, we have probed possible differences across European economies in their vulnerability to a shift in global imbalances. While there is substantial variation in the extent of trade and financial linkages between individual European countries and the United States and Asia, the scale of such linkages is limited even for the most exposed countries (with the possible exception of Ireland). If this shift were to be accompanied by a less benign international financial environment, characterized by higher spreads on debtor countries and less bountiful capital flows, some countries in Central and Eastern Europe may be forced to undergo a sharp adjustment in their external accounts.

Discussion

Paolo Pesenti
Federal Reserve Bank of New York, NBER and CEPR

This paper fills an important gap in our understanding of the implications of global rebalancing. The focus is on Europe, usually the innocent (and marginal) bystander in the debate on current account adjustment. The key message of the paper is that a global hard-landing scenario would have comparatively smaller wealth effects in Europe than in other parts of the world, but its implications for European real and financial markets would be highly asymmetric across countries.

To some extent there is a risk that this paper will be judged more on the basis of its methodology than its bottom line. But it is worth emphasizing that its general direction of analysis is fully convincing, and the basic message pervasive. At a very minimum, readers will find value added in the detailed quantitative projections presented here, estimates that represent the benchmarks against which any future investigation will be compared.

For most analysts, current and future trajectories of global imbalances basically represent a tale of two regional blocs: the United States on the borrowing side, vis-à-vis a constellation of net lenders typically identified with emerging Asia and the oil exporters. According to the conventional wisdom, Europe (and Japan, for that matter) have relatively little to do with the dynamics of world saving gluts or investment shortages. And in those rare cases in which Europe is mentioned in the context of the debate, its role is confined to two main issues. First, it is argued that European structural reforms would help to spur world growth and allow the United States to spread the 'economic engine' burden over a larger set of importer countries. Second, as long as rebalancing requires a dollar adjustment in effective terms, the more limited is exchange rate flexibility in emerging Asia, the stronger needs to be the appreciation of the European currencies against the dollar (an argument that some – including myself – find misleading but others consider self-evident: it all depends on whether the extent of dollar adjustment is taken as an exogenous *datum* rather than as an endogenous variable).

The paper has something to say about these issues, as the role of structural reforms is investigated in the so-called 'policies' scenario, and limited exchange rate flexibility in emerging Asia is incorporated in all simulation analyses of European currencies. But the paper covers broader ground, as it considers a series of rebalancing scenarios in the global economy, some involving a smooth macroeconomic adjustment, some characterized by sharper movements in asset prices, and investigates thoroughly the role of trade and financial linkages between Europe and the rest of the world.

The paper does not develop its own simulation model. Instead, it follows a 'hybrid' approach. It starts by considering current account scenarios obtained by using the Global Economy Model (GEM), the multi-country model developed at the

International Monetary Fund. Next, it uses these scenario projections as a kind of 'conditioning assumption' to forecast paths of financial variables and valuation effects excluded from GEM. The assessment of capital gains and losses is carried out by accounting for data on financial asset composition in 2005 and projecting gross inflows and outflows over time, in such a way that net flows are consistent with the GEM simulations. The shares of currency denomination are assumed to remain constant over time. This approach allows tackling issues left virtually unexplored in the literature, such as the quantitative implications of wealth effects in the process of current account and exchange rate adjustment in Europe.

Is this approach successful?

I am not sure I can be an impartial judge, as I have quite a few vested interests here. I share with Douglas Laxton the main responsibility for the design of GEM, and I have been directly involved in elaborating some of the aforementioned rebalancing scenarios, which first appeared in a series of research papers and in the IMF's *World Economic Outlook*. From my (biased) vantage point, what the authors do is very clever. Of course, it is also slightly problematic. Ideally, macroanalyses of wealth effects and asset prices should be designed with an eye to analytical consistency, modifying the simulation model as appropriate to incorporate new elements and desired features (or, perhaps, should rely on a new model tout-court). But this strategy is bound to be highly costly given time and resource constraints, and – frankly – it is unclear whether at the end of the day the net gains relative to the hybrid approach would be sizeable enough.

There are very good reasons to adopt the GEM projections as a starting point. Because of its general-equilibrium structure, GEM guarantees the internal coherence of the simulations, both at the intratemporal level (thanks to its integrated system of balance of payments accounting across countries) and the intertemporal one (solvency/sustainability considerations, consistent expectations, etc.). Far from embracing theoretical unorthodoxies, GEM is a representative model within its class (a medium-scale, multi-country, multi-sector dynamic macroeconomic model), and its properties and calibration are similar to most outstanding policy evaluation models, including SIGMA at the Board of Governors, NAWM at the European Central Bank, etc.

Also, GEM has been designed to incorporate satisfactory solutions to a large array of analytical problems arising in multi-country macromodels. As an example, consider the choice of long-term elasticity of import substitution.

As mentioned in Section 3.2, high values for this elasticity are inconsistent with macro evidence, but low values are inconsistent with trade/micro studies.

According to the GEM steady-state calibration this elasticity is relatively high (2.5). The paper states that 'as a result, the adjustment in real effective exchange rates associated with reduced external current account imbalances is generally smaller relative to other model-generated estimates in the literature'.

But this needs to be clarified: in fact, GEM's analytical framework includes specific real rigidities (in the form of import adjustment costs) that reduce the effective import elasticities in the short term, allowing for realistic projections of short-term swings in international prices. It is true that the implied paths for real exchange rates in the GEM scenarios are less exorbitant than the ones implied by some back-of-the-envelope calculations or small-scale model exercises in the literature. Whether this is a pitfall of GEM, or rather a desirable feature, can be debated. It is perhaps worth highlighting that the GEM-based projections are qualitatively consistent with event studies on the limited role of real exchange rates in rebalancing episodes in industrialized countries (see e.g. Freund and Warnock, 2007).

Having said that, there is no question of course that some features of the GEM scenarios are open to improvement. For instance, Japan and the euro area are lumped together in one regional bloc. Partially this reflects limits to the technology of GEM at the time the scenarios were elaborated. Partially it can be argued that Europe and Japan overlap to some extent in key structural characteristics – low productivity growth, very low inflation (or deflation), and structural rigidities, particularly in the labour market. But in the two regions the pattern of net asset accumulation may turn out to be rather dissimilar going forward, and a more disaggregated analysis would be useful. Also, some of the scenarios may be strongly affected by assumptions about policy responses, in particular the weights assigned to inflation and output gaps in the description of the policy rules in the different country blocs. And, of course, the structure of international financial markets embedded in GEM is far from sophisticated, although the vast majority of open-economy dynamic stochastic general-equilibrium models share similar simplifying assumptions.

If there is a reason for concern about the methodology of the paper, this stems from the fact that the projected paths for exchange rates are assumed to be invariant to the specification of the scenario analysis, thus to the characteristics of the asset markets. To clarify this point, consider two models, one with valuation effects (e.g., with gross assets and liabilities denominated in different currencies) and the other one without. Assume that in both cases the dollar adjusts to generate a path for the trade balance consistent with sustainability. Consider a fall in the external value of the dollar today. Without valuation effects, there is no change on impact in the value of US net debt. The trade balance must improve over time to be consistent with sustainability, and further dollar depreciation after the initial jump may be required. But if valuation effects are considered, the fall of the dollar today reduces the US net debt position on impact, possibly by a sizeable amount. Thus, future trade balances need to improve by less without jeopardizing solvency. In this case, the dollar is expected to depreciate less relative to the trajectory predicted by the alternative model.

The point is that if we take the exchange rates projections generated by a model without valuation effects (such as GEM) and use them without any modification to predict the extent of valuation effects, the estimated capital gains and losses may be biased upward. In fact, if we had used the correct model with valuation effects from the very beginning, the simulated degree of currency volatility would have been endogenously lower relative to the baseline projections, other things being equal.

A related problem with the approach of the paper is that it is not possible to assess how sensitive are consumption and investment behaviours to the estimated wealth effects. In fact, the methodology of the paper allows for no feedback from asset price changes to macroeconomic variables.

These methodological issues notwithstanding, my feeling is that the key results of the paper are quite robust. It is worth summarizing them briefly.

The United States mostly gains from valuation effects, while the rest of the world (including Europe, but especially China and Japan) suffers extensive capital losses under the disruptive scenario. A disruptive scenario implies capital losses, partially offset by capital gains in the banking sector. The weakening of the dollar reduces the value of European-owned dollar-denominated claims, although wealth effects are comparatively smaller than in Asia. This is because the trade channel is of limited importance (for most European countries the direct weight of the United States and Asia in trade is relatively small, with the partial exceptions of Ireland and the United Kingdom). Also, the level of dollar exposure (and vulnerability to hard landing in currency markets) is relatively small for most countries in the euro area. As most countries have negative net debt, global rebalancing with higher interest rates would raise the cost of leveraging almost anywhere in Europe.

However – and this is possibly the most pervasive part of the paper – there is considerable heterogeneity in the macroeconomic responses within Europe. For Italy (and Austria, Finland, Greece, Portugal) exposure is relatively low. For France, Germany (and Belgium), the degree of exposure is intermediate. Exposure is high in Ireland, Luxembourg, the Netherlands, but especially outside EMU, in countries such as the United Kingdom and Switzerland. And there is dispersion in size (and sign) of current account balances and net asset positions.

The bottom line is that a global hard landing would represent an asymmetric shock in Europe, requiring bilateral real exchange rate movements through inflation differentials or, more likely, cyclical slowdowns in debtor countries such as Spain and Central Europe relative to surplus countries such as Germany. Outside the euro area, there would be scope for bilateral exchange rate adjustment. In Central Europe this may well lead to a tension between need for adjustment and desire to maintain stable exchange rates.

Global adjustment and increased risk aversion may reduce capital flows to European countries outside the euro area. Although it is difficult to gauge the effective implications (and implied risks) for saving/investment behaviours in Europe, there is little disagreement on the validity and robustness of these conclusions.

Federico Sturzenegger
Harvard University and Universidad Torcuato Di Tella

In this paper Philip Lane and Gian Maria Milesi-Ferretti address the issue of how valuation adjustments in foreign assets may affect the adjustment to global imbalances with particular attention to understanding how it would affect European countries individually. An important aim of the paper is to show that in spite of the fact that Europe as a whole appears to be fairly balanced there may be substantial heterogeneity among European countries and that some should prepare for adjustments in the event of an unwinding of global imbalances.

It is clear, according to the authors, that the world is seeing large global imbalances and that these imbalances will have to be corrected sooner or later. They do not take position on how these imbalances will be resolved, but they certainly assume that they will. They point out that global imbalances have come with large increases in gross asset positions, so that valuation effects may play an important role on how the adjustment does actually play out.

In a nutshell the paper concludes that asset positions, while heterogeneous across countries, imply a Europe that is long the dollar, though exposure is not very large. Still, however, Europe should brace for an adjustment, though this may be dwarfed by what is in store for China and Japan.

I would group my concerns to the exercise in two major themes. One has to do with whether the exercise as postulated makes sense from a conceptual point of view. The other has to do with the technical aspects of how the exercise is conducted. As I will try to argue, the paper has problems on both of these dimensions, something that may not be entirely surprising given the difficulty of what is attempted.

Let us start with the conceptual issues, i.e. the motivation and underlying assumptions which are necessary to make the exercise meaningful. First, the paper takes as a fact that global imbalances need to be corrected. It is somewhat surprising that the authors just take this as a given considering the substantial literature that claims that such imbalances respond to underlying fundamentals that may make it quite persistent (see the work of Dooley *et al.*, 2004; Caballero *et al.*, 2005; Engel and Rogers, 2006; Mendoza, 2006; and Hausmann and Sturzenegger, 2006, 2007). Of course the authors are free to analyse any future path they choose to, but by failing to acknowledge that the current configuration is potentially sustainable, their exercise becomes one-sided, ignoring those cases where the measured disequilibria may remain or even increase (as has been the case since the authors presented the first version of their paper), potentially moving exchange rates move in opposite directions to the ones assumed here (which has not been the case since they presented the first version of this paper).

But even if we buy into this logic we need to acknowledge that countries hold an international asset position to diversify risks. As a result sometimes the value of these assets changes, creating winners and losers. Measuring the valuation changes from exchange rate changes does not imply either that the original portfolio was not optimal, nor that countries will want to change their portfolios from learning what would happen to their asset values if the exchange rate moves in a given direction. I tend to believe portfolios are optimal given an expected distribution of possible valuation and exchange rate changes. Or are Lane and Milesi-Ferretti assuming that countries buy into inevitable capital losses? I am not completely sure what we should read from the exercise once we acknowledge that exchange rates may move in the opposite direction and winners become losers and vice versa. In the end, would anybody want to change their portfolio as a result of seeing the exercise produced in this paper? Unlikely.

Let us move now to methodological issues. This entails reviewing the assumptions that are required for the current exercise to work. The paper is based on an off-the-shelf use of the IMF's GEM model. The GEM model is a multi-country dynamic stochastic general equilibrium model that relies on individual optimization. The model considers four regions: the United States; the euro area and Japan (jointly); emerging Asian economies; and the rest of the world. The key contribution of the paper is the addition of valuation effects that are not considered in the original framework. To estimate these valuation effects they need to track asset positions going forward by accumulating inflows and outflows. Because only the net amounts are predicted by GEM, predicting the evolution of flows types becomes extremely difficult; so the authors, starting from the actual positions, need to make some assumptions. For example, they assume that 'Inflows and outflows of specific types – direct investment, portfolio equity, portfolio debt, other investment flows, and reserves – are assumed in most cases to remain constant as a share of GDP, broadly reflecting recent trends'. This assumption is certainly odd, as one would expect the composition of flows to change significantly across the different adjustment scenarios suggested by the authors. Additionally, it is assumed that the currency composition does not change over time, which also seems at odds with the large expected changes in exchange rates predicated by the model. GEM does not run into these contradictions because there is a single international bond, but as a result appears to be a set-up that is quite inappropriate to tackle the issue of the effect of valuation changes.

At a more basic level, because the authors tag on valuation changes to a model that does not allow for valuation changes they implicitly make two key assumptions. First, that asset prices do not change as valuation changes (e.g., as a result of exchange rate changes) occur. This, for example, implies that foreign equity prices do not respond to the dollar depreciation. However, Campbell *et al.* (2006) show that there are important co-movements between stock markets and the dollar. These relationships seem to have been ignored. Second, perhaps more importantly, that consumption choices do not change in response to changes in aggregate wealth. I see this as a violation of the basic principle of consumer optimization which states that consumption needs to be on the budget constraint. Omitting this suggests a very cavalier approach to macroeconomic modelling. The authors acknowledge this in the paper, but refer to future work to sort out the issue.

These problems refer to the intellectual consistency of the exercise, but even if we are willing to accept a model where consumption and asset prices do not change in the face of changes in wealth, a decision has to be made still on how the valuation changes will be measured. This also requires making heroic assumptions. Lane and Milesi-Ferretti suggest for equities, to provide an example, that stock values be updated by

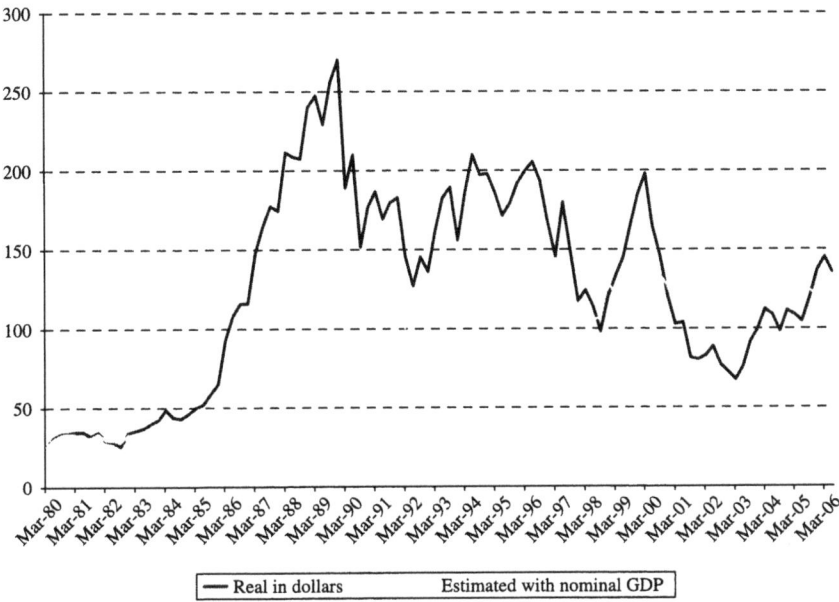

Figure 9. Real and estimated Nikkei in dollars (1980–2006)

Source: Global Financial Data, and IFS.

(real) GDP and then adjusted by the exchange rate. It is difficult to assess how good this approximation will be going forward. But one potential check is to see how it would have performed in the past. Figures 9, 10 and 11 show how it would have done for Japan, the United Kingdom and Brazil, three countries sufficiently different that allow us to assess the validity of the assumption in different contexts. What I do is to take the value of the stock market, increase it by nominal output growth and then convert it to dollars, presumably what the authors are doing as they extrapolate asset values forward.[34] I compare these numbers with actual dollar stock prices. While the assumption works pretty well for the stagnant Japanese stock market, it does not work well for the United Kingdom and Brazil. As we know the UK and Brazilian stock market have had significant rallies, as both economies became increasingly globalized during the last decade. As a result the estimation that bases capital gains on current output growth potentially underestimates in a very substantial way the valuation changes that may occur. The reason is simple: valuation changes represent present value improvements and thus magnify dramatically current output changes. If globalization persists in accelerating world output growth the suggested valuation changes will be dwarfed by real changes. On the other hand, if the world jumps into a global crisis and recession, then valuation drops will be much larger than predicted in this setup.

---

[34] It is not clear if they use nominal or real GDP. Nominal GDP should be used for the exercise to make sense.

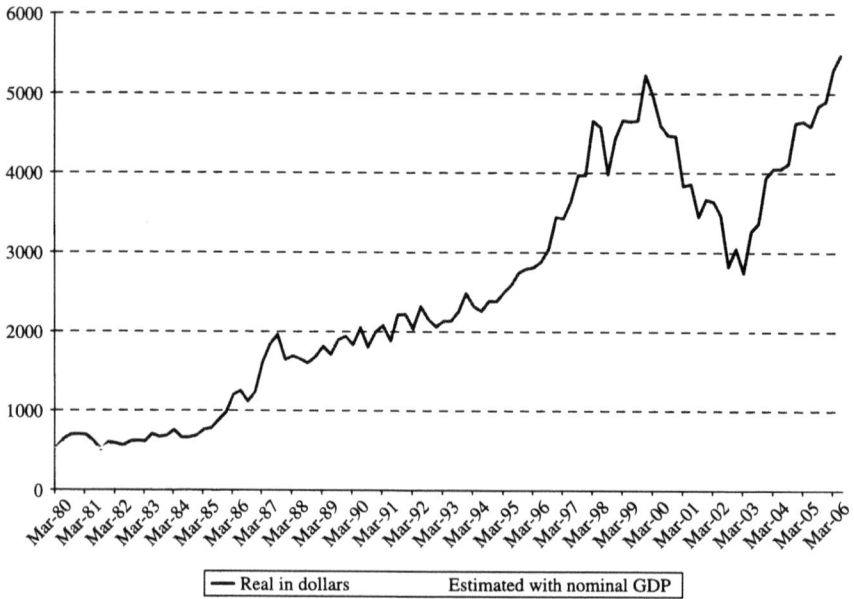

Figure 10. Real and estimated FTSE in dollars (1980–2006)

Source: Global Financial Data, and IFS.

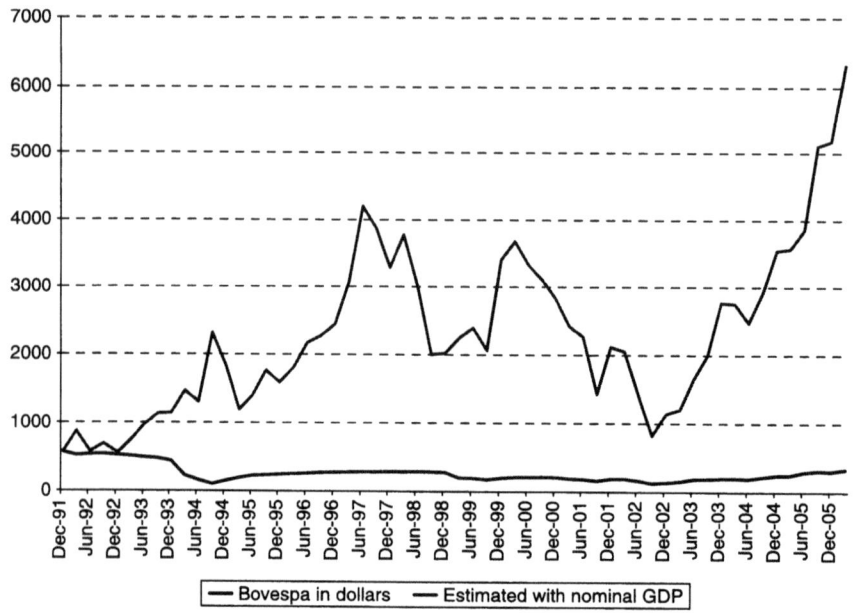

Figure 11. Real and estimated Bovespa in dollars (1980–2006)

Source: Global Financial Data, and IFS.

In concluding, we return to the issue of global imbalances. They are currently large and asset values will play a fundamental role in their adjustment. But today nobody truly knows how the adjustment will play out.

Panel discussion

Paul Krugman wondered about the negative output effects in the disruptive scenario. The results suggest that monetary policy is not loose enough in appreciating countries, and inappropriately tight in depreciating countries. So one possible policy implication of the paper is that monetary policies should respond more adequately to the US current account adjustment if this is identified as a one-time event.

Roubini noted the extent of the heterogeneity within the EU in terms of current account surpluses and deficits but also in terms of housing bubbles. For those countries with housing bubbles (Spain for example) the swing in the dollar can be very painful. Linda Goldberg also stressed the heterogeneity of European countries in terms of the flexibility to switch resources across sectors.

APPENDIX 1. DECOMPOSITION OF CHANGES IN NET FOREIGN ASSETS

In earlier work, we have developed an accounting framework that is helpful in thinking about the dynamics of external positions (Lane and Milesi-Ferretti, 2005, 2007b). We provide a brief presentation of this framework in this appendix.

The change in the net foreign asset position B can be written as follows:

$$B_t - B_{t-1} = CA_t + KG_t + E_t \tag{1}$$

where B_t is the net foreign asset position, CA_t is the current account balance, KG_t is the capital gain or loss on net foreign assets (equal to the change in stocks minus the underlying flows) and the term E_t includes factors such as capital account transfers (the so-called capital account balance) and errors and omissions that drive a wedge between a country's current account and net inflows of capital. In turn, the current account CA_t equals the sum of the balance on goods, services, and current transfers $BGST_t$ and the investment income balance $i_t^A A_{t-1} - i_t^L L_{t-1}$, where A and L are external assets and liabilities, respectively, and i_t^A, i_t^L are the nominal yields on these assets and liabilities.[35]

Indicating ratios to GDP with lower-case letters, we can express (1) as follows:

$$b_t - b_{t-1} \equiv bgst_t + \frac{i_t^A A_{t-1} - i_t^L L_{t-1}}{Y_t} + \frac{KG_t}{Y_t} - \frac{g_t + \pi_t}{(1 + g_t)(1 + \pi_t)} b_{t-1} + \varepsilon_t \tag{2}$$

---

[35] We incorporate international labour income in the term BGST.

where g_t is the growth rate of real GDP, π_t is the inflation rate, and the term ε includes the ratio of capital transfers and errors and omissions to GDP. The second and third term on the right-hand side of Equation (2) captures the effect of nominal returns on external assets and liabilities on the evolution of the external position. To see this more clearly, define $kg_t^A (kg_t^L)$ as the ratio of the capital gain on external assets (liabilities), measured in domestic currency, to the outstanding stock of external assets (liabilities) at the beginning of the period, so that $kg_t^A A_{t-1} - kg_t^L L_{t-1} = KG_t$. Then the real rate of return on foreign assets, measured in domestic currency, will equal $r_t^A = (1 + i_t^A + kg_t^A)/(1 + \pi_t) - 1$, and an analogous definition will hold for the rate of return on foreign liabilities r_t^L. Using these definitions, we can re-write (2) as follows:[36]

$$b_t - b_{t-1} \equiv bgst_t + \frac{r_t^L - g_t}{1 + g_t} b_{t-1} + \frac{r_t^A - r_t^L}{1 + g_t} a_{t-1} + \varepsilon_t \qquad (3)$$

This framework delivers several important insights. First, the trade balance is only one factor in determining the aggregate evolution of the net foreign asset position: the 'intrinsic dynamics' of net foreign assets depend on the difference between the rate of return on liabilities and the growth rate, captured by the second term on the right-hand side of (3), which is familiar from the standard debt accumulation equation. The importance of this effect depends on a country's net foreign asset position – an increase in the rate of return improves the net foreign asset position of a creditor but is adverse for a debtor.

Second, when rates of return on external assets and liabilities differ, the gross scale of external assets and liabilities matters in addition to the net position, as shown by the last term on the right-hand side of Equation (3). Differences in rates of return between external assets and liabilities can arise for various reasons:[37]

- In larger advanced economies, assets tend to be denominated in foreign currency and liabilities mostly in domestic currency. Consequently, an unexpected exchange rate depreciation (not reflected in *ex ante* interest differentials) will increase the domestic-currency rate of return on external assets and hence improve the net foreign asset position. More generally, differences in the portfolio composition of external assets and liabilities (for example, differences in the debt-equity mix) can imply differences in rates of return.
- In contrast, for emerging markets that are net debtors and whose external liabilities are primarily denominated in foreign currency, a real exchange rate depreciation raises the domestic-currency burden of foreign liabilities. In recent years, however, a trend towards a larger share of external liabilities denominated in domestic currency is at play in emerging markets as well, driven in particular by the increased importance of foreign FDI and portfolio equity investment.

---

[36] The same equation can be written using real rates of return in dollars, rather than domestic currency, using the equivalence $1 + r_t^\$ = (1 + r_t)(1 + s_t)$ where s_t is the rate of real domestic-currency appreciation vis-à-vis the US dollar.

[37] See also the extended discussion in Lane and Milesi-Ferretti (2005).

- Differential changes in asset prices (for example, in stock prices) across countries will tend to drive a wedge between returns on external assets and liabilities.

APPENDIX 2. ESTIMATING THE CURRENCY COMPOSITION OF NET FOREIGN ASSETS

This appendix summarizes the methodology used to estimate the currency composition of net foreign assets for the euro area, as well as for China, Japan and the United States.

The euro area

We rely on a variety of sources, described more in detail below, and we focus in particular on holdings denominated in US dollars and in euros.

External assets

For *foreign direct investment abroad* and *portfolio equity investment assets*, we assume that investment in each country is denominated in the currency of that country. In particular, all euro area holdings in the United States and half of FDI in offshore centres are assumed to be denominated in dollars. Data on the geographical breakdown of the euro area's International Investment Position at end-2004 comes from the August 2006 ECB Bulletin. The share of investment in dollars is assumed to be unchanged in 2005.

For *portfolio debt assets*, ECB (2005) reports the currency breakdown between euro and other currencies at end-2004. To estimate the weight of the dollar in other currencies, we use statistics on the currency composition of portfolio debt holdings by euro area Monetary and Financial Institutions (MFIs), reported by the ECB, and assume that the dollar share in non-euro currencies is the same for non-MFI portfolio debt holdings. In light of the 6 percentage point decline in the share of euro-denominated portfolio debt holdings by MFIs between end-2004 and end-2005, we assume a 5% decline in the share of total euro-denominated holdings in 2005 relative to 2004.

For *other investment assets*, we assume that all euro area investment in the United States and half of the investment in offshore centres is denominated in dollars, with the remainder assumed to be denominated in euros. We again rely on the geographical breakdown of the euro area International Investment Position at end-2004 from the August 2006 ECB Bulletin.

For *foreign exchange reserves*, we assume a 90% weight for the US dollar.

External liabilities

For *foreign direct investment* and *portfolio equity investment* in the euro area, we assume that all liabilities are denominated in euros.

For *portfolio debt liabilities*, we use the currency breakdown between euro and other currencies at end-2004 reported in ECB (2005). We assume that the dollar share in non-euro debt liabilities is 60%, in line with BIS data on the currency composition of international banking liabilities in the euro area.

For *other investment liabilities*, we assume that the share denominated in dollars is 25%, with the remainder denominated in euros. This assumption ensures that the net dollar position in the 'other investment' category is broadly balanced.

China

We have virtually no direct information on the currency composition of China's external position, and hence our assumptions are subject to significant uncertainty.

External assets

For *foreign direct investment abroad* and *portfolio equity investment assets*, we assume for simplicity that Chinese holdings in the United States are zero. The United States currently reports 2005 FDI holdings by China at historical cost of around US$0.5 billion.

For *portfolio debt assets and other investment assets*, we assume that all Chinese overseas holdings are denominated in US dollars.

For *foreign exchange reserves*, we assume a 75% weight for the US dollar and a 25% weight for the euro.

External liabilities

For *foreign direct investment* and *portfolio equity investment* in China, we assume that all liabilities are denominated in renmimbi.

For *portfolio debt and other investment*, we assume that all liabilities are denominated in US dollars.

Japan

We rely primarily on data from the Bank of Japan.

External assets

For *foreign direct investment abroad* and *portfolio equity investment assets*, we assume investment in each country is denominated in the currency of that country. In particular, all Japanese investment in the United States and half of Japan's FDI in offshore centres is assumed to be denominated in dollars. Data on the geographical breakdown of Japan's portfolio equity and FDI assets comes from the CPIS and the Bank of Japan, respectively.

For *portfolio debt assets*, we use Bank of Japan's data on the currency composition of portfolio debt holdings by Japanese residents (available at http://www.boj.or.jp/en/type/stat/boj_stat/bop/pip/pip2005.zip)

For *other investment*, we assume that the net position (assets minus liabilities) – which is negative at 3–4% of GDP – is denominated in US dollars.

For *foreign exchange reserves*, we assume a 75% weight for the US dollar and a 25% weight for the euro.[38]

External liabilities

For *foreign direct investment* and *portfolio equity investment* in Japan, we assume that all liabilities are denominated in yen.

For *portfolio debt liabilities*, we assume that a 90% share is denominated in yen and a 10% share in US dollars. Data from the US Treasury Report on US Portfolio Holdings of Foreign Securities indicates that 95% of US portfolio debt claims in Japan are yen-denominated.

For *other investment liabilities*, see the discussion of the 'other investment' category above.

United States

Our primary sources are Nguyen (2006), who reports details on the US International Investment Position, and Tille (2005), who describes available sources for determining the currency composition of the US external portfolio. We focus in particular on the determination of the net dollar position and the net foreign-currency position.

External assets

For *foreign direct investment abroad*, we rely on the geographical data at historical cost published by the Bureau of Economic Analysis (2006), and approximate the market value by multiplying historical cost holdings by the ratio of aggregate market value to historical cost value. We assume that FDI in each country is denominated in the currency of that country.

For *portfolio equity assets*, we rely on the US Treasury report on US Portfolio Holdings of Foreign Securities at end-2004 (http://www.treas.gov/tic/shc2004r.pdf), which reports the geographical distribution of US portfolio holdings, assuming that portfolio equity holdings in each country are denominated in the currency of that country. We update the data to 2005 by assuming that the individual country shares of total portfolio equity holdings remain unchanged.

For *portfolio debt holdings* we rely on the same report, which also contains information on the currency composition of these holdings (Tables 21 and 22).

---

[38] Truman and Wong (2006) argue that the weight of the dollar is likely to exceed 80%.

Table A1. Assumptions on the composition of capital flows (2006–2015)

Type of flow	Assumptions	Avg value (%)
United States		
Direct investment abroad	Constant ratio of GDP	1.4
Portfolio equity investment abroad	Constant ratio of GDP	1.0
Portfolio debt investment abroad	Constant ratio of GDP	0.4
Other investment abroad	Constant ratio of GDP	2.5
Reserves	None	0
Direct investment in the country	Constant ratio of GDP	1.4
Portfolio equity invest. in the country	Constant ratio of GDP	1.0
Portfolio debt invest. in the country	Residual to ensure that net capital flows=CA balance	5.4
Other investment in the country	Constant ratio of GDP	2.5
Euro area		
Direct investment abroad	Constant ratio of GDP	2.5
Portfolio equity investment abroad	Constant ratio of GDP	1.5
Portfolio debt investment abroad	Residual to ensure that net capital flows=CA balance	3.2
Other investment abroad	Constant ratio of GDP	3.5
Reserves	None	0.0
Direct investment in the country	Constant ratio of GDP	2.5
Portfolio equity invest. in the country	Constant ratio of GDP	1.5
Portfolio debt invest. in the country	Constant ratio of GDP	3.0
Other investment in the country	Constant ratio of GDP	3.5
Japan		
Direct investment abroad	Constant ratio of GDP	1.0
Portfolio equity investment abroad	Constant ratio of GDP	1.0
Portfolio debt investment abroad	Residual to ensure that net capital flows=CA balance	2.8
Other investment abroad	Constant ratio of GDP	1.0
Reserves	Constant ratio of GDP	0.5
Direct investment in the country	Constant ratio of GDP	0.2
Portfolio equity invest. in the country	Constant ratio of GDP	1.0
Portfolio debt invest. in the country	Constant ratio of GDP	1.0
Other investment in the country	Constant ratio of GDP	1.0
China		
Direct investment abroad	Gradually increasing ratio of GDP	0.6
Portfolio equity investment abroad	Gradually increasing ratio of GDP	0.5
Portfolio debt investment abroad	Gradually increasing ratio of GDP	0.4
Other investment abroad	Constant ratio of GDP	0.8
Reserves	Residual to ensure that net capital flows=CA balance	8.0
Direct investment in the country	Gradually declining ratio of GDP	3.0
Portfolio equity invest. in the country	Constant ratio of GDP from 2007	0.9
Portfolio debt invest. in the country	Gradually increasing ratio of GDP	0.4
Other investment in the country	Constant ratio of GDP	0.9

Notes: The average value for the residual category of capital flows changes across scenarios (because the current account balances change). The reported value corresponds to the baseline scenario.

For *other investment assets*, we use the reported currency breakdown between dollar and foreign currencies for bank claims (Nguyen, 2006, Table D) and assume that the breakdown for non-bank claims has the same currency composition. Bank claims account for around three-quarters of total other investment assets.

For *foreign exchange reserves*, we use data from the US Treasury (available at the link http://www.treas.gov/press/releases/20061119281827487.htm).

External liabilities

For *foreign direct investment* and *portfolio equity investment* in the United States, we assume that all liabilities are denominated in US dollars.

For *portfolio debt liabilities*, we use data published in the Report on Foreign Portfolio Holdings of US Securities as of 30 June 2005 (http://www.treas.gov/tic/shl2005r.pdf), which provides the currency composition of long-term debt securities, and apply the same currency share to short-term debt securities. The currency shares are assumed to have remained constant between June and December 2005.

For *other investment liabilities*, we use the reported currency breakdown between dollar and foreign currencies for claims reported by banks (Nguyen, 2006, Table I) and assume that the breakdown for the remaining claims has the same currency composition. Claims on banks account for around 70% of total other investment liabilities.

REFERENCES

Bayoumi, T., J. Lee and S. Jayanthi (2005). 'New rates for new weights', IMF Working Paper 05/99, May.

Blanchard, O. (2006). 'Adjustment within the euro: The difficult case of Portugal', mimeo, MIT.

Blanchard, O., F. Giavazzi and F. Sa (2005). 'International investors: The U.S. current account, and the dollar', *Brookings Papers on Economic Activity*, 1, 1–65.

Caballero, R., E. Farhi and P.O. Gourinchas (2005). 'An equilibrium model of "global imbalances" and low interest rates', mimeo, MIT, September.

Campbell, J., K. Serfaty-de Medeiros and L. Viceira (2006). 'Global currency hedging', mimeo, Harvard University.

Cavallo, M., and C. Tille (2006). 'Could capital gains smooth a current account rebalancing?', Federal Reserve Bank of New York Staff Report 237.

Chinn, M., and J. Frankel (2007). 'Will the euro eventually surpass the dollar as leading international reserve currency?' in R. Clarida (ed.), *G7 Current Account Imbalances: Sustainability and Adjustment*, Chicago University Press, Chicago, 283–322.

Coeurdacier, N. (2006). 'Do trade costs in goods market lead to home bias in equities?', Essec Business School.

Devereux, M.B., and C. Engel (2006). 'Expectations and exchange rate policy', mimeo, University of British Columbia and University of Wisconsin.

Devereux, M.B., and A. Sutherland (2006). 'Country portfolios in open economy macro models', mimeo, University of British Columbia and St Andrews University.

Dooley, M., D. Folkerts-Landau and P. Garber (2004). 'The revised Bretton Woods system', *International Journal of Finance and Economics*, 9(4), 307–13.

Eichengreen, B., and Yung Chul Park (2006). 'Global imbalances: Implications for emerging Asia and Latin America', mimeo, UC-Berkeley.

Elliott, J., and E. Wong Min (2004). 'The external balance sheet of the United Kingdom: *recent developments*', *Bank of England Quarterly Bulletin*, Winter.

Engel, C., and A. Matsumoto (2006). 'Portfolio choice in a monetary open-economy DSGE model', NBER Working Paper 12214, May.

Engel, C., and J. Rogers (2006). 'The U.S. current account deficit and the expected share of world output', *Journal of Monetary Economics*, 53, 1063–93.

Erceg, C., L. Guerrieri and C. Gust (2005). 'SIGMA: A new open economy model for policy analysis', Federal Reserve Board, International Finance Discussion Paper 835.

ECB (European Central Bank) (2005). *Review of the International Role of the Euro*, Frankfurt, Germany: European Central Bank (http://www.ecb.int/pub/pdf/other/euro-international-role200512en.pdf).

European Economic Advisory Group (2006). *Report on the European Economy 2006*, CESifo.

Faruqee, H. (2004). 'Global rebalancing of current accounts: A euro-area perspective', in *Euro Area Policies: Selected Issues*, IMF Country Report 04/235, August.

Faruqee, H., D. Laxton, D. Muir and P. Pesenti (2007). 'Smooth landing or crash? Model-based scenarios of global current account rebalancing', in R. Clarida (ed.), *G7 Current Account Imbalances: Sustainability and Adjustment*, Chicago University Press, Chicago, 377–451.

— (2006). 'Would protectionism defuse global imbalances and spur economic activity? A scenario analysis', NBER Working Paper No. 12704.

Freund, C., and F. Warnock (2007). 'Current account deficits in industrial countries: The bigger they are the harder they fall?', in R. Clarida (ed.), *G7 Current Account Imbalances: Sustainability and Adjustment*, University of Chicago Press, Chicago, 133–62.

Ghironi, F., J. Lee and A. Rebucci (2006). 'The valuation channel of external adjustment', mimeo, International Monetary Fund.

Gourinchas, P.-O., and H. Rey (2005). 'International financial adjustment', NBER Working Paper 11155, August.

— (2007). 'From world banker to world venture capitalist: US external adjustment and the exorbitant privilege', in R. Clarida (ed.), *G7 Current Account Imbalances: Sustainability and Adjustment*, University of Chicago Press, Chicago, 11–55.

Hau, H., and H. Rey (2006). 'Exchange rates, equity prices and capital flows', *Review of Financial Studies*, 19(1), 273–317.

Hausmann, R., and F. Sturzenegger (2006). 'Why the US current account is sustainable', *International Finance*, 9(2), 223–40.

— (2007) 'The valuation of hidden assets in foreign transactions: Why "dark matter" matters', *Business Economics*, January, 29–35.

Hunt, B., and A. Rebucci (2005). 'The U.S. dollar and the trade deficit: What accounts for the late 1990s?' *International Finance*, 8(3), 399–434.

IMF (International Monetary Fund) (2005a). 'Globalization and external imbalances', *World Economic Outlook*, Chapter III, April, International Monetary Fund, Washington DC.

— (2005b). 'How Will Global Imbalances Adjust?', *World Economic Outlook*, Appendix I.2, September, International Monetary Fund, Washington DC.

— (2006). *World Economic Outlook*, Box 1.3, September, International Monetary Fund, Washington DC.

Krugman, P. (2007). 'Will there be a dollar crisis?', *Economic Policy*, 51, 435–67.

Kumhof, M., D. Laxton and D. Muir (2005). 'The consequences of U.S. fiscal consolidation for the current account', in *United States: Selected Issues*, IMF Country Report No. 05/258, International Monetary Fund, Washington DC.

Lane, P.R., and G.M. Milesi-Ferretti (2001). 'The external wealth of nations: Measures of foreign assets and liabilities for industrial and developing countries', *Journal of International Economics*, 55, 263–94.

— (2003). 'International financial integration', *IMF Staff Papers*, 50 (Special Issue), 82–113.

— (2005). 'Financial globalization and exchange rates', IMF Working Paper 05/03, January.

— (2006). 'The external wealth of nations Mark II', IMF Working Paper 06/169, March (forthcoming, *Journal of International Economics*).

— (2007a). 'Capital flows to Central and Eastern Europe', *Emerging Markets Review*, 8(2), May, 106–23.

— (2007b). 'A global perspective on external positions', in R. Clarida (ed.), *G7 Current Account Imbalances: Sustainability and Adjustment*, Chicago University Press, Chicago, 67–98.

Martin, P., and H. Rey (2000). 'Financial integration and asset returns', *European Economic Review*, 44, 1327–50.

—— (2004). 'Financial super-markets: Size matters for asset trade', *Journal of International Economics*, 64(2), 335–61.
Mendoza, E., V. Quadrini and V. Rios Rull (2006). 'Financial integration, financial deepness and global imbalances', mimeo, University of Maryland.
Nguyen, E.L. (2006). 'The international investment position of the United States at yearend 2005', *Survey of Current Business*, July, 9–19.
Obstfeld, M., and K. Rogoff (2000). 'Perspectives on OECD capital market integration: Implications for U.S. current account adjustment', in *Global Economic Integration: Opportunities and Challenges*, Federal Reserve Bank of Kansas City, 169–208.
—— (2005). 'Global current account imbalances and exchange rate adjustments', *Brookings Papers on Economic Activity*, 1, 67–146.
—— (2007). 'The unsustainable US current account position revisited', in R. Clarida (ed.), *G7 Current Account Imbalances: Sustainability and Adjustment*, Chicago University Press, Chicago, 339–66.
Thomas, C.P., F.E. Warnock, and J. Wongswan (2004). 'The performance of international portfolios', International Finance Discussion Paper 817, Board of Governors of the Federal Reserve System.
Tille, C. (2003). 'The impact of exchange rate movements on U.S. foreign debt', *Current Issues in Economics and Finance*, 9(1), Federal Reserve Bank of New York.
—— (2005). 'Financial integration and the wealth effect of exchange rate fluctuations', Federal Reserve Bank of New York Staff Report No. 226.
Truman, E.M., and A. Wong (2006). 'The case for an international reserve diversification standard', Institute for International Economics Working Paper 06-2, May.
Warnock, F. (2006). 'How might a disorderly resolution of global imbalances affect global wealth?', IMF Working Paper 06/170, July.

Assessing China's exchange rate regime

SUMMARY

The IMF Articles of Agreement forbid a country from manipulating its currency for unfair advantage. The US Treasury has been legally required since 1988 to report to Congress biannually regarding whether individual trading partners are guilty of manipulation. One part of this paper tests econometrically two competing sets of hypothesized determinants of the Treasury decisions: (1) legitimate economic variables consistent with the IMF definition of manipulation – the partners' overall current account/GDP, its reserve changes and the real overvaluation of its currency, and (2) variables suggestive of domestic American political expediency – the bilateral trade balance, US unemployment and an election year dummy. The econometric results suggest that the Treasury verdicts are driven heavily by the US bilateral deficit, though other variables also turn out to be quite important.

In 2005 China announced a switch to a new exchange rate regime. The exchange rate would be set with reference to a basket of other currencies, with numerical weights unannounced, allowing a movement of up to ± 0.3% within any given day. Although this step was originally accepted at face value in public policy circles, scepticism is in order. The second econometric part of the paper evaluates what exchange rate regime China has actually been following. We use the technique introduced by Frankel and Wei (1994): one regresses changes in the value of the local currency, in this case the RMB, against changes in the values of the dollar, euro, yen and other currencies that may be in the basket. We find that within 2005, the de facto regime remained a peg to a basket that put virtually all weight on the dollar. Subsequently there has been a modest but steady increase in flexibility with some weight shifted to a few non-dollar currencies – but not those one might expect. In any case, the weight on the dollar was still fairly heavy in 2006. The paper tests whether the decline in the implicit weight on the dollar is related to the pressure from US officials. It also considers whether the increase in flexibility that we have seen, small though it is, has been gradually accelerating, at a rate that would suggest the likelihood of some genuine flexibility in the not-so-distant future.

— Jeffrey A. Frankel and Shang-Jin Wei

Assessing China's exchange rate regime

Jeffrey A. Frankel and Shang-Jin Wei
Harvard University and National Bureau of Economic Research

1. INTRODUCTION

The issue of the regime governing the Chinese exchange rate – and specifically whether the currency is moving away from the *de facto* peg that for ten years had tied it to the US dollar – is much more than just another application, to a particular country, of the long-time question of fixed versus floating exchange rates. It is a key global monetary issue. It bears directly on China's surpluses in the current account and in the overall balance of payments, which are major counterparts to US deficits. The question even bears more broadly on what may well become one of the key issues of international political economy in the 21st century, perhaps the primary such issue: the rise of China and its likely long-run challenge to the global hegemony of the United States.

Exchange rate regimes in emerging markets have been a primary concern of international economists and policy-makers since the 1990s cycle of record capital

---

This paper was prepared for the 44th Panel Meeting of *Economic Policy*, 12 February 2007. The authors would like to thank Yuanyuan Chen, Ellis Connolly and Chang Hong for outstanding research assistance; and to thank also for comments Jahangir Aziz, Jianxiong He, Yun Jung Kim, Sunyoung Lee, Katharine Moon, Nouriel Roubini and John Williamson. Frankel would also like to thank a number of officials in the Clinton and (current) Bush Treasury Departments, at all levels, for discussion regarding the biannual reports to Congress. Neither they, nor any institutions with which the authors are associated, bear any responsibility for any views expressed in this paper, which are those of the authors alone.

The Managing Editor in charge of this paper was Philippe Martin.

flows to these countries followed by widespread crises. Most emerging market countries switched to more flexible exchange rate regimes in that episode. China is by far the largest developing country to continue to cling to a currency peg even after the Argentine and Turkish crises of 2001. That may have something to do with the fact that the peg appears to have served China well. The country was one of the few in Asia not to succumb to the crises of 1997–8. Indeed, it was praised by the United States and others at the time for not letting its currency devalue. The Chinese currency, known both as the yuan and the Renminbi (RMB; 'People's currency'), stayed fixed against the dollar into the new phase of global capital inflows to emerging markets that began around 2003.

It is another angle, however, that gives global importance to the issue of the yuan-dollar exchange rate. The attention of policy-makers and researchers in international economics in the current decade has switched to the large and rising deficits that the United States is running in its current account and overall balance of payments. The emerging markets have by now grown so large that they are major players in the world economy. This is particularly true of China, which is on track to surpass Germany around 2008 as the world's third largest economy, even if GDP is evaluated at current exchange rates. China's importance in net international financial flows is even greater. The counterparts to those rising US external deficits are surpluses among Asian countries and major oil producers – rather than in Europe, as in the 1960s. Of these surplus countries, China has received by far the most attention.

There is a rapidly growing literature on the positive question of what are the causes of the Chinese surpluses and US deficits, as well as on the normative question of whether China should move to a more flexible exchange rate, either in its own interest, or in the interest of others, or both. The present paper does not deal with these issues. For what it is worth, we, like many others, come down on the side that China should increase its exchange rate flexibility in its own interest, but that the US deficits should not be blamed on China.

The present paper deals, instead, with two questions that, while perhaps appearing narrow and technical, lie at the heart of the debate. First, do the bi-annual US Treasury reports to Congress base their findings with regard to whether China and other trading partners are 'manipulating' their currencies on 'manipulation' in the sense of the IMF Articles of Agreement? Or, rather, on criteria that come from domestic US politics? Second, is the precise exchange rate regime that China has put into place since 2005 a genuine departure from the earlier dollar peg, in the direction of flexibility? Is it a basket peg with the genuine possibility of cumulatable daily appreciations, as was announced at the time?

The question of US findings regarding manipulation and the question of the nature of the current Chinese regime are directly connected. The connections run in both directions. Going from the first question to the second, the US political pressure has been fairly intense, and may have been an important factor behind the 2005 announcement of a change in policy, notwithstanding attempts by China's leaders to avoid the appearance of being swayed by the US push. In the paper, we test if there are timing connections between US political rhetoric and Chinese steps toward flexibility. Going in the opposite direction, if China has not in fact changed its *de facto* pegging policy, as it has its official policy, such a finding might provide ammunition for a renewed US campaign, particularly in the form of threatened Congressional legislation. If, on the other hand, the change in regime was genuine, perhaps the RMB/dollar problem is being solved, with no need for further outside intervention.

The headline empirical findings for each of our two questions might not be surprising to some knowledgeable experts and insiders. But in both cases the findings are at odds with what routinely appears in the press, even the highest quality financial press, which often reports at face value both the US Treasury findings regarding manipulation and the Chinese government's announcements regarding moves toward increased exchange rate flexibility. And in the case of the estimated weights in the new currency basket, even most experts are unable to guess correctly the identities of the non-dollar currencies to which the Chinese authorities have begun to shift.

1.1. The US Treasury as a catalyst for RMB speculation

Political pressure from the US Treasury may have played a role in the origin of the entire economic question of yuan appreciation. Although China had already been running (small) balance of payments surpluses for several years before September 2003, there had not been a tremendous amount of speculation, either in the press or in the markets, regarding the possibility of yuan appreciation. Figure 1 shows the forward exchange rates from the NDF (non-deliverable forwards) market. The yuan had actually been selling at a small forward discount against the dollar. Then, in October

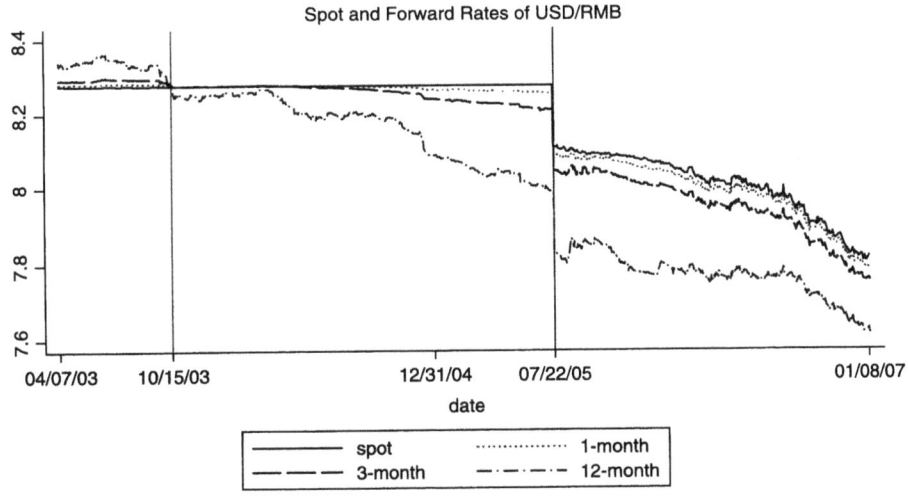

Figure 1. Prices of non-deliverable forwards (NDFs)

2003, it flipped to a forward premium. If we can use words that anthropomorphize the market, before October 2003 the NDF market expected future depreciation, but after that date it came to expect future appreciation. What happened around that time? In September 2003, Treasury Secretary John Snow travelled to China to meet with its leaders. He was reported to have browbeaten them over the currency issue and to have extracted a promise eventually to allow the RMB to trade freely on international markets. On 24 September, he successfully enlisted the support of the G-7 at a meeting in Dubai behind a new position for increased exchange rate flexibility, aimed at China. On 1 October, Undersecretary John Taylor testified before Congress in favour of a more flexible RMB. On 30 October, when the semi-annual Treasury report was released to Congress, with the finding for the first time in 9 years that concerns regarding China's currency merited bilateral negotiations, Secretary John Snow's accompanying testimony repeated 'China now has an opportunity to show leadership on the important global issue of exchange rate flexibility.' In short, the timing is right to implicate the US Treasury in the flipped sign that appears in Figure 1.

The forward premium started out small, but widened substantially in 2004. By July 2005, the one-year forward rate had moved to 8 yuan per dollar – representing a 3% forecasted revaluation that was in fact soon realized. The rate of accumulation of reserves by the People's Bank of China, that is, the balance of payments surplus, accelerated thereafter, without a concomitant rise in the trade balance or in foreign direct investment. In other words, much of the increase in the BOP surpluses is explained by inflows of (unmeasured) portfolio capital including a dramatic reversal of Chinese capital flight (Prasad and Wei, 2005). The implication of the timing in Figure 1 was that the Treasury campaign may have been the catalyst for speculation that underlay these portfolio inflows – speculation regarding future appreciation.

This is not to say that the Treasury campaign was necessarily the fundamental underlying cause of the speculative capital inflows. In the first place, the opposition political party, particularly candidates in the US presidential campaign, picked up the theme of an undervalued yuan in 2004. It is reasonable to assume they would have done so even in the absence of Administration initiatives, and that the latter were indeed an attempt to pre-empt the former. In the second place, the economic fundamentals, particularly current account surpluses in China and deficits in the United States, pointed in the direction of an eventual decline in the yuan/dollar rate and speculators would sooner or later have noticed this. Nevertheless, it is interesting to 'speculate' that China's speculative inflows and soaring reserve levels, which became the world's highest in 2006, might have been substantially more moderate were it not for the US public pressure.

1.2. Origins of the language of manipulation

Article IV of the IMF Articles of Agreement deals with Obligations Concerning Exchange Arrangements. After the Members of the Fund ratified the move to floating exchange rates in the Jamaica Communiqué of January 1976, they agreed a framework for mutual surveillance under what is called the '1977 Decision on Surveillance over Exchange Rate Policies', and they amended Article IV in 1978. Principle (A) of the 1977 Decision and Clause 3 of Section 1 of Article IV both require that each member shall 'avoid manipulating exchange rates or the international monetary system in order to prevent effective balance of payments adjustment or to gain an unfair competitive advantage over other members.' We should realize that these were themselves politically negotiated documents.[1]

In theory, the obligation is meant to fall on countries seeking to keep the values of their currencies down so as to preserve a balance of payments surplus, as much as to those seeking to keep the values of their currencies up, thereby preserving a balance of payments deficit.[2] In practice, however, the economic and political pressure on a surplus country to allow the value of its currency to adjust upward has always been far less than the pressure on a deficit country to allow the value of its currency to adjust downward. Many countries have been pushed into devaluing or floating downward. But since the end of the Bretton Woods system there have been few cases – and no important ones – of countries having been successfully pushed into revaluing or floating upward.

The once-obscure question of Chinese exchange rate policy is today one of the hottest topics in the world of international monetary policy issues. The United States has since 2003 been pressuring China to abandon its peg to the dollar and allow the RMB to appreciate, and some have claimed that China's refusal to do so constitutes unfair manipulation of the currency for competitive advantage. The motivation evidently stems from concerns over the US trade deficit, where China is following closely in the path of scapegoat that was earlier tread by Japan and Korea. American firms that have trouble competing against China are of course a source of political pressure. The Chinese have largely resisted the pressure to appreciate, even though many economists think an abandonment of the peg may be in their own interest.[3]

The meaning of the word 'manipulation' is open to dispute, since it plays no role in economic theory. The 1977 Decision refers to the intent behind the actions of the authorities. Some claim that a country that has in the past made the decision to fix its exchange rate cannot now be accused of manipulation. No deliberate action has been taken. Etymologically, the root of the word is the Latin for 'hand', which suggests active steps rather than a passive acceptance of developments. In this view,

---

[1] Boughton (2001, p. 68). The leitmotif over the decades in negotiations over the world monetary system is that the United States has favoured free-floating exchange rates and the French have opposed them. The history of the 1970s negotiations is in de Vries (1986).

[2] International Monetary Fund (2006b, p. 15): 'the term "in order to prevent balance of payments adjustment" is sufficiently broad to cover situations where a member is manipulating its exchange rate in a manner that makes it either overvalued or undervalued.'

[3] Frankel (2006a) presents the arguments, and gives references to other recent writings. In its Article IV consultation of October 2006, the International Monetary Fund took the position that the RMB was undervalued as well.

if a country opts to peg, it cannot be accused of manipulation. This is so even when future developments leave the currency 'undervalued', whether because such factors as the Balassa–Samuelson effect or low inflation have rendered a once-appropriate exchange rate level no longer appropriate, or because the anchor currency, in this case the dollar, has in the meantime depreciated against other relevant currencies. A fixed exchange rate is a legitimate choice for any country under Article IV. It is pointed out that smaller countries with long-time fixed exchange rates, say the Côte d'Ivoire, would never be accused of manipulation.

Some, on the other side, claim that China's decision to cling to a peg when the currency could as easily be allowed to appreciate is a deliberate choice with the intent to gain competitive advantage on world markets, and that it frustrates balance of payments adjustment, with adverse effects on the rest of the world (e.g., Goldstein, 2003, 2004, 2007; and Goldstein and Lardy, 2003, 2005). They point out that 'protracted large-scale intervention in one direction in the exchange market' is one of the criteria the 1977 Decision specifies the Fund shall consider 'as among those which might indicate the need for discussion' with a member over its exchange rate policy.

Although the US Treasury must report to Congress biannually regarding whether individual trading partners are manipulating currencies for unfair advantage, it has resisted Congressional pressure to name China as an outright currency manipulator. Section 2 of this paper tests econometrically two competing hypotheses regarding the determinants of the Treasury decisions. The first hypothesis is that the determinants are legitimate economic variables. The second hypothesis is that the determinants are variables suggestive of domestic US political expediency. The econometric results suggest that the Treasury verdicts are driven heavily by the US bilateral deficit with the country in question, though some of the other legitimate variables also turn out to be quite important. Partly as a result, China runs a relatively high danger of being named a manipulator.

An interesting question in international law arises. On the one hand, the US Congress did legally mandate that the bilateral balance should be an important consideration. On the other hand, the bilateral balance does not appear as a criterion in the 1977 Decision or Article IV of the International Monetary Fund, the original source of the 'manipulation' language. The Fund, rather, emphasizes instead the factors described as 'legitimate economic variables' under (1) above. We shall return at the end to the potential importance of manipulation definitions that diverge between the United States and the Fund.

1.3. The new regime

China announced the switch to a new exchange rate regime in July 2005. The exchange rate – after a minor initial revaluation of 2.1% – would be set with reference to a basket of other currencies (with numerical weights unannounced), allowing a movement of up to ± 0.3% in bilateral exchange rates within any given day. In theory

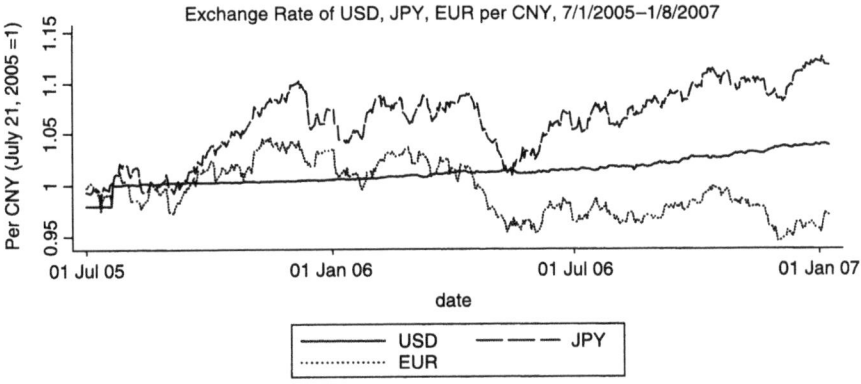

Figure 2. Value of the yuan in terms of other major currencies: whole sample

this daily band could cumulate at the maximum to a strong trend of 6.4% per month, which would require both that movement among the major currencies is low and that the Chinese authorities make maximum use of the 0.3% band. In practice, the cumulative trend has been only a small fraction of this.[4] The trend has been dwarfed by movements in the dollar against the euro, yen and other currencies, as Figure 2 shows.

Although the announced change in official policy was originally taken at face value in public policy circles, it is clear that, at least for the remainder of 2005, the currency remained closely linked to the dollar. More recently, the RMB has indeed started to give some weight to some other currencies with the result that the cumulating trend against the dollar has gradually accelerated, but the process is very slow.

The second econometric task of this paper is to analyse precisely what exchange rate regime China put in place after July 2005. We take account of the likelihood that the regime has evolved even over the short span of time since then. Fortunately, abundant exchange rate data are available daily, or even intra-daily, which makes it possible to answer the question. The basic approach uses the technique introduced by Frankel and Wei (1994): one regresses changes in the value of the local currency, in this case the RMB, against changes in the values of the dollar, euro, yen and other currencies that are candidate constituents of the basket. If China is following a perfect basket peg, it should be easy to recover precise estimates of the weights. The fit should be perfect, an extreme rarity in econometrics: the standard error of the regression should be zero, and $R^2 = 100\%$. Far more likely, the basket peg is not perfect, but one can still expect to estimate the weights with fairly tight standard errors. The real questions are how wide the band is, how great is the estimated weight on non-dollar currencies and how strong is the trend term.

---

[4] A cumulative 6% appreciation of the RMB against the dollar by the end of 2006 – one-seventeenth of the maximum possible trend – has been widely reported. But this number fails to distinguish between appreciation against a basket and appreciation against the dollar due to changes in the cross rates of currencies within the basket. Indeed, the effective exchange rate has hardly changed at all during this period.

2. DOES THE US TREASURY BASE DETERMINATION OF MANIPULATION ON VALID ECONOMICS OR POLITICAL EXPEDIENCY?

Since they were first mandated in 1988, there have been 33 biannual reports from the US Treasury regarding whether individual trading partners – particularly those in Asia – were manipulating currencies for unfair advantage (see Box 1).

Box 1. Brief history of the semi-annual Treasury reports

The US Congress mandated in its Omnibus Trade and Competitiveness Act of 1988 biannual reports from the US Treasury regarding whether trading partners were manipulating currencies. More specifically, in Section 3004, the Treasury is required to 'consider whether countries manipulate the rate of exchange between their currency and the United States dollar for purposes of preventing effective balance of payments adjustments or gaining unfair competitive advantage in international trade.' The law says the United States must hold talks with governments deemed to be breaking the rules. Fred Bergsten had originally instigated in 1986 the idea of pushing the newly industrialized economies of Asia to revalue, at a time when a large depreciation of the dollar against the yen and other traditional major currencies had not yet produced the promised improvement in the US trade balance. The US campaign was successful in persuading Korea and Taiwan to let their currencies appreciate in the late 1980s. (For the Korean case, see Bergsten, 1989 and Frankel, 1993a, b. There was an earlier precedent in the yen-dollar talks of 1983–84, in which the US Treasury pressured Japan to open its capital markets, with the motive of allowing appreciation of the yen, and reducing the pattern of capital flowing from surplus Japan to deficit America – see Frankel, 1984.)

In the first of the Reports to Congress on International Economics and Exchange Rate Policy, filed in October 1988, Korea and Taiwan, Province of China, were found to be guilty of manipulation, while Singapore and Hong Kong SAR 'got off with a warning' in that policy changes were recommended. In subsequent years, those countries pronounced manipulators, or given warnings, have always been Asian. From May 1992 to July 1994 China was the primary target. Ironically, in January 1994, China engineered a devaluation of its official exchange rate against the US dollar, unifying its dual exchange rate system. In the late 1990s, the mechanism fell somewhat into disuse: none of the countries investigated in 1996 was found to be a problem, and the reports were not filed at all after January 1997, until January 1999. These were the years of the East Asia crises, in which the concern had abruptly shifted to whether countries had been artificially keeping the value of their currencies too high rather than too low. From May 2002 to May 2003, Treasury did not even identify any countries as having been investigated. (A table in the appendix to the working paper lists the findings of all the Treasury reports, according to our classification scheme.) During this period, judged from the black market exchange rates on China's streets, the RMB was deemed overvalued.

The intense pressure on China from US politicians of both parties to revalue its currency upward began in 2003. There are plenty of good arguments pro and con, whether China should move in the direction of increasing exchange rate flexibility and/or allowing its currency to appreciate. This is true whether the criterion is China's own economic interest, or facilitating an orderly unwinding of record global current account imbalances. (Bergsten, 2006; Frankel, 2006a, 2006a; Goldstein, 2003, 2004; Goldstein and Lardy, 2003, 2005; and Roubini, 2007 are among those in favour of increased flexibility and/or revaluation for the yuan. McKinnon and Schnabl, 2004, 2006; Mundell, 2004; and Cooper, 2005 are among those opposed.) But it is clear that much of the pressure is political, tied to the record US trade deficits and loss of jobs in manufacturing.

Much of the pressure on the Treasury to name China a manipulator comes from Capitol Hill. Congressmen had entered the subject – usually considered arcane – of a trading partner's exchange rate regime. The Schumer–Graham Bill, originally proposed in February 2005, has received the most attention. It would impose WTO-illegal tariffs of 27.5% against all Chinese goods if China does not substantially revalue its currency. On 28 March 2006, Senators Baucus and Grassley proposed another Bill substituting the phrase 'currency misalignment' in place of 'unfair manipulation'. Schumer and Graham subsequently withdrew their Bill and suggested that they might return with a WTO-legal version. (By now Schumer and Graham have backed off approximately three times: first after a week-long visit to China where they became more familiar with the situation; second after China's July 2005 announcement of a change in regime, and third in 2006 when Henry Paulson was named Treasury Secretary.)

The response of the US Treasury has been measured. But ever since October 2003 – as the US entered a presidential election year – the semi-annual reports have again designated two countries as meriting recommendations or discussion: China plus one other (either Japan or Malaysia). As already noted, China announced a change in the exchange rate regime in July 2005, an abandonment of its *de facto* peg against the dollar. But perhaps in recognition that not that much had yet changed in reality, the Treasury gave China the same designation in its reports of November 2005, April 2006 and December 2006. (The reports are often submitted one or more months later than they are officially due. Perhaps busy Treasury officials do not relish devoting resources to producing a document that, at best, is ignored, and, at worst, becomes the grist for attacks by grandstanding Congressmen.) Speculation mounted that the Treasury was likely to name China a manipulator outright.

We now examine the statistical pattern of designations in the historical record since 1988. The primary goal is to assess two different interpretations of the driving force behind the Treasury reports. First, one could take the 1988 legislation and the subsequent reports at face value, as an attempt to evaluate the economics of currency undervaluation. The IMF Articles of Agreement prohibit member countries from manipulating their currencies for their own competitive advantage. The IMF has seldom in practice exercised this sort of surveillance. Only twice has the IMF found that a country has deliberately undervalued its currency, while it has found hundreds of cases of countries overvaluing their currencies.* Thus one could interpret the US Congress and Treasury as stepping in to enforce this principle on their own. The biannual Treasury reports submitted during the period when John Snow was secretary have included appendixes that are thoughtfully written to explain the economics of exchange rates and trade balances, and the way the department makes its decisions. The US Treasury (2005, Appendix) lists six important indicators that factor into its decision. They include trade and current account balances, rapid foreign exchange reserve accumulation, and measures of undervaluation and real effective exchange rate movements. The list explicitly does not include bilateral trade balances among the criteria, and the document explains why they are not economically relevant.

Second, one could interpret the biannual reports as a manifestation of political pressures within the United States. While economists do not believe that bilateral trade deficits are of much economic significance, they clearly do matter politically. Bilateral deficits are blamed for loss of US jobs, especially in manufacturing, and politicians compete to see who can use the tougher rhetoric. (Fortunately the actual policy actions of whoever holds the White House tend to some extent to be tempered by offsetting lobbying from US firms that benefit from cheap imports and by realities of international economics and politics.) The focus was on Japan 20 years ago and Korea 15 years ago. The spotlight is now on China, with India perhaps waiting in the wings, auditioning for the scapegoat role.

* This paper focuses on the US legislation and Treasury reports, more than the wisdom of IMF surveillance. The authors personally incline to the view that this provision in the Articles of Agreement has been used so rarely, and findings of manipulation are so subjective (especially when the country in question is seeking to maintain a peg), that the language of 'unfair manipulation' is not appropriate even for a country with massive, persistent, and undesirable surpluses on its current account or overall balance of payments. 'Unfairness' should be alleged rarely, and only when on firm ground, such as allegations of violations of international trade agreements.

In recent years, parallel to calls from American politicians to allow the RMB to appreciate against the dollar, the Treasury has recommended policy changes and indicated that it has commenced discussions with the Chinese government. There has been speculation that the Treasury could go to the next step, and name China as an outright currency manipulator, as it did in the early 1990s, and as it did to Korea and Taiwan, Province of China in the late 1980s. This part of the paper seeks to test two competing hypotheses: (1) that the Treasury decisions are determined by legitimate economic variables – the partners' overall current account/GDP, its reserve changes and the real overvaluation of its currency, and (2) that the Treasury decisions are determined by variables suggestive of domestic American political expediency – the bilateral trade balance,[5] US unemployment and an election year dummy.

As already noted, we use three variables to capture the first hypothesis, that the Treasury findings are motivated by genuine international economics: the overall current account surplus of the trading partner (as a percentage of its GDP), the change in the partner's reserve holdings (using its GDP as the scale variable, along with a few alternative denominators), and the value of the partner currency (relative to the IMF's concept of the PPP exchange rate). We also use three variables to capture the second hypothesis, that the reports are motivated by US politics: the bilateral balance of the United States with the partner in question, the US unemployment rate and a dummy variable for a presidential election year.

The sample consists of 63 US trading partner countries, observed in each of the 34 reports through November 2006. The variable to be explained is ordinal. Let Y denote the Treasury's decision, which can take one of the four values:

0 = country not investigated
1 = examined as a potential manipulator
2 = policy changes recommended / conducting discussions
3 = found to be manipulating its exchange rate.

Here we apply to the problem the technique of ordered probit.[6] Let us assume that Y depends on the value of a latent variable Y^*, which in turns depends on a set of observables:

$$Y^* = \mathbf{X}\beta + \varepsilon$$

and

$Y = 0$ if $Y^* < k1$
$Y = 1$ if $k1 \leq Y^* < k2$
$Y = 2$ if $k2 \leq Y^* < k3$
$Y = 3$ if $k3 \leq Y^*$

---

[5] In an exercise roughly analogous to this one, Noland (1997) found that bilateral trade imbalances explain the judgments of partners' trade policies that are made in annually mandated reports to Congress by the US Trade Representative.

[6] Less sophisticated estimation techniques were reported in the working paper version in addition to ordered probit: a linear specification, and a probit with a dichotomous dependent variable. They are omitted here to save space.

where $k1$, $k2$ and $k3$ are 'cutoff points' and $k1 < k2 < k3$ and residual ε is assumed to follow a standard normal distribution. Vector **X** includes US bilateral trade balance with the country in question, the partner country's overall current account balance (as a share of GDP), the extent of the partner's currency overvaluation, the scaled change in the partner's reserve position, US unemployment and a dummy for US election year. In some regressions we also include period dummies, to capture a changing economic or political environment generally. In this case, US unemployment and election year dummy are dropped out as they are linear combinations of the period dummies. The cutoff points and β can be estimated by maximum likelihood.

2.1. Estimates from ordered probit analysis

The results are presented in Tables 1–3. We report standard errors that are clustered by country.

The first column shows estimation on the complete sample of 63 trading partners. Two variables stand out as consistently stronger than any others: the US bilateral trade balance with the country in question, and the partner's overall current account as a share of GDP. Both show coefficients that are of the hypothesized sign and highly significant. The only other variable that is significant, even at the 10% level is the US election year dummy. The partner reserves variable[7] – essentially its balance of payments surplus – generally appears statistically insignificant.

The second column reports our preferred estimation. It omits from the sample nine oil-exporting countries, because this is what the Treasury says it does.[8] Now the effect of the partner's real exchange rate rises above the 10% significance level, as does the US unemployment rate. The election year dummy loses its significance. There were only five presidential elections during this period, so lack of observations may explain the lack of statistical significance of this variable.

Columns (3) and (4) use the US unemployment rate interacted with the election year dummy, instead of entering them separately. The interactive variable is significant at the 5% level, with either the full sample or the non-oil countries sample. Evidently the domestic politics become more important, not in all election years, but in those election years when the electorate is worried about job loss.[9]

---

[7] Table 3 in the Working Paper (i.e. Frankel and Wei, 2007) suggests that the best scale variable for the change in reserves is GDP, not the level of imports or the level of reserves itself. Thus we report only that measure of reserves here.

[8] Since virtually all the attention has been on Asian countries, we have also tried narrowing the sample further, first to 15 Asian countries, and then to the 8 who are actually named in the reports (not reported here). Reducing the sample size in this way gives similar point estimates on all the variables, but deprives them of much of their statistical significance. That the Treasury reports choose to focus on Asia is itself important information, and there seems little justification for throwing it away. We give a taste of the smaller samples in Table 3.

[9] When we include unemployment and the election dummy separately alongside their interaction, although all tend to lose significance, the interaction term dominates (not reported here). Indeed the coefficient on regular election years is not even positive. Particularly among the Asian countries that are the usual targets, high-unemployment election years are the ones that have the significant effects.

Table 1. Determinants of US Treasury findings with unemployment and election dummy ordered probit, October 1988–December 2006

Variable	(1) Full sample		(2) Excluding oil exporters		(3) Full sample		(4) Excluding oil exporters		(5) SD of variable	(6) Standardized response = Coeff.est. from (4) × SD from (5)
US bilateral goods trade balance with partner country (tb)	−2.205***	(0.363)	−2.121***	(0.384)	−2.163***	(0.360)	−2.047***	(0.374)	0.157	−0.321
Partner country's current account/GDP ratio (ca)	0.048***	(0.016)	0.090***	(0.022)	0.045***	(0.016)	0.083***	(0.020)	5.159	0.427
Partner's real exchange rate relative to PPP (ppp)	−0.616	(0.415)	−0.745*	(0.424)	−0.591	(0.411)	−0.694*	(0.413)	0.350	−0.243
Partner country's change in reserves/GDP ratio (res)	0.006	(0.021)	−0.015	(0.025)	0.008	(0.020)	−0.008	(0.022)	3.050	−0.025
US unemployment rate	0.092	(0.078)	0.149*	(0.082)						
Election year dummy	0.107*	(0.056)	0.096	(0.062)						
US unemployment rate × Election year dummy					0.022**	(0.010)	0.022**	(0.011)	2.604	0.059
Period dummies	no		no		no		no			
Observations	2009		1721		2009		1721			
Pseudo R-squared	0.17		0.21		0.17		0.20			

Notes: Robust standard errors in parentheses (clustered by country).

(1) Using all 63 countries.

(2) Excludes Algeria, Kuwait, Mexico, Nigeria, Norway, Russia, Saudi Arabia, United Arab Emirates and Venezuela.

* Significant at 10%; ** significant at 5%; *** significant at 1%.

Table 2. Adding previous report's finding ordered probit, October 1988–December 2006

Variable	(1) Full sample		(2) Excluding oil exporters		(3) Asian 15		(4) SD of variable	(5) Standardized response = Coeff.est. from (2) × SD from (4)
US bilateral goods trade balance with partner country (tb)	−0.724**	(0.301)	−0.719**	(0.307)	−0.593***	(0.230)	0.1568	−0.1127
Partner country's current account/GDP ratio (ca)	0.039***	(0.010)	0.060***	(0.017)	0.043**	(0.018)	5.1593	0.3082
Partner's exchange rate relative to PPP (ppp)	−0.263	(0.239)	−0.363	(0.246)	−0.088	(0.318)	0.3495	−0.1267
Partner country's change in reserves/GDP ratio (res)	0.031***	(0.012)	0.019	(0.013)	0.007	(0.012)	3.05	0.059
US unemployment rate	0.219**	(0.102)	0.280***	(0.104)	0.262**	(0.133)	0.9721	0.2718
US election year dummy	0.223	(0.139)	0.213	(0.148)	0.212	(0.156)	0.4497	0.0957
Finding in preceding report[a]	3.212***	(0.231)	3.156***	(0.233)	2.715***	(0.194)	0.2143	0.6764
Period dummies	no		no		no			
Observations	2009		1721		473			
Pseudo R-squared	0.58		0.59		0.46			

Notes: Robust standard errors in parentheses (clustered by country).
(1) Using all the 63 countries.
(2) Excludes Algeria, Kuwait, Mexico, Nigeria, Norway, Russia, Saudi Arabia, United Arab Emirates and Venezuela.
(3) Includes Bangladesh, China, Hong Kong SAR, India, Indonesia, Japan, South Korea, Malaysia, Pakistan, Philippines, Russia, Singapore, Sri Lanka, Taiwan, Province of China and Thailand.

[a] Dummy equals one if a country was investigated during last US Treasury report.
* Significant at 10%; ** significant at 5%; *** significant at 1%.

Table 3. Ordered probit regressions with period dummies, October 1988–December 2006

	(1) Full sample	(2) Excluding oil exporters	(3) Asian 15	(4) Asian 8	(5) Standard deviation of variable	(6) Standardized response = Coeff.est. from (2) × SD from (5)
US bilateral goods trade balance with partner country (tb)	−1.109*** (0.234)	−1.212*** (0.192)	−1.049*** (0.274)	−0.827*** (0.307)	0.177	−0.215
Partner country's current account/GDP ratio (ca)	0.059*** (0.017)	0.092*** (0.028)	0.078*** (0.030)	0.059** (0.027)	5.171	0.474
Partner's exchange rate relative to PPP (ppp)	−0.540** (0.213)	−0.675*** (0.242)	−0.534* (0.279)	−0.743** (0.303)	0.504	−0.340
Partner country's change in reserves/GDP ratio (res)	0.063*** (0.017)	0.047** (0.020)	0.033 (0.022)	0.025 (0.023)	3.038	0.144
Finding in preceding report[a]	4.060*** (0.383)	3.952*** (0.400)	3.666*** (0.401)	3.477*** (0.426)	0.215	0.849
Period dummies	Yes	Yes	Yes	Yes		
Observations	2072	1775	488	290		
Pseudo R-squared	0.67	0.68	0.58	0.53		

Notes: Robust standard errors in parentheses (clustered by country).

(1) Using all the 63 countries.
(2) Excludes Algeria, Kuwait, Mexico, Nigeria, Norway, Russia, Saudi Arabia, United Arab Emirates and Venezuela.
(3) Includes Bangladesh, China, Hong Kong SAR, India, Indonesia, Japan, South Korea, Malaysia, Pakistan, Philippines, Russia, Singapore, Sri Lanka, Taiwan, Province of China and Thailand.
(4) Includes China, Hong Kong SAR, Japan, South Korea, Malaysia, Russia, Singapore and Taiwan, Province of China.

[a] Dummy equals one if a country was investigated during last US Treasury report.

* Significant at 10%; ** significant at 5%; *** significant at 1%.

2.2. Assessing the relative importance of different factors

How can one assess the relative quantitative importance of the different factors in the Treasury decisions? One way is according to level of statistical significance. Here the bilateral trade balance is the clear leader. But another way to approach the problem – at least for variables that pass the threshold of statistical significance – is to look at the estimated size of the effect of a regressor on the latent variable Y^*. One does not want to compare the point estimates of the coefficients directly, because their scales are arbitrary. Instead, we re-scale a given point estimate by the relevant regressor's standard deviation in the sample. The last column in each table reports the predicted change in the latent variable in response to a one-standard deviation increase in a regressor. We only report such coefficients corresponding to the regression in Column 4 (to avoid overcrowding in the tables). One may read the absolute size of this coefficient as a way to assess the relative importance of various regressors that cause the Treasury to move a country up the ladder in the findings. By this criterion, in Table 1 the partner's current account beats out the bilateral balance by a fairly small margin: a one-standard-deviation increase in the partner's current account has a larger effect than a one-standard-deviation increase of the US bilateral deficit. The US unemployment-election variable comes third in importance, whether judged by statistical significance or standardized response (among the variables that are significant).

2.3. Controlling for findings of preceding Treasury reports

It would not be surprising to find some persistence over time in the Treasury findings. That is, if it chooses to investigate a country for possible manipulation in one period, it is likely to do so again in the next period (possibly due to omitted variables). To check this, we augmented the basic model by including in the **X**-vector a new dummy that indicates whether $Y > 0$ in the previous report. This conjecture is confirmed in Table 2: the goodness of fit (pseudo R^2) increases sharply and the variable is highly significant in all cases. Its presence also boosts the strength of some of the other estimated coefficients, notably the change in partner reserves. Also the US unemployment rate is now highly statistically significant on its own.

We also tried interacting the previous report variable with the other determinants. Our findings (not reported here) are that a high US bilateral deficit this period, or high partner surplus on the current account or overall balance of payments, counts significantly less if the partner was already investigated last period.

2.4. Other extensions of results

It appears that the Treasury is eager not to single out one country for unique opprobrium. There has never been a case where a single country is left completely exposed on its own. Other things equal, the country with the top ranking in terms of the combination of economic and political variables is less likely to be named than if it had some other country to hide behind, while the second-ranked and third-ranked countries are more likely to be moved up, to give the leader company. These results are highly significant statistically.[10]

As a final robustness check, in Table 3 we added time period dummies. This would allow, for example, for different approaches under different presidents or Treasury secretaries. The disadvantage is that we lose the US political variables, unemployment and the election dummy, since these vary only over time and not by trading partner.

The result is that all variables are highly significant statistically: the bilateral balance, the partner's current account, the real exchange rate and the partner's change in reserves. Their significance survives the narrowing of the sample better than it did when there were no time dummies: only the reserves variable becomes insignificant on the Asia-only samples.

2.5. Conclusions from the analysis of the Treasury reports

There is evidence for both hypotheses. The variables that an economist would recognize as legitimate have a statistically significant effect on the decisions in the Treasury reports – particularly the partners' overall current account/GDP, and sometimes also the overvaluation of its currency relative to PPP, and its reserve changes. But variables that an economist would not recognize as legitimate also matter. In particular the bilateral trade balance is the most consistently and strongly significant. It is generally significant at the 1% level of significance. The US unemployment rate is often significant, though not always. When the presidential election dummy is interacted with US unemployment, it is more highly significant.

Overall, three aspects of the regression results suggest that the domestic political variables are as important determinants of the Treasury decision as the legitimate global manipulation criteria: the absence of a clear role for reserve accumulation by the partner country as mandated by the IMF criteria, the significance of US unemployment (especially in election years), and the very high significance of the bilateral balance notwithstanding that the Treasury deliberately excludes this indicator from its list of criteria (US Treasury Department, 2005). If it was the IMF interpreting the criteria in the Articles of Agreement, rather than the Treasury interpreting the criteria in the 1988 US law, then consistent uni-directional intervention in the foreign exchange market would receive a lot more emphasis, and the US-specific variables such as the bilateral trade balance and US unemployment would not appear at all.

It should be noted that the law governing the Treasury reports mandates both sorts of tests: 'If the Secretary considers that such manipulation is occurring with respect to countries that (1) have material global current account surpluses; and (2) have

---

[10] Table 5 of the Working Paper (Frankel and Wei, 2007).

significant bilateral trade surpluses with the United States, the Secretary of the Treasury shall take action to initiate negotiations . . .' In that sense, to interpret evidence (that the bilateral balance numbers drive the Treasury decision to accuse a country of manipulation) as political, requires assigning the political motivation to the Congress, which passed the law, rather than to the Treasury that merely has to follow it. Alternatively, one could argue that the legally operative criterion lies in the interpretation of the ambiguous word 'manipulation', that many of the 185 members of the IMF currently satisfy conditions (1) and (2) above – most of whom are never mentioned in the Treasury reports – and that therefore Treasury does genuinely have the latitude necessary to exercise its judgment. Others, however, would argue that the phrase 'material global current account surpluses' means that the country in question must have a big share of the global surplus, as China does but Côte d'Ivoire does not, to qualify as a manipulator.

A third hypothesis should also be noted: that the US Treasury (in any administration) walks a fine line. On the one hand, it needs to placate vote-conscious Congressmen who are in danger of passing protectionist legislation more damaging than anything likely to come out of a Treasury report. On the other hand, it needs to take into account the constraints of international diplomacy (too much pressure on China would backfire politically) and of international markets (the danger of sparking a hard landing for the dollar, in which the dollar falls abruptly, interest rates rise and securities prices fall).

US politicians could come to regret it, if China finally followed their advice, because the result could well be an abrupt upward movement in US interest rates when the Chinese authorities stopped intervening in the market by buying dollar securities. The same could be the result if the Chinese authorities were to switch the composition of their reserves away from the dollar, perhaps in line with the ongoing shift in the currency composition of their reference basket away from the dollar. Our recommendation to the Treasury, if it finds it impossible to resist the political pressure from the Congress to name China a manipulator, is to invoke the provision in the last sentence of Section 3004: 'The Secretary shall not be required to initiate negotiations in cases where such negotiations would have a serious detrimental impact on vital national economic and security interests . . .' The Secretary would then explain to Congress that the detrimental economic impact would fall on his ability to sell Treasury securities (and the detrimental security impact would fall on the US Government's ability to enlist China's help on higher priority goals such as defusing the North Korean nuclear threat).

3. WHAT IS THE CURRENT EXCHANGE RATE REGIME IN CHINA?

If a country announces the adoption of a basket peg but does not reveal the exact weighting of the component currencies, how would one verify if the authorities' actions are consistent with their words? We apply a simple methodology first developed more than a decade ago[11] to the case of the RMB currency basket to study its evolution since 21 July 2005.

To summarize our findings from the outset, we find that the Chinese currency continues to assign heavy weight to the US dollar, but that there are signs of some modest but steady increase in flexibility since the spring of 2006. We also look at the possibility of US pressure being a cause of steps toward increased flexibility, by counting complaints from US officials about the RMB as reported in the press. There is some evidence that US officials' complaints tend to be associated with gradual reductions in the weight of the dollar in the RMB currency basket. This trend is modest, however, and there is no evidence that such complaints have led the Chinese to revalue the RMB relative to the currency basket.

3.1. Uncovering the secrets in an opaque currency basket

The Chinese currency had been effectively pegged to the US dollar at the rate of 8.28 RMB/dollar from 1997 until 21 July 2005, when the Chinese central bank announced the switch to a managing float regime 'with reference to a basket of currencies'. The announcement was billed as a major regime change. (Incidentally, however, China's official policy has never been a pegged exchange rate. This just goes to show the common divergence between *de jure* and *de facto* exchange rate regimes and the importance of inferring the true regime from observed data, a point that is by now well understood.)

3.1.1. What is publicly announced and what is not.
As is often the case with currency baskets, the weights were not made public. Speculation ensued after the announcement about which currencies were in the new reference basket and what their weights were. Jen (2005), for example, guessed that the weight on the dollar was 85%.

On 9 August 2005, Central Bank Governor Zhou Xiaochuan (2005) disclosed a list of 11 currencies as constituents of the reference basket, in a speech in Shanghai marking the opening of the central bank's second headquarters. In particular, he stated that the major currencies in the basket are the US dollar, the euro, the yen and the Korean won. We will label these four as the first-tier currencies in the basket. In addition, Governor Zhou stated that the rest of the currencies in the basket are the Singapore dollar, the British pound, the Malaysian ringgit, the Russian ruble, the Australian dollar, the Thai baht and the Canadian dollar. The last seven will be labelled as the second-tier currencies. The governor said that these currencies were chosen because of their economies' importance for China's current account.

---

[11] Frankel (1993c) and Frankel and Wei (1994, 1995). The approach has since been used by others, including Bénassy-Quéré (1999), Ohno (1999), Frankel *et al.* (2000), and Bénassy-Quéré *et al.* (2004). For the RMB: Eichengreen (2006), Shah *et al.* (2005), and Yamazaki (2006, p. 8). Haldane and Hall (1991) had earlier regressed the British pound exchange rate against the dollar and the Deutschemark; but their equation did not have a theoretical basis as estimation of basket weights, as the pound was not on a basket peg system.

Still not announced were the weights on these currencies, or the frequency and the criteria with which these weights might be altered.[12]

3.1.2. A picture is worth a thousand words.

Before we turn to regression-based estimation, it may be useful to inspect some simple time series plots. Some perspective can be gleaned from Figure 1, the graph that traces out the spot and three forward rates (from 1, 3 and 12 months non-deliverable forward contracts, respectively) of the USD/RMB exchange rate from April 2003 to January 2007. Interestingly, even though the actual regime change came in July 2005, the market had been expecting an RMB revaluation as reflected in the forward rate ever since October 2003. In fact, on 20 July 2005, the day before the actual regime change, the 12-month forward contract was forecasting an exchange rate of 8 RMB/US dollar, which implied a higher magnitude of appreciation than what actually happened the day after, but which turned out to be relatively close to the actual spot rate a year later (20 July 2006).

To see how the RMB's value has evolved relative to major currencies, we turn to Figure 2, the one that plots the value of the yuan in units of US dollars, euros and yen, respectively, since 1 July 1995. The three exchange rate series are rescaled to be equal to one on the first day (21 July 2005) after the exchange rate regime reform, so that one can easily see subsequent percentage changes. A number of features stand out. First, in spite of the announced abandonment of the dollar peg, the link to the US dollar even after 21 July 2005, is clearly much stronger than to either the euro or the yen. Second, one can discern a gradual (and very slow) strengthening of the RMB against the dollar, accumulating a total of another 4% of appreciation from 21 July 2005 to the end of 2006. Third, the value of the RMB against the euro and the yen fluctuates a lot, mostly a reflection of the fluctuation in the value of the US dollar against these other two currencies. Relative to 20 July 2005, the day before the exchange rate reform, the RMB had by April 2006 appreciated by about 12% against the yen, but was at about the same level against the euro. Then by the end of 2006, the yuan was down against the yen as much as it was up against the euro. In other words, the action has been in the euro and yen.

To get a sense of the evolving range of the dollar/RMB movement, Figure 3 plots the percentage changes (the first differences in the log) of the exchange rate since 22 July 2005. Up to the spring of 2006, most of the daily movement was within 0.05%, with occasional movements approaching or exceeding 0.1% especially in the more recent period. In other words, the daily movement of the dollar/RMB had been tiny, despite the announced switch to a managed floating exchange rate. Since the spring of 2006, however, there has been a visible increase in the daily movement, with daily changes exceeding 0.1% frequently.

---

[12] According to a 2006 report, which may not be reliable, Governor Zhou put the dollar weight at 'much less than 50 percent' (http://www.forbes.com/markets/feeds/afx/2006/01/26/afx2481184.html).

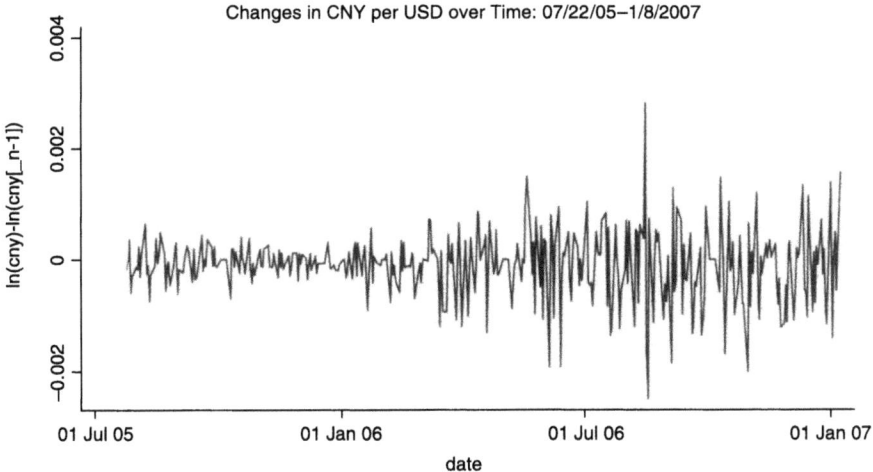

Figure 3. Fluctuations in CNY/USD exchange rate

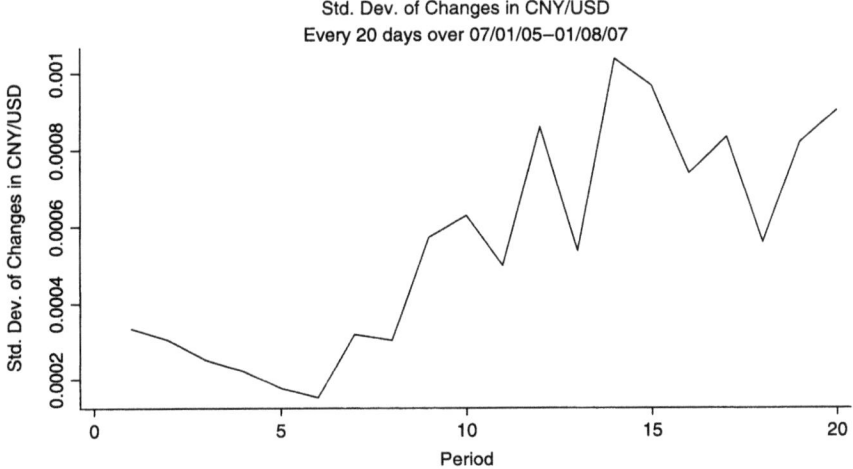

Figure 4. Variability in yuan/dollar exchange rate

As another way to see the evolving flexibility, Figure 4 plots the standard deviation of the daily exchange rate movement over a sequence of rolling 20-day sample since 22 July 2005. After some initial moderate gyration in the rate following the announced regime change, the fluctuations die down in the last few months of 2005 and the beginning of 2006. The standard deviation then trends upward after the beginning of 2006, reaching around 0.08% by the end of 2006, a tripling relative to the magnitude in the immediate aftermath of the regime change announcement. In order not to lose sight of the big picture, we note again that, in spite of the visible increase in exchange rate flexibility, the absolute magnitude of the movement has been small so far.

3.1.3. Implicit weights in the currency basket.
Assuming that the value of the RMB is indeed determined by a currency basket, how does one uncover the currency composition and weights in the basket? This is a problem to which ordinary least squares (OLS) regression is unusually well suited. If we know the list of currencies, of which the ones used in the basket can be a subset, then we regress changes in the log value of the RMB against changes in the log values of the candidate currencies.

The reason to work in terms of changes rather than levels is the likelihood of non-stationarity. Concern for non-stationarity goes beyond the common refrain of modern time series econometrics, the inability to reject statistically a unit root, which in many cases can be attributed to insufficient power. One of the most important hypotheses we are testing is that the authorities have allowed the yuan to drift away from a basket, perhaps via an upward trend. Thus it is important to allow for non-stationarity. Working in terms of first differences is the cleanest way to do so. We should include a constant term to allow for the likelihood of a trend appreciation in the RMB, whether against the dollar alone or a broader basket. Algebraically, if the RMB is pegged to currencies $X1, X2, \ldots$ and Xn, with weights equal to $w1, w2, \ldots$ and wn, then

$$\log RMB(t+s) - \log RMB(t) = c + \Sigma\, w(j)\, [\log X(j, t+s) - \log X(j, t)] \qquad (1)$$

If the exchange rate is truly governed by a strict basket peg, then we should be able to recover the true weights precisely, so long as we have more observations than candidate currencies, and the equation should have a perfect fit.

Shah *et al.* (2005) adopted this methodology to study the Chinese currency basket after 21 July 2005 and found that the RMB is still tightly pegged to the dollar, and no other currencies. However, they only consider four candidate currencies in the RMB basket (the dollar, the yen, the euro and the pound), probably unaware of the 11-currency disclosure made by the Chinese central bank. In addition, their sample was only the initial few months after 21 July 2005. Frankel and Wei (2006) extended to 11 the components of the basket, but found that the RMB regime in the second half of 2005 was still a tight dollar peg – as tight as that of the Hong Kong SAR regime. Ogawa (2006) found the same. Eichengreen (2006, pp. 22–25) had daily observations of data that ran from 22 July 2005 to 21 March 2006, and found a dollar weight around 0.9, but with no evidence of a downward trend in the weight, and no significance on non-dollar currencies. Each of these four papers was too early to catch the evolution in 2006. Yamazaki (2006, p. 8) updated the estimation and found some weight had shifted to the euro, yen and won; but he estimated the equation in terms of levels rather than changes (risking non-stationarity), did not allow for a trend, did not allow for the other currencies on the list, and had a relatively small number of (bimonthly) observations.

One methodological question must be addressed, before we turn to the new results. How do we define the 'value' of each of the currencies? This is the question of the numeraire.[13] If the exchange rate is truly a basket peg, the choice of numeraire currency is immaterial; we estimate the weights accurately regardless.[14] If the true regime is more variable than a rigid basket peg, then the choice of numeraire does make some difference to the estimation. Some authors in the past have used a remote currency, such as the Swiss franc (e.g., Frankel and Wei, 1994). But a weighted index such as a trade-weighted measure or the SDR (Special Drawing Right, an IMF unit composed of a basket of most important major currencies) is probably more appropriate. Here is why. If the true regime is a target zone or a managed float centred on a reference basket, where the authorities intervene to an extent that depends on the magnitude of the deviation – and this seems the logical alternative hypothesis in which a strict basket peg is nested – then the error term in the equation represents shocks in demand for the currency that the authorities allow to be partially reflected in the exchange rate (but only partially, because they intervene if the shocks are large). Then one should use a numeraire that is similar to that used by the authorities in measuring what constitutes a large deviation. The authorities are unlikely to use the Swiss franc or Canadian dollar in thinking about the size of deviations from their reference point. They are more likely to use a weighted average of major currencies. If we use a similar measure in the equation, it should help minimize the possibility of correlation between the error term and the numeraire. Similarly, if there is a trend in the exchange rate equation (a constant term in the changes equation) representing deliberate gradual appreciation of the currency, then the value of the RMB should be defined in terms of whatever weighted exchange rate index the authorities are likely to use in thinking about the trend. These considerations suggest a numeraire that is itself composed of a basket of currencies. We choose here the SDR.

Using daily exchange rates (from 21 July 2005 to the beginning of 2007) and the SDR as the numeraire currency, we implement a sequence of estimations for the whole sample. Bilateral exchange rates are observed at the same moment in the day. Column 1 of Table 4 reports the result for the entire sample period. Of the 11 currencies that are supposedly in the basket, only two currencies receive weights that are steady enough throughout the sample period to show up with positive and statistically significant weights: the US dollar (90% weight) and Malaysian ringgit (5% weight). Surprisingly, the two major non-dollar currencies, the euro and the yen, receive zero weight in the basket. (These results stay the same when we switch the numeraire currency from SDR to Swiss franc or gold as a robustness check.) It appears that the Chinese authorities are more concerned with preserving trade competitiveness

---

[13] Frankel (1993c) used purchasing power over a consumer basket of domestic goods as numeraire; Frankel and Wei (1995) used the SDR; Frankel and Wei (1994, 2006), Ohno (1999), and Eichengreen (2006) used the Swiss franc; Bénassy-Quéré (1999), the dollar; Frankel et al. (2000), a GDP-weighted basket of five major currencies; and Yamazaki (2006), the Canadian dollar.

[14] If the linear equation holds precisely in terms of any one 'correct' numeraire, then add the log exchange rate between that numeraire and any arbitrary unit to see that the equation also holds precisely in terms of the arbitrary numeraire. This assumes the weights add to one, and there is no error term, constant term, or other non-currency variable.

Table 4. Estimating the implicit basket weights in determining the yuan, 22 July 2005–1 August 2007 (numeraire currency = SDR)

Sub-period	Whole sample	(1)	(2)	(3)	(4)	(5)	(6)
US dollar	0.904** (0.021)	0.997** (0.034)	0.968** (0.031)	0.695** (0.050)	0.947** (0.045)	0.867** (0.134)	0.886** (0.087)
Euro	−0.006 (0.014)	−0.008 (0.015)	−0.006 (0.011)	−0.049* (0.023)	0.005 (0.040)	0.005 (0.100)	0.039 (0.064)
Japanese yen	0.008 (0.009)	0.010 (0.013)	−0.008 (0.006)	−0.017 (0.013)	0.052* (0.026)	0.019 (0.044)	0.007 (0.030)
Korean won	0.002 (0.009)	−0.001 (0.013)	0.019** (0.007)	0.033** (0.016)	−0.076** (0.029)	−0.024 (0.040)	−0.002 (0.029)
Singapore dollar	−0.018 (0.021)	−0.043 (0.028)	−0.005 (0.021)	−0.065* (0.037)	0.002 (0.055)	−0.054 (0.077)	−0.108* (0.061)
British pound	−0.004 (0.011)	−0.007 (0.013)	0.010 (0.009)	0.012 (0.018)	−0.043 (0.032)	0.003 (0.041)	−0.026 (0.041)
Malaysia ringgit	0.053** (0.015)	−0.015 (0.026)	0.032 (0.028)	0.239** (0.058)	0.076** (0.033)	0.122 (0.084)	0.057 (0.041)
Russia ruble	−0.018 (0.021)	0.005 (0.027)	−0.016 (0.013)	0.126** (0.040)	−0.030 (0.053)	−0.165 (0.217)	−0.108 (0.124)
Australian dollar	−0.003 (0.008)	0.012 (0.010)	−0.006 (0.007)	−0.008 (0.012)	0.003 (0.020)	−0.013 (0.033)	0.012 (0.028)
Thailand baht	0.006 (0.010)	0.010 (0.019)	−0.014 (0.012)	0.047** (0.016)	0.036 (0.031)	−0.023 (0.040)	0.017 (0.020)
Canadian dollar	0.003 (0.008)	−0.011 (0.008)	0.005 (0.008)	−0.005 (0.016)	−0.040** (0.017)	0.014 (0.034)	0.025 (0.028)
Constant	0.00009** (0.00003)	0.00005 (0.00003)	0.00004 (0.00003)	−0.00008 (0.00006)	0.00009 (0.00008)	0.00022** (0.00010)	0.00015* (0.00009)
Observations	382	72	66	63	66	66	71
Root MSE	0.00055	0.00027	0.0002	0.00037	0.00061	0.0008	0.00064
R-squared	0.95	0.99	1.00	0.98	0.97	0.81	0.90

Notes: Standard errors in parentheses. Change in the log value of the target currency is regressed on changes in the log values of other currencies.

(1) First sub-period: 22 July 2005–31 October 2005
(2) Second sub-period: 1 November 2005–31 January 2006
(3) Third sub-period: 1 February 2006–28 April 2006
(4) Fourth sub-period: 1 May 2006–31 July 2006
(5) Fifth sub-period: 1 August 2006–31 October 2006
(6) Sixth sub-period: 1 October 2006–8 January 2007

* Significant at 10%; ** significant at 5%.

Data source: Bloomberg daily closing price, New York.

against major Asian rivals than with minimizing variability vis-à-vis the world's most important currencies or China's most important export markets.

Despite the official pronouncement that China has ceased its particular link to the US dollar, the sample-wide estimated weight on the dollar is still 90%. Further, the regression has a tight fit, with R^2 of 0.95 and root mean squared errors (MSE) of 0.03%, suggesting a tight peg to the basket. This finding is in contrast to the official position that the link to the basket (whatever its composition) is loose, that it is just a reference point. For comparison, we implement the same methodology on a currency that is clearly floating, namely the Japanese yen and another currency that is known to be pegged to the US dollar, namely, the Hong Kong dollar. The R^2 is 0.54 for the Japanese yen, much lower than that of the RMB. It is 99% for the Hong Kong dollar, not that much different from the RMB. Similarly, the root mean squared error is 0.36% for the yen, an order of magnitude bigger than for the RMB, but is 0.02% for the Hong Kong dollar, virtually the same as the RMB. It is striking that the behaviour of the Chinese RMB since 21 July 2005 closely resembles that of a known dollar pegger, the HK dollar, but is very far from a known floater, the yen.

We implemented the methodology on three other East Asian currencies as well: the Singapore dollar, the Malaysian ringgit and the Korean won (reported in the Working Paper, Frankel and Wei, 2007). They constitute intermediate cases. Of the three, the Singapore dollar and Malaysian ringgit both appear to be following loose basket pegs. The weights on the dollar are lower, and the fit looser, than in the case of the RMB. Nevertheless, considering that the Malaysian currency appears to be the only important non-dollar currency in the Chinese basket, it is striking that the ringgit itself gives 0.5 weight to the dollar (also 0.1 weight, each, to the Taiwan dollar, Philippine peso and Indian rupee). It means there is even less scope for yuan appreciation against the dollar.

Some have reacted to our results by pointing to high multicollinearity and reverse-causality among the regressors in the RMB equation and wondered whether the coefficient estimates are biased. After all, we have just seen that the Malaysian dollar is highly correlated with the US dollar, and have suggested that this is deliberate policy on the part of Kuala Lumpur. But the independent significance of the US and Malaysian dollars in the RMB equation suggests that the relationship is strong enough to prevail over the multicollinearity. (Of course, that is what multivariate regression is designed to discover.) And the tightness of the fit suggests that the existence of another simultaneous equation determining the ringgit would not much bias the estimates in the RMB equation. Recall that, in the limit, a perfect basket peg will produce perfect coefficient estimates: the error term cannot be correlated with right-hand side variables if there is no error term.

3.2. Evolution of the basket

The situation is changing rapidly over time. Estimates that impose unchanging coefficients could well be misleading.

3.2.1. Estimates from the sub-samples. To allow for evolution of the Chinese exchange rate regime since the 21 July 2005 policy change, we divide the sample into six approximately equal-sized sub-periods: (1) 22 July–31 October 2005, (2) 1 November 2005–31 January 2006, (3) 1 February–28 April 2006, (4) 1 May–31 July 2006, (5) 1 August–31 October 2006, and (6) 1 October 2006–8 January 2007.[15]

The estimation by sub-periods reveals some interesting shifts. In the first two sub-samples, the regime is virtually a US dollar peg, after the initial 2.1% revaluation. The weight on the dollar is 0.997 in the first sub-sample and 0.968 in the second sample. Neither estimate differs statistically from one. Except for a tiny weight (0.02) on the Korea won in the second sub-sample, no other currency in the basket receives weight. The R^2 is essentially 100%. So for these sub-periods, the regime was simply a dollar peg masquerading as a basket.

After January 2006, however, the dollar weight falls. In the sub-period February–April 2006, the estimated weight on the US dollar is only 0.70. A few other currencies, notably the Malaysian ringgit, the Korean won, the Russian rubble and the Thai baht, receive positive weights in the basket. The yen and euro continue to receive no positive weight. The root MSE increases marginally from 0.02–0.03% in the first two sub-samples to 0.04% in the third sub-period.[16]

The estimated weight on the dollar returns to 0.95 during May–July 2006, but then declines to 0.87 and 0.89 in the last two sub-periods. Interestingly, none of the other currencies such as the ringgit, the won, the yen, or the euro, received a positive weight that is statistically significant. In other words, the relaxed association between the RMB and the dollar in the last five months of 2006 is not accomplished by shifting more weights to other non-dollar currencies in the basket, but by a looser association between the RMB and the entire currency basket. These are also the first two sub-periods when the trend is statistically significant: a trend appreciation of 0.0002 per day, which is 0.001 per week, or 5.2% per year. This is far less than the maximum allowable under the announced band, but is nonetheless large enough to be important.

To summarize, in the first 6 months following the announced shift by the Chinese central bank to a managed floating regime with reference to a basket of 11 currencies, China made such a heavy reference to the US dollar that it was indistinguishable from a dollar pegger. However, since February 2006, there are signs of increased flexibility. First, in the spring of 2006, some weight in the basket was shifted to other currencies, particularly the Malaysian ringgit, the Korean won, the Russian ruble and the Thai baht. Surprisingly, throughout the sample, there is not an iota of evidence

---

[15] The last sub-period overlaps with the previous one for a month in order to ensure enough observations in the sample.

[16] When similar regressions are done for other currencies, most are seen to switch, from assigning significant weights to the US dollar in the first two sub-samples, to none in the third sub-sample. The exceptions are Malaysia, which reduces its dollar weight from 0.964 in the first sub-period to 0.608 in the last sub-period, and Hong Kong SAR, the institutionally fixed currency, which as expected continues to assign nearly 100% weight to the US dollar. These non-RMB results are reported in the Working Paper (Frankel and Wei, 2007), but are omitted here to save space.

of any positive weight assigned to the yen or the euro. Second, since the fall of 2006, in addition to the lesser weight on the dollar (an estimated weight of 0.9 rather than 1.0 as in the earlier periods), the association between the RMB and the reference currency basket has become looser. There is a non-negligible trend of appreciation against the basket, and slightly looser fit.

3.2.2. Robustness with respect to numeraire currency.
We have chosen to emphasize estimates that use the Special Drawing Right as the numeraire currency. We noted earlier that the choice of the numeraire is irrelevant if the currency is strictly pegged to a currency basket. However, if the value of the currency relative to the basket is allowed to fluctuate, different numeraires might generate different point estimates. For this reason, we examined if the conclusions are robust with respect to the choice of numeraires, repeating the regressions using the price of gold as an alternative numeraire.

The gold-based regression results are reported in the working paper. Although the exact point estimates vary somewhat, the same qualitative results as before emerge clearly. First, in the initial 8 months after 21 July 2005, the Chinese exchange rate regime is best characterized as a virtual peg to the US dollar. The goodness-of-fit measure and RMSE for the Chinese RMB are closer to those of the Hong Kong dollar, than to currencies known to have some flexibility. Second, there are signs of increased flexibility since February 2006. The weight on the US dollar declines (though the estimated magnitude of the decline is not as large as when the SDR is used as the numeraire). Third, as before, there is no evidence of a positive weight assigned to either the euro or the yen.

3.2.3. Allowing for steady acceleration in the shift.
Several considerations suggest it would be useful to return to estimation over the entire 18-month sample period but to allow for steady escalation of the various flexibility parameters. First, everything we know about Chinese government officials, from their history of economic reforms to their own words, points to policy change that is gradual. Second, looking simply at the yuan/dollar exchange rate in Figure 2, there is a gradual trend appreciation that visually accelerates. Third, looking at the econometric estimates across our sub-samples, all three flexibility parameters loosen up as we move from 2005 to late 2006: the weight on the dollar tends to fall, the appreciation trend becomes positive and significant, and the fit becomes looser. All these considerations presume very little movement in the short-term, but suggest signs of a pattern of acceleration that if extrapolated a few years into the future could imply substantial flexibility.

Allowing for a time trend of appreciation that is linear in the log of the exchange rate is easy; that is the constant term that has been in the changes regression all along. Allowing for a steadily accelerating time trend requires adding some function of time to the changes equation. The simplest is to add time itself. Allowing for there to be a time trend in weight placed on the dollar versus non-dollar currencies is trickier. We add to the equation time-dependent terms that interact with the changes in currency values, to see how the weights change over time. We begin with a simple linear trend specification for these time-dependent terms as well, even though linearity here is less realistic than for the trend in the log of the RMB exchange rate itself.

The penultimate row of estimates in Table 5 shows a highly significant downward linear trend in the weight placed on the dollar.[17] The constant term is still highly significant statistically as well, but the implied estimated trend appreciation against the basket (0.0001 per day, or 2.5% per year) is now half what it was before. Interestingly, there is only weak evidence here of an acceleration of the trend appreciation *per se* (third to last row of estimates in Table 5). Apparently the visual impression of accelerating appreciation in, for example, Figure 2, is primarily due to the (quite modest) shift in weight to non-dollar currencies at a time when they have been appreciating against the dollar.

3.2.4. Pressure from the US and the movement of the Chinese currency.

We now turn to a question that links the two parts of the paper: Do complaints about the Chinese exchange rate from US Treasury officials or other US officials lead China to respond by appreciating its currency relative to the basket and by reducing the weight of its currency on the dollar?

The change of the currency regime on 21 July 2005, came after two years of complaints from the United States (and a few other countries). Complaints from US officials and politicians continued thereafter, perhaps because as we have seen there had been so little *de facto* change to match the announcement. To document the official US pressure systematically, we searched an electronic database of news reports (FACTIVA/NewsPlus) and recorded the number of news stories in all English-language newspapers in Washington DC, New York City and Los Angeles, in which US officials are reported to have asked China to speed up the exchange rate flexibility/revaluation from 1 July 2005 to 8 January 2007.

To see whether Chinese exchange rate behaviour is related to the complaints, Table 6 reports a sequence of currency weight regressions that have added the cumulative US complaints and their interactions with the weight on the dollar as extra regressors. There is no evidence of an association between the complaints from US officials and appreciation of the RMB relative to the currency basket. There is evidence that cumulative complaints are associated with a reduction in the RMB basket's weight on the US dollar. An attempt to distinguish between the effect of complaints from Treasury officials versus other US officials suggests that the former may have carried more punch.[18]

---

[17] We have also allowed for non-linear trends, which would slow down with the passage of time. The basic results were little changed.

[18] Results reported in the Working Paper (Frankel and Wei, 2007). When estimated separately, the effects of Treasury and non-Treasury complaints were not statistically significant (let alone the difference between the two), probably because they are collinear.

Table 5. Trend appreciation of the yuan and trend change in the dollar weight; whole sample (22 July 2005–8 January 2007, numeraire currency = SDR)

	(1)	(2)	(3)	(4)	(5)	(6)	(7)	(8)	(9)
US dollar	0.904**	0.990**	0.991**	0.926**	1.017**	1.017**	0.891**	0.979**	0.980**
	(0.021)	(0.029)	(0.029)	(0.011)	(0.020)	(0.020)	(0.015)	(0.026)	(0.026)
Euro	−0.006	−0.006	−0.006	−0.022**	−0.015**	−0.015**	−0.018**	−0.014**	−0.014**
	(0.014)	(0.013)	(0.013)	(0.008)	(0.006)	(0.006)	(0.008)	(0.006)	(0.006)
Japanese yen	0.009	0.009	0.009	0.009			0.005		
	(0.009)	(0.008)	(0.008)	(0.008)			(0.008)		
Korean won	0.003	0.000	0.001				0.001	0.001	0.001
	(0.009)	(0.009)	(0.009)				(0.009)	(0.008)	(0.008)
Singapore dollar	−0.020	−0.017	−0.019						
	(0.020)	(0.020)	(0.020)						
British pound	−0.004	−0.008	−0.008						
	(0.011)	(0.011)	(0.011)						
Malaysia ringgit	0.052**	0.036**	0.035**				0.050**	0.036**	0.034**
	(0.015)	(0.015)	(0.015)				(0.015)	(0.015)	(0.015)
Russia ruble	−0.017	−0.014	−0.013						
	(0.021)	(0.021)	(0.021)						
Australian dollar	−0.004	−0.001	−0.002						
	(0.008)	(0.008)	(0.008)						
Thailand baht	0.006	0.008	0.008						
	(0.010)	(0.009)	(0.009)						
Canadian dollar	0.004	0.001	0.003						
	(0.008)	(0.007)	(0.007)						
Trend	0.004		0.004	0.004		0.004	0.004		0.004
	(0.003)		(0.003)	(0.003)		(0.002)	(0.003)		(0.002)
Dollar × Trend		−4.473**	−4.459**		−5.106**	−5.089**		−4.407**	−4.409**
		(1.058)	(1.056)		(1.007)	(1.005)		(1.041)	(1.040)
Constant	0.00001	0.00009**	0.00001	0.00002	0.00009**	0.00001	0.00001	0.00008**	0.00001
	(0.00006)	(0.00003)	(0.00006)	(0.00006)	(0.00003)	(0.00006)	(0.00006)	(0.00003)	(0.00006)
Observations	383	383	383	383	383	383	383	383	383
Root MSE	0.00055	0.00054	0.00054	0.00056	0.00054	0.00054	0.00055	0.00054	0.00054
R-squared	0.954	0.955	0.956	0.952	0.954	0.955	0.953	0.955	0.955

Notes: Trend = observation/10 000. Standard errors in parentheses. Change in the log value of the target currency is regressed on changes in the log values of other currencies.

* Significant at 10%; ** significant at 5%.

Data source: Bloomberg daily closing price, New York.

Table 6. Pressure from the US as a determinant of the Chinese exchange rate; whole sample (22 July 2005–8 January 2007, numeraire currency = SDR)

	(1)		(2)		(3)	
US dollar	0.904**	(0.021)	0.983**	(0.030)	0.983**	(0.030)
Euro	−0.006	(0.014)	−0.006	(0.014)	−0.006	(0.014)
Japanese yen	0.009	(0.009)	0.009	(0.009)	0.010	(0.009)
Korean won	0.003	(0.009)	0.000	(0.009)	0.001	(0.009)
Singapore dollar	−0.020	(0.020)	−0.018	(0.020)	−0.019	(0.020)
British pound	−0.004	(0.011)	−0.008	(0.011)	−0.007	(0.011)
Malaysia ringgit	0.053**	(0.015)	0.037**	(0.016)	0.037**	(0.016)
Russia ruble	−0.017	(0.021)	−0.015	(0.021)	−0.014	(0.021)
Australian dollar	−0.004	(0.008)	−0.001	(0.008)	−0.002	(0.008)
Thailand baht	0.006	(0.010)	0.009	(0.010)	0.009	(0.010)
Canadian dollar	0.004	(0.008)	0.002	(0.007)	0.003	(0.007)
US Complaint	0.004	(0.003)			0.004	(0.003)
US Complaint × USD			−4.493**	(1.219)	−4.508**	(1.217)
Constant	0.00002	(0.00006)	0.00009**	(0.00003)	0.00001	(0.00006)
Observations	383		383		383	
Root MSE	0.00055		0.00054		0.00054	
R-squared	0.95		0.95		0.96	

Notes: Standard errors in parentheses. Treasury in columns (1)–(6) are: Cumulative Treasury report/1000. Other in Columns (1)–(6) are: Cumulative Other report/1000. US Complaint = Treasury Complaint + Other Complaint.
* Significant at 10%; ** significant at 5%.

Since the complaint series is by construction a non-decreasing function of time, one could wonder if it simply picks up a trend effect. We add a time trend and its interaction with the dollar weight as the additional regressors. The results are little changed. Again, there is evidence of a gradual decline in the RMB's weight on the US dollar, but there is no evidence of a steady appreciation of the RMB relative to the whole basket.

3.2.5. Constraining the basket weights to sum to one.
There is a good argument for constraining the weights on the currencies to add up to one. However weak one thinks the link to the reference basket might be, or however large or small the weight on the dollar, the authorities must view movements in the RMB through the metric of distance from some reference rate or effective exchange rate. The easiest way to implement the adding up constraint is to run the regressions with the changes in the log yuan value on the left-hand side of the equation transformed by subtracting off the changes in the log value of one of the currencies, say the dollar, and the changes in the values of the non-dollar currencies on the right-hand side transformed in the same way.

To see this, we repeat Equation (1):

$$\Delta \log RMB_t = c + \Sigma \, w(j) \, [\Delta \log X(j)_t]$$
$$= c + \alpha \, \Delta \log \$_t + \beta(1) \, \Delta \log €_t + \beta(2) \, \Delta \log £_t + \beta(3) \ldots$$

We want to impose the adding up constraint $\alpha = 1 - \beta(1) - \beta(2) - \beta(3) \ldots$

We implement it by running the regression Equation (2):

$$[\Delta \log RMB_t - \Delta \log \$_t]$$
$$= c + \beta(1)[\Delta \log €_t - \Delta \log \$_t] + \beta(2)[\Delta \log £_t - \Delta \log \$_t] + \beta(3) \ldots \quad (2)$$

The results are reported in the Working Paper (Frankel and Wei, 2007). One can recover the implicit weight on the dollar by adding the estimated weights on the non-dollar currencies, and subtracting the sum from one. We learn, for example, that the weight on the dollar is one minus the weights on the won (0.02) and ringgit (0.07), which is 0.91. These are very similar to the corresponding estimates when no constraint was imposed on the weights. The increase in the root MSE is tiny, suggesting that a test would not reject the constraint that the weights sum to one. But imposing the constraint sharpens the estimates a bit; for example, the coefficient on the Korean won now appears statistically significant not just when gold is used as numeraire but also in the preferred case where the SDR is used as numeraire. The basic findings are unchanged: significant weights only on the same two non-dollar currencies, a trend appreciation against the basket, and gradually diminishing linear weight on the dollar.

When we impose the adding-up constraint in the equation where we test the role of official US complaints, the results are again little changed; but the complaints have an even stronger negative effect on the dollar weight. There is little evidence that they lead to an immediate appreciation, however small, *per se*.

3.2.6. Allowing for non-linear trends in the weights.

In Sections 3.2.3 and 3.2.4 we allowed for a downward trend in the weight assigned to the dollar in the basket of reference currencies. But the specification was a linear trend. Since the currency weights are logically bounded by 0 and 1, a linear functional form for the trend in the weights, which has the undesirable property that the weights eventually breech the limits of 0 or 1, is not the best specification. Instead, the term designed to capture the possible shifting of weight toward non-dollar currencies can be assumed proportionate to $[1 - \exp(-\delta t)]$, which runs from 0 to 1 as required. The parameter δ helps to capture the speed of the shift.

We can continue to impose the constraint that the weights sum to one, not just at $t = 0$ but throughout the period, implementing the constraint by subtracting the change in the value of an arbitrary currency from all currency variables (i.e., from both the change in the RMB value and the change in the values of other candidate currencies in the basket). Algebraically, if $X(j)$ is the value of currency j in the basket, and $w(j)$ is the weight on that currency, then

$$\Delta \log RMB_t = f(t) + \Sigma\, w(j)\, \Delta X(j)_t$$

To impose the constraint that $\sum_1^J w(j) = 1$, we only need $w(1) = 1 - \sum_2^J w(j)$.

Now we choose euro as the first currency. The constraint on the weights implies that:

$$[\Delta \log RMB_t - \Delta \log_t] = f(t) + \sum_{2}^{J} w(j)(\Delta X(j)_t - \Delta \log_t)$$

where $w(j)$ can be anything between zero and one.

Now let us add the time-dependent weight terms, using the exponential functional form for the weights $w(j)$. We consider four different ways to specify and/or estimate the trend terms. The choice depends on how one feels about non-linear estimation.[19]

Specification 1: let $w(j) = b0(j) + b1(j)* t, f(t) = c0 + c1*t$.

This is the simplest specification and is estimated with OLS.

Specification 2: let $w(j) = b0(j) + b1(j)* [1 - \exp(-d\, t)], f(t) = c0 + c1*t$.

We set $d = 0.00001$. While the trend on the currency weights is non-linear, by selecting a particular value for d we keep the specification still linear in the parameters to be estimated. Therefore, this equation can be estimated with OLS as well.

Specification 3: let $w(j) = b0(j) + b1(j)* [1 - \exp(-d\, t)], f(t) = c0 + c1*t$

Instead of imposing a value, d is a parameter to be estimated. A non-linear least squares method is used for estimation. However, $b1(US)$ turns out not to be identified in the estimation.

Specification 4: let $w(j) = b0(j) + b1(j)* [1 - \exp(-d\, t)], f(t) = c0 + c1*t$

This time, we set $b1(USD) = -28.9$, which is the point estimate of $b1(USD)$ from specification 2. The parameter d is still to be estimated, which we do by a non-linear least squares method.

The results, reported in Table 7, are probably the most important for distinguishing whether the gradual appreciation of the yuan against the dollar is attributable to a shift of weights in the basket away from the dollar, or rather to an appreciation against the basket. The table confirms that in the immediate aftermath of the policy change in July 2005, the weight on the dollar was an estimated 0.98, statistically indistinguishable from 1. It also confirms a downward trend in the weight on the dollar (this time estimated in a realistic non-linear functional form). While it is less clear which of the other currencies are receiving the reallocation of weight, an upward trend in the weight on the Malaysian ringgit appears the strongest statistically. Under the technique of non-linear least squares, the ringgit trend acquires statistical significance (the last two columns in the table). Strikingly, there is no statistical significance to the trend of appreciation against the basket, let alone to acceleration in that trend. Rather the action comes from the decline in the weight on the dollar.

---

[19] We tried also imposing the constraint that the relative importance of the non-dollar weights vis-à-vis each other remains constant over time, while still allowing the upward trend in their collective importance. But this constraint was not supported by the data, and those results are not included here.

Table 7. Allowing for trends in level and (nonlinearly) in the currency weights, while imposing throughout the constraints that the weights sum to 1

	(1) OLS	(2) OLS	(3) Non-linear LS	(4) Non-linear LS
US dollar	0.982**	0.982**	0.982***	0.982***
	(0.042)	(0.042)	(0.042)	(0.042)
Japanese yen	0.0004	0.0004	0.0004	0.0004
	(0.0165)	(0.0165)	(0.0165)	(0.0165)
Korea won	0.0114	0.0114	0.0114	0.0114
	(0.0179)	(0.0179)	(0.0179)	(0.0179)
Malaysia ringgit	0.0155	0.0154	0.0155	0.0154
	(0.039)	(0.039)	(0.039)	(0.039)
US dollar × Trend	−0.00029*	−28.91*	Not identified	−28.9
	(0.00017)	(16.79)		(imposed)
Japanese yen × Trend	0.00002	1.946	6.874	1.945
	(0.00008)	(8.284)	(29.5)	(8.341)
Korea won × Trend	0.00004	4.005	14.2	4.003
	(0.00009)	(8.750)	(29.7)	(8.409)
Malaysia ringgit × Trend	0.0002	20.2	71.5*	20.2*
	(0.0001)	(15.0)	(29.7)	(8.4)
Trend2 × 10E+6	0.3	0.3	0.3	0.3
	(0.3)	(0.3)	(0.3)	(0.3)
Constant × 10E+4	0.167	0.167	0.167	0.167
	(0.592)	(0.592)	(0.592)	(0.592)
d × 10E+4			0.028	0.100**
			(0.016)	(0.058)
Observations	383	383	383	383
R-squared	0.987	0.987	0.987	0.987

Notes: Standard errors reported in parentheses. The constraint that the weights sum to 1 is imposed by subtracting the change in € from all exchange rates.
Equation (1) OLS, Trend = Trend2 = $t(j)$, $t = 0$ (for 22 July 2005), 1, 2, etc.
Equation (2) OLS, Trend = $1 - \exp(-d * t)$, where d is set to be 0.00001, Trend2 = t.
Equation (3) Non-linear least squared estimation.
Equation (4) Non-linear LS. Set the coefficient on US dollar × trend = −28.9 (which is the point estimate in column 2).
* Significant at 10%; ** at 5%; ** at 1%.

Could the steady decrease in the dollar weight that we find produce important flexibility in the future if it continues? It is hard to judge the importance of the parameter estimates by just looking at them, especially for estimates from a non-linear specification. So we calibrate what the implied path for the weight on the dollar would be out into the future, extrapolating the trend of our sample period based on the last column in the table. Figure 5 reveals the shift away from the dollar to be painfully slow over a five-year period: starting at 0.98 in 2005, the dollar weight would fall only to 0.87 by 2010.

3.3. Other extensions

Some extensions of the empirical estimates allow us to gain more confidence in the findings.

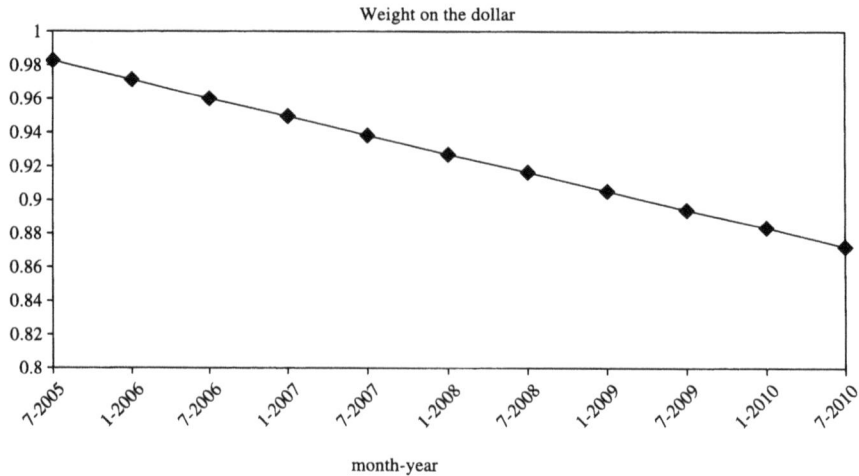

Figure 5. Extrapolation of the estimated non-linear time trend in the weight on the dollar in the Chinese basket

Notes: Weight on the dollar over time = $b0(USD) + b1(USD)[1 - \exp(-d*t)]$ where $b0(USD) = 0.982$, $b1(USD) = -28.9$, and $d = 0.00001$, based on the estimates from a non-linear regression, reported in column (4) of Table 7.

3.3.1. Method of moments. Bénassy-Quéré et al. (2004) propose a modification of the Frankel–Wei methodology based on a method of moments approach. The advantage of the modification is that it does not depend on the choice of a numeraire currency. As a robustness exercise, we apply the Bénassy-Quéré et al. approach to the Chinese currency data. We take as given the 11 currencies that the Chinese central bank says are in the basket, impose the restriction that the weights in the basket sum to one, and estimate by GMM. We experimented with different sets of lagged regressors as the instrumental variables (skipping the first lag to avoid contamination from possible first-order serial correlation). Unfortunately, it is generally difficult for the estimation to converge in our sample.

As an alternative, we focus on the set of first-tier currencies in China's announced basket, namely, the dollar, the yen, the euro and the Korean won. This time, we do obtain convergence. There is also a decline in the weight on the US dollar by this approach, though the decline is more moderate than in the previous estimation, from 0.97/0.98 in the first and second sub-periods to 0.91 in the last sub-period. As before, the Korean won receives some positive weight, especially in the latest sub-period, and there is little sign of positive weight on the euro or yen.

3.3.2. Intra-daily movements. It is possible that the RMB regime governing intra-day exchange rate movement is different from that governing day-to-day or month-to-month movement. In particular, the regime announced in July 2005 sets a limit on intra-day movement, leaving the possibility that the rules governing the change from daily close to the following day's open quotes could be different. Unfortunately, as

RMB trading is relatively thin, there are generally too few observations to perform a regression based on one day's data. So we have to pool intra-day data together.

We have collected intra-day data (quotes at 15-minute intervals) for two periods: 22 July–25 August 2005, and 16 February–17 May 2006. In a given 15-minute interval, say, 10:00–10:15 a.m., the exchange rate is the last quote during the interval. If there is no active quote available, then the most recently available quote is used. For a very active currency, say the euro, the quote is likely to take place at or close to 10:15 a.m. However, for a thinly traded currency, such as the RMB, the actual time of the quote could be much earlier. It is useful to bear in mind that this potential mismatch in timing among the different exchange rates introduces noise into our estimation.

Table 8 reports a sequence of estimation using 15-minute exchange rates and the SDR as the numeraire currency.[20] If one focuses on the four first-tier currencies in the Chinese basket, one sees that the weight on the dollar is very high throughout the sample, virtually 99–100% in all sub-periods. If one uses all 11 currencies as candidate currencies in the basket, then the weight on the dollar fluctuates (between 0.51 in the very last sub-period to nearly one in the second-to-the last sub-period).[21]

These results are consistent with the interpretation that the intra-day RMB regime may be somewhat different from the day-to-day or month-to-month regime. Within a day, the dollar weight is likely to be high and close to one, now as in 2005. However, from day to day, the dollar weight may have declined subsequent to the first months after the July 2005 announcement.

3.4. Conclusions regarding the recent Chinese exchange rate regime

To summarize our findings, within 2005 there was very little change in the *de facto* regime despite the announced policy change in July of that year. Not only did the true weight on the dollar in the basket remain close to one, but the tightness of the fit was similar to that of the Hong Kong dollar, which is on a currency board![22] In 2006, the *de facto* regime began to put a significant, but still small, weight on some non-dollar currencies. These were not primarily the yen or euro as one would expect, but rather the currencies of other Asian developing countries (the won and the ringgit) which themselves do not float freely against the dollar. Moreover, these weights were still small and the peg was still tight. The small increase in flexibility that we have seen could be important only if it were a harbinger of more to come. This is likely, as Chinese leaders gradually become more comfortable with the idea.

---

[20] The SDR rate is reported once a day by the International Monetary Fund. However, since its composition is fixed in the sample except for a one-time discrete adjustment of the currency weights on 1 January 2006, we can compute its intra-day rate vis-à-vis the dollar based on the intra-day exchange rates of the currencies that make up the SDR.

[21] Table 23A in the Working Paper (Frankel and Wei, 2007) repeats these estimations but using the Swiss franc as the numeraire currency.

[22] As often with countries said to be on a currency board, Hong Kong SAR's regime differs in some ways from a pure idealized currency board.

Table 8. Intra-day regressions for RMB (15-minute intervals, numeraire currency = SDR)

	(1)	(2)	(3)	(4)	(5)	(6)	(7)	(8)	(9)	(10)
	All data		21 July–25 August 2005		16 February–16 March 2006		17 March–17 April 2006		18 April–17 May 2006	
US dollar	0.867**	0.921**	0.702**	1.000**	0.754**	0.842**	1.012	0.954**	0.507*	0.968**
	(0.033)	(0.009)	(0.186)	(0.007)	(0.072)	(0.013)	(1.085)	(0.027)	(0.282)	(0.021)
Euro	−0.048*	−0.010	−0.270	0.004	−0.096*	−0.035**	0.068	−0.026	−0.361	−0.024
	(0.026)	(0.008)	(0.168)	(0.007)	(0.052)	(0.013)	(0.853)	(0.023)	(0.232)	(0.020)
Japanese yen	−0.024**	−0.010**	−0.102*	−0.002	−0.046**	−0.022**	0.020	−0.011	−0.123*	−0.011*
	(0.009)	(0.003)	(0.061)	(0.003)	(0.018)	(0.005)	(0.268)	(0.007)	(0.073)	(0.006)
Korean won	0.063**	0.063**	−0.000	−0.000	0.110**	0.110**	0.013**	0.012**	−0.001	0.004
	(0.001)	(0.001)	(0.001)	(0.001)	(0.001)	(0.001)	(0.005)	(0.005)	(0.003)	(0.003)
Singapore dollar	−0.000		0.000		−0.014**		−0.006		0.016**	
	(0.003)		(0.002)		(0.005)		(0.007)		(0.005)	
British pound	−0.015*		−0.092		−0.032*		0.031		−0.113	
	(0.009)		(0.056)		(0.018)		(0.270)		(0.075)	
Malaysia ringgit	0.010**		−0.008**		0.019**		0.063**		0.036**	
	(0.004)		(0.003)		(0.008)		(0.011)		(0.007)	
Russia ruble	0.005		0.002		0.011**		0.007		−0.001	
	(0.003)		(0.002)		(0.005)		(0.009)		(0.007)	
Australian dollar	0.003**		0.001		0.002		0.005*		−0.001	
	(0.001)		(0.001)		(0.003)		(0.003)		(0.003)	
Thailand baht	−0.003*		−0.000		−0.003		0.001		0.005	
	(0.002)		(0.002)		(0.002)		(0.004)		(0.004)	
Canadian dollar	−0.002		−0.001		0.001		0.000		−0.001	
	(0.002)		(0.001)		(0.003)		(0.004)		(0.004)	
Observations	12087	12087	3428	3428	2748	2748	2976	2976	2935	2935
R-squared	0.96	0.96	0.99	0.99	0.99	0.99	0.87	0.87	0.93	0.93

Notes: Standard errors in parentheses. All currencies are valued in units of SDR.
* Significant at 10%; ** significant at 5%.
Data source: Bloomberg intra-day closing price, New York.

Reporting in the financial press has focused on the appreciation of the RMB against the dollar. The focus is understandable, both because this is the question of political interest, and because looking at a graph of the dollar/yuan exchange rate (e.g. in Figure 2) seems to tell a clean story of an appreciation trend that, though starting out very small, has been gradually escalating in an exponential way. If this accelerating trend were in fact deemed part of the current regime, one could extrapolate it and predict more serious appreciation in the future.

Our results, however, suggest that the regime probably is not best described as a dollar peg with a trend appreciation, let alone a gradually accelerating trend. The findings of Section 3.2.6 are the sharpest on this point. Rather, the regime is better described as a basket peg with weights on non-dollar currencies that, though starting out very small in 2005, rose gradually in 2006. The difference in characterizations of the regime could make a big difference for the future. Our results suggest that if the Korean won and Malaysian ringgit stop appreciating against the dollar, or even begin to reverse, so will the Chinese currency. In any case, the evidence supports the hypothesis of small steps away from the dollar link more than small steps toward appreciation *per se*. This ultimately may not be enough to appease the US Treasury or, especially, the US Congress.

This adds to the onus on the IMF to deal with the yuan/dollar question. Multilateral institutions and international law are more relevant to this issue than is the case with most big-power issues realistically speaking. The IMF was given the mandate in the spring of 2006, both by its governing body and – perhaps more importantly – by the G-7, to reconsider the 1977 Decision and thereby expand the surveillance described in the Articles of Agreement beyond the World Economic Outlook and bilateral Article IV consultations, and to look into the issue of global current account imbalances through a multilateral consultation process. In practical terms, this means that the US Treasury in 2006 passed the RMB hot potato on to the IMF, giving that institution a rare potential opportunity to pass judgment or at least help broker a multilateral agreement over the Chinese currency and also G-7 imbalances.[23] Many economists identify G-7 imbalances as far more a result of deficient US national saving than of China's support of the dollar against its own currency.[24] A cooperative agreement would entail concrete steps by the US government to raise national saving, together with a decision by China jointly with other Asian countries, and oil-exporters which are running even larger surpluses, to allow their currencies to appreciate simultaneously. Europe would have a role as well. Negotiations over such an agreement cannot take

---

[23] To Mervyn King (2006), the IMF either takes this opportunity or else is out of a job. The US Treasury also supported a strengthening of IMF surveillance: in Adams (2006) and US Treasury (2006), e.g., by making more explicit the definition of 'protracted large-scale intervention'. The IMF Managing Director responded to the new mandate with a process to review surveillance, both bilateral and multilateral, as part of his Medium-Term Strategy for the Fund.

[24] Frankel (2006b) considers the various arguments.

place in the G7 because China, Korea, and the others are not members. The IMF is the logical place.[25]

Agreeing on such multilateral cooperation will not be easy. Both sides will be reluctant to make the necessary concessions. The United States is not likely to give up easily on the politically attractive idea that China bears some responsibility for its trade deficit, represented numerically by the bilateral deficit. Congress deliberately intended to legitimize the bilateral deficit in the 1988 law, however the IMF Articles of Agreement define manipulation. China for its part is not likely to give up easily on the idea that it has the sovereign right to move as slowly on currency reform as it deems in its interest. But both sides also have something important to lose if the issue is not settled. China's leaders run the danger of losing free access to a very large and important export market. The US leaders run the risk of the political momentum behind the scapegoat strategy backfiring, in the form of either self-inflicted protectionist legislation or a hard landing for the dollar and US securities in global financial markets. The RMB/dollar rate and associated imbalances constitute a better subject for multilateral surveillance and international cooperation than any subject to come along in many years, and it is more likely to be amenable to progress in the forum of the IMF than anywhere else. If nothing else, this process might help delay and deflect protectionist fervor in the US Congress.

Discussion

Linda Goldberg
Federal Reserve Bank of New York and NBER[26]

Overview

Jeff Frankel and Shang-Jin Wei have put together a topical and very interesting analysis of China's exchange rate regime combined with a focus on related themes in the political economy of US policy discussions of country exchange rate choices. The paper has three main broad goals. The first goal is to provide an overview of China's currency policies. The second goal of the authors is to provide an empirical

---

[25] The outcome of the IMF's multilateral consultation on global imbalances, as reported to the semi-annual meeting of Fund members in April 2007, followed this approach rhetorically. European policy-makers were assigned their well-rehearsed role of agreeing to make their goods and labour markets more flexible. Perhaps a more realistic European contribution to the package could be an agreement to stand by in the event that the dollar goes into uncontrolled freefall, ready to buy up dollars to put a reasonable floor under its value. Talk of a 'new Plaza Agreement' could be dangerous unless there is also a 'new Louvre Agreement' waiting in the wings. The truly worrisome aspect of the 2006–07 multilateral consultation, however, was the acceptance at face value of authorities' rhetorical claims: US claims to be raising national saving on the one hand, and Chinese claims to have increased the flexibility of the RMB exchange rate, on the other hand.

[26] The views in this paper are those of the author and do not necessarily reflect the position of the Federal Reserve Bank of New York or the Federal Reserve System.

analysis in the spirit of Frankel and Wei (1994) that delivers *de facto* currencies and weights in the renminbi basket and their progression over time. The third broad goal is to explore International Monetary Fund (IMF) and Treasury positions on what constitutes 'currency manipulation' and consider if US decisions on naming currency manipulators are driven by legitimate economic variables or political expediency.

This is a very informative paper that provides substantial insights into both the Chinese exchange rate regime and the decisions by the Treasury on whether China and other countries have been currency manipulators. These two analyses relate well to each other, especially since China is the country most frequently assigned currency manipulator status, with regular appearances on the related watch list. The Frankel and Wei decomposition of the components of China's *de facto* currency basket helps us to discern the facts from fictions in China's stated approach to implementation of a basket peg. Indeed, my main reaction to this work is to ask for more details and interpretation. The authors could take this discussion further, as they have done in other papers, and provide a more extensive treatment of the consequences of the basket currency weight choices for China and what are the potential paths going forward.

The more provocative part of the paper is its extensive analyses of the themes of currency manipulation and associated 'namings' by the US Treasury of countries to some form of currency manipulator status, as manipulators or on a watch list. Given the novelty of this focus, most of my discussion will pertain to this topic of the US Treasury naming countries as currency manipulators. In the Frankel and Wei approach, the main question asked is: when *does* this naming happen? I will argue that, while this question is interesting, the analysis could be expanded to address other highly relevant questions: when *should* this happen? Have the decisions been *appropriate?* Frankel and Wei also could address whether the Treasury decisions *have been consequential and accomplished some goals*, particularly with regard to China.

Assessing China's exchange rate regime

What is the regime? Frankel shows that China's exchange rate regime is recently characterized by more flexibility, but is not a dramatic change from past practices. There remains a high basket weight on the US dollar.

The question of whether the renminbi is still undervalued is left somewhat open. It is noteworthy that consensus has not emerged among the researchers of this issue. This lack of a common view arises in part because the literature on this topic utilizes a range of approaches and horizons for the discussion. The studies that rely on macroeconomic balance (current account) or extended purchasing power parity models have an accordingly wide variance in estimates of 'equilibrium' exchange rates and in resulting real exchange rate changes that would eliminate imbalances. See, for example, studies by Dunaway *et al.* (2006), Prasad *et al.* (2005), and Yin-Wong Cheung *et al.* (2007).

What is a currency manipulator?

The 1988 Act states that currency manipulation is said to occur 'for purposes of preventing effective balance of payments adjustments or gaining unfair competitive advantage in international trade'. This definition is broad enough to lend itself to potentially inconsistent use. Indeed, one of the key findings by Frankel and Wei is that political forces play a role in whether a country is named a currency manipulator. The stated consequence of naming a country as a currency manipulator is that the United States must then take action to initiate negotiations to ensure that such countries regularly and promptly adjust the rate of exchange in order to eliminate the unfair advantage. Frankel and Wei give a nice empirical description of the US practice of naming currency manipulators. One of their fundamental observations is that an objective statement of criteria for such status is lacking. Given this observation, Frankel and Wei set out to examine which criterion – political or economic – appears to have been most important in determining which countries are named.

While this type of investigation is certainly revealing and interesting, it does not address another key and fundamental issue, namely when is it that a country *should* be named a currency manipulator, as opposed to when they *have* been named a manipulator? I would like to know whether the decision to name a country is motivated in part by the expectation of accomplishing some specified economic objectives. It might be the case, for example, that the bilateral exchange rate between the US and the country in question becomes the focal point of policy attention and adjustment, perhaps erroneously, when the underlying issue is rising productivity in manufacturing industries in countries elsewhere.

Which country has been named, and to what avail?

To shed light on the features of the countries named, and the consequences of being deemed a currency manipulator of some type, I examined the composition of countries that have appeared in the currency manipulator discussions. First, it is interesting to note that all countries named have been in Asia, except Russia. China, Taiwan and South Korea together accounted for more than three-quarters of all announcements of some type of currency manipulator status as reported in Frankel and Wei.

	China	Taiwan	South Korea
Share of total announcements	27.9%	26.7%	23.3%

A key question that arises is: what did these announcements of currency manipulator status do to the key variables targeted by the policy, namely, exchange rates and bilateral trade conditions? Below I report the results of a simple empirical description of whether the action was associated with currency revaluations by the named country, or with a slower rate of appreciation of the named currency. I also consider whether there were changes in bilateral trade imbalances in a direction consistent

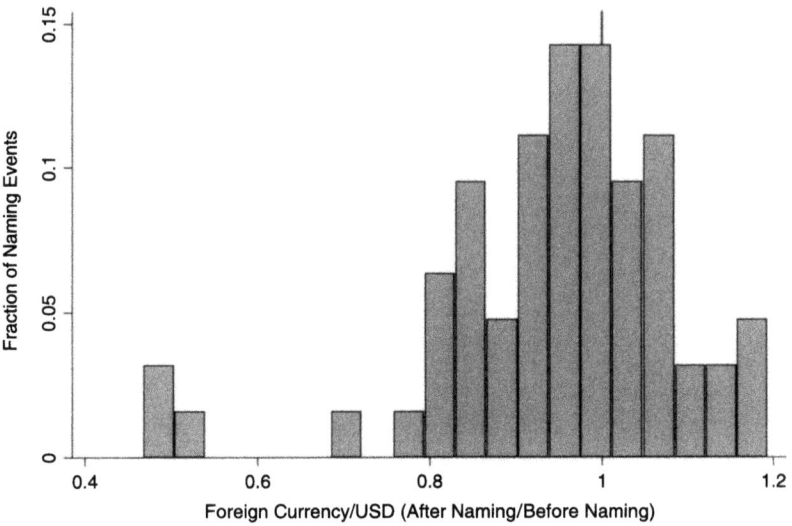

Figure 6. Does the foreign currency become stronger after naming?

with what is presumably the 'desired' outcome of the status, either reductions in bilateral trade surpluses with the United States or a slowing of the rate of growth of these country trade surpluses. In each case, the period for comparison is one year before the announcement, contrasted with one year after the announcement. The actual paths of these variables are shown in Figures 6–9, with shading indicating the values of the indicator variables for status as a manipulator as used in Frankel and Wei.[27] For 'namings' I use those instances where Frankel and Wei assigned a country a numeric value of (2) or (3), meaning that for (2) policy changes are recommended and discussions being conducted, or for (3) the country is found to be manipulating its exchange rate.[28] The following findings result from this simple analysis:

1. Real exchange rates of the manipulating countries did not systematically appreciate after namings. The post-naming exchange rate appreciated against the US dollar in less than 40% of the naming incidents. This is depicted in the histogram showing the exchange rates after naming events compared with prior exchange rates (Figure 6).

2. Rates of real exchange rate depreciation of the foreign currency against the US dollar did not systematically slow (or rates of appreciation rise) after countries were named as currency manipulators. In just 44% of the naming episodes were rates of real depreciation slower or rates of appreciation greater in the 12 months after the naming, compared with the 12 months before the naming. (See Figure 7.)

---

[27] The values are: 0 = country not investigated; 1 = examined as a potential manipulator; 2 = policy changes recommended/conducting discussions; 3 = found to be manipulating its exchange rate.

[28] Because Russia was never assigned a value of 2 or 3, shading for these charts indicates an assignment of (1).

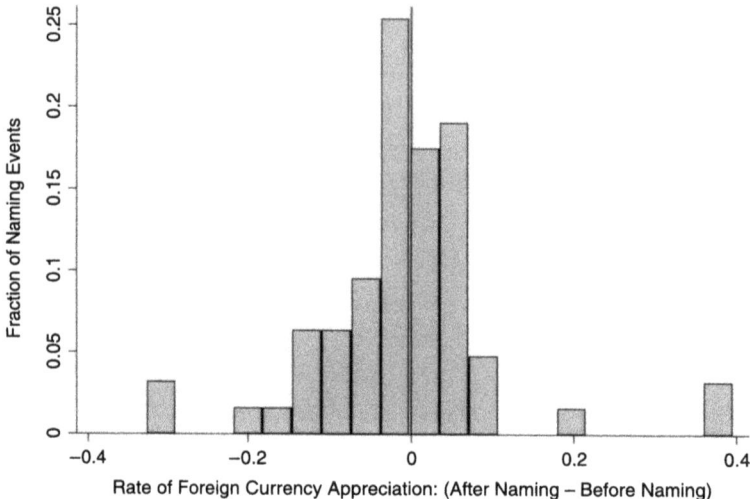

Figure 7. Does currency appreciation speed up after naming?

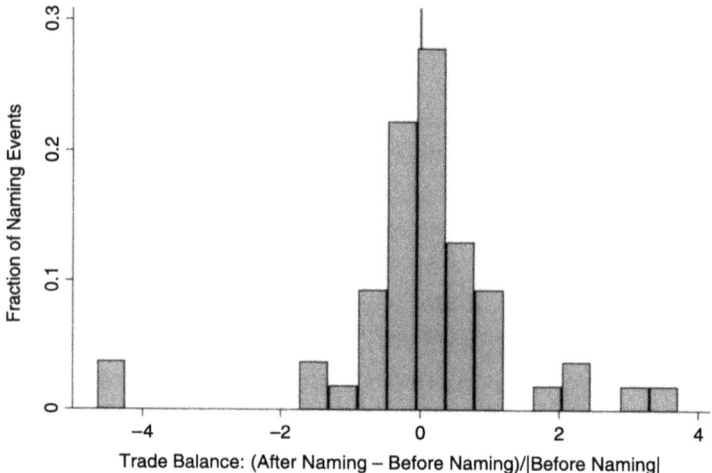

Figure 8. Does the bilateral trade surplus with the US decline?

3. Country bilateral trade surpluses with the United States did not systematically decline after countries were given some currency manipulator status. Figure 8 shows the mass of occurrences when the country trade surplus with the United States grew or declined over the course of a year. In 57% of the cases the trade surplus increased.

4. The growth of the bilateral trade surplus of the country relative to the United States did not systematically slow after the naming event. In roughly half the cases, the growth rate of the bilateral trade surplus was higher after the naming than before the naming. (See Figure 9.)

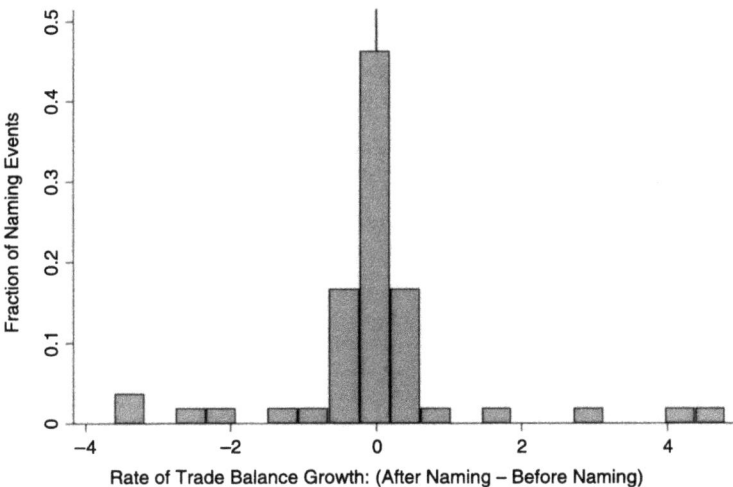

Figure 9. Does growth of the bilateral trade surplus with the US slow?

Clearly, the naming events could have been associated with measurable improvements in bilateral conditions between the United States and counterparty countries in ways that are fully missed by this simplistic empirical exercise. However, this exercise does point to the potential contributions that Frankel and Wei can make via a careful 'after action review' of naming countries as currency manipulators, providing us with information on what these namings have accomplished. This analysis would help with an understanding of the US Treasury approach to using this policy instrument of naming some level of manipulator status, as has occurred numerous times with respect to China.

Bottom line

To conclude, this is an original paper and the authors have taken a fresh approach at tackling interesting themes relevant for discussions of China's exchange rate policy. They conclude that renminbi behaviour has changed, but not dramatically. They also provide evidence that Treasury decisions have some political as well as economic underpinnings.

Given the interest in and focus on the issue of whether a country is, in some way, being named a currency manipulator by the United States, at the end of the day it also would be useful for Frankel and Wei to provide their assessment of whether Treasury decisions had been 'correct' historically, given the goals of these decisions. Moreover, have these decisions 'mattered' for the policies that are pursued by the 'offending countries' or mattered for real outcomes in the United States? As pertains to China, regardless of the Treasury decisions on currency manipulator status, it would be useful to have clearer and careful evidence provided on what a revaluation of the renminbi is expected to mean for the United States.

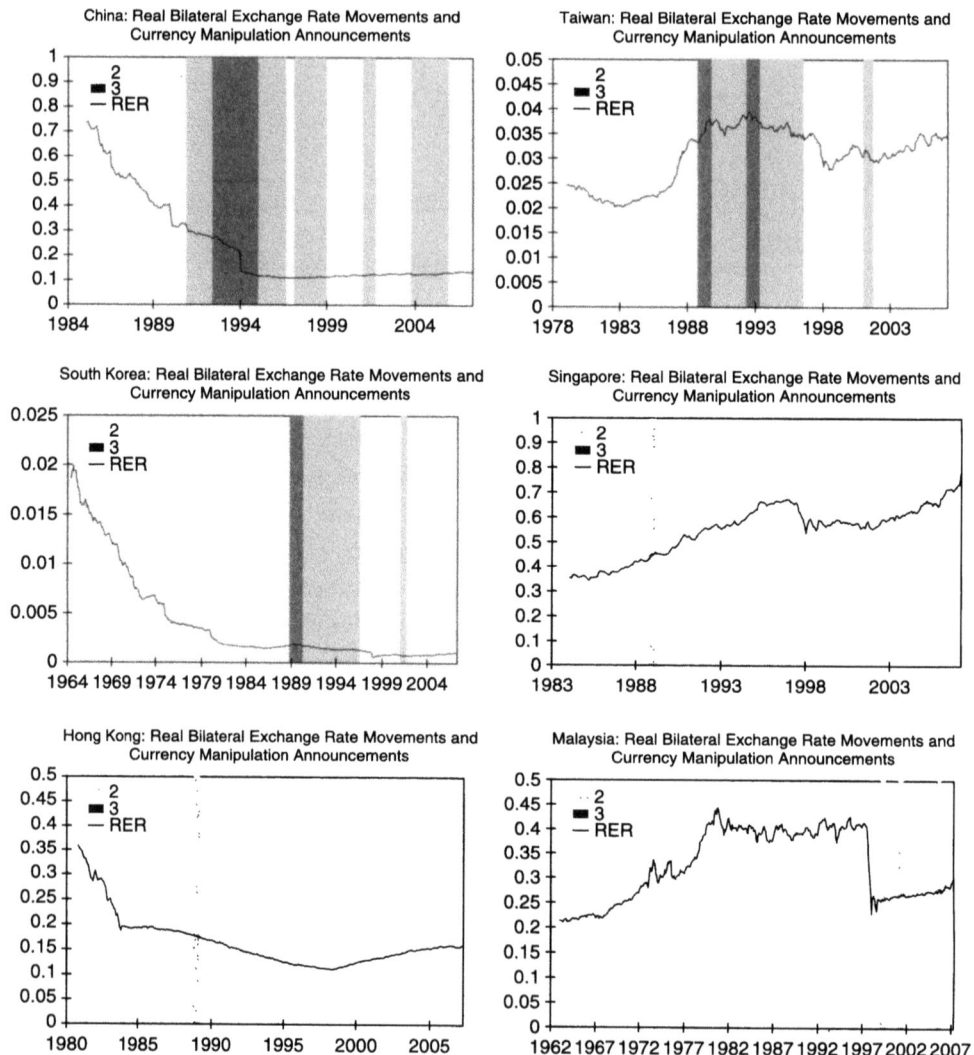

Figure 10. Real bilateral exchange rate movements and currency manipulation announcements; and real bilateral trade balances.

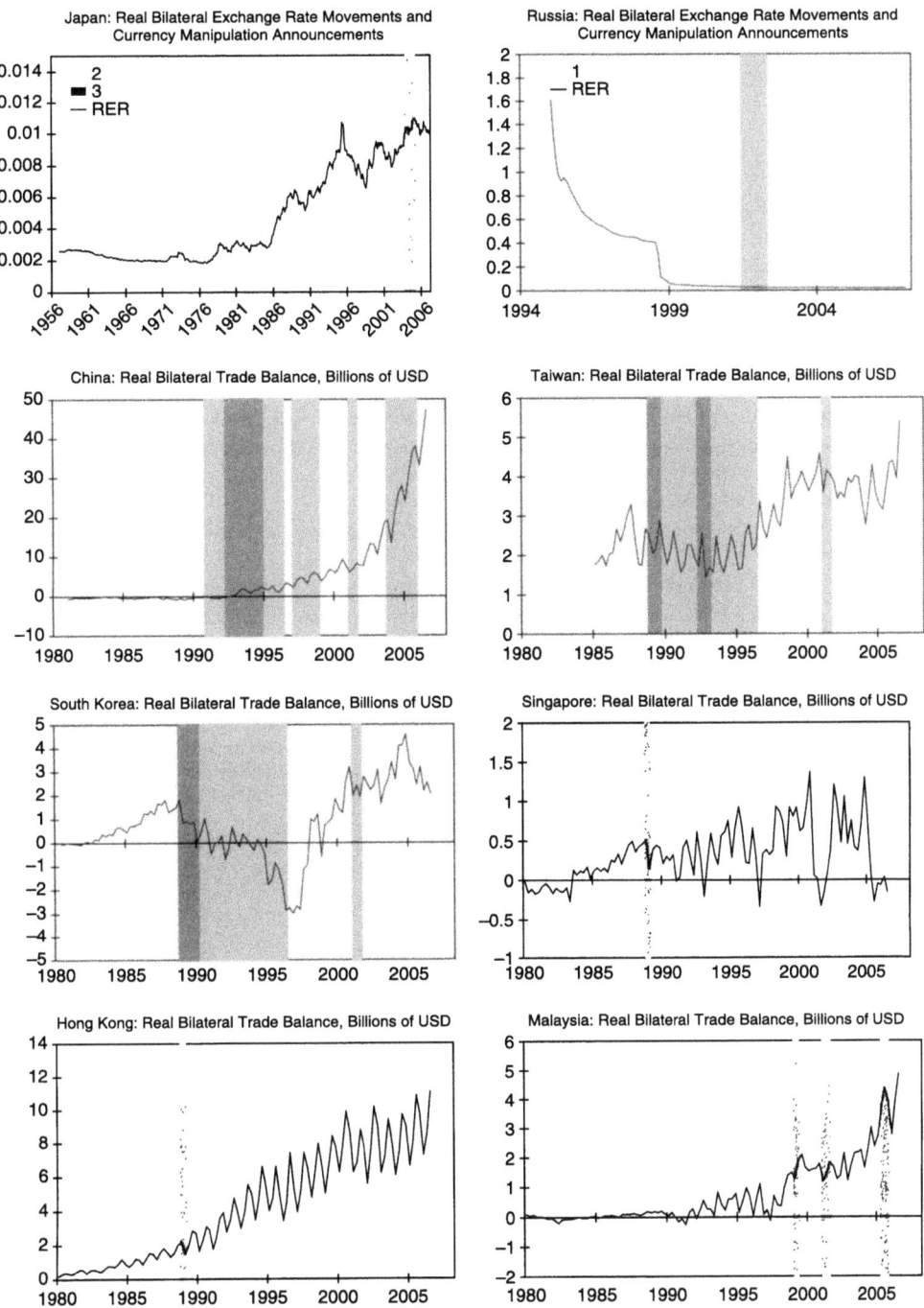

Figure 10. *Continued*

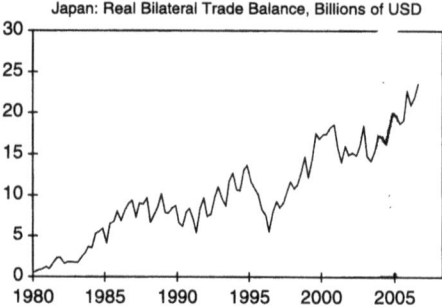

Figure 10. *Continued*

Data notes:

- Exchange rates are real bilateral exchange rates in US dollars per unit of foreign currency.
- Trade balances are real bilateral trade balances (exports-imports) in billions of 2000 US dollars from the perspective of the named country and vis-à-vis the United States.
- 'Namings' are episodes where the country was listed as a 2 or 3.
- ER_rate_change = (% change in exchange rate over the 12 months after each naming) − (percentage change in exchange rate over the 12 months before each naming).
- ER_level_change = (exchange rate 12 months after each naming) / (exchange rate 12 months before each naming).
- TB_rate_change = (percentage change in trade balance over the four quarters after each naming) − (percentage change in trade balance over the four quarters before each naming).
- TB_level_change = (trade balance four quarters after each naming − trade balance four quarters before each naming) / (|trade balance four quarters after each naming|).
- Naming events occurring in 2005Q4 (China and Malaysia) are excluded from the trade balance histograms due to data availability. Outliers where changes from before to after were greater than 500% were also dropped from the trade balance histograms. Seven outliers were dropped from each trade balance histogram: China (1992q2, 1993q4), South Korea (1991q2, 1992q4, 1994q3, 1995q3, 1995q4).

Panel discussion

Drazen argued that the question is not whether politics matter because they obviously do but whether the political reaction is excessive. It would also be interesting to better understand whose voice (industrial sector, region and so on) the Treasury represents when making the choice. Portes noted that there is nothing in economic theory that says that countries with fixed exchange rate manipulate the exchange rate (Panama is an example). A further difficulty is that there is no consensus on whether the RMB is actually undervalued.

DATA APPENDIX

Treasury Department Report to Congress on International Economic and Exchange Rate Policy

Thirty-one reports have been released since 1988. Recent reports are available on the Treasury website (http://www.ustreas.gov/offices/international-affairs/

economic-exchange-rates/) while older reports were obtained from the American Statistics Index (ASI) Microfiche Library held in the Government Documents section of the Lamont Library at Harvard. They are catalogued under the number 8002-14 for each year.

We classify as zero countries that are not identified in the Treasury reports as having been examined at all. Potential exchange rate manipulators can be broken down into three categories. (1) 'economies were closely examined as potential exchange rate manipulators if they had significant global current account surpluses and bilateral surpluses with the United States and maintained a fixed or actively managed exchange rate system during the period of this report' (this is the language used in the reports from 1999 to 2001). For some of these economies, (2) Treasury recommends policy changes or indicates that it has commenced discussions with their governments. Finally, (3) Treasury can escalate to officially designating an economy as a currency 'manipulator'. These categories have been applied to eight economies since publication of the reports commenced in 1988: China, Taiwan, Province of China, South Korea, Singapore, Hong Kong SAR, Malaysia, Japan and Russia. The data are included in Table A1.

In the Probit specification in Table 6, the limited dependent variable is defined in two ways. In the first two columns of the table, the dependent variable is whether the economy has been named as an exchange rate manipulator (mapping from the classification in the data appendix table, Table A1: value of 0 if 0, 1 or 2; value of 1 if 3). In the last two columns of the table, the dependent variable is whether Treasury has at least recommended policy changes or is conducting discussions with the government (value of 0 if 0 or 1; value of 1 if 2 or 3). The ranks for April 2006 are based on the predicted values using data for the period up to December 2005. The probability next to each ranked country refers to the probability of a positive outcome in April 2006. Table 7 reports that China is generally a higher probability target than any other country.

Explanatory variables

The 63 countries/economies included in the dataset are: Algeria, Argentina, Australia, Austria, Bangladesh, Belgium, Brazil, Canada, Chile, China, Colombia, Costa Rica, Denmark, Dominican Republic, Ecuador, Egypt, El Salvador, Germany, Finland, France, Gabon, Greece, Guatemala, Honduras, Hong Kong SAR, Hungary, India, Indonesia, Ireland, Israel, Italy, Ivory Coast, Jamaica, Japan, Korea, Kuwait, Malaysia, Mexico, Netherlands, New Zealand, Nigeria, Norway, Pakistan, Panama, Peru, Philippines, Poland, Portugal, Russia, Saudi Arabia, Singapore, South Africa, Spain, Sri Lanka, Sweden, Switzerland, Taiwan, Province of China, Thailand, Trinidad and Tobago, Turkey, United Arab Emirates, United Kingdom and Venezuela.

The data are for the period reviewed by a particular report rather than the release date of the report to acknowledge the lags in real time data release. For example, the

Table A1. Economies examined as potential currency manipulators

Date of release	China	Taiwan Prov of China	South Korea	Singapore	Hong Kong SAR	Malaysia	Japan	Russia
Oct 1988	0	3	3	2	2	0	0	0
Apr 1989	0	3	3	0	0	0	0	0
Oct 1989	0	2	3	0	0	0	0	0
Apr 1990	0	2	2	0	0	0	0	0
Nov 1990	2	2	2	0	0	0	0	0
May 1991	2	2	2	0	0	0	0	0
Nov 1991	2	2	2	0	0	0	0	0
May 1992	3	3	2	0	0	0	0	0
Dec 1992	3	3	2	0	0	0	0	0
May 1993	3	2	2	0	0	0	0	0
Nov 1993	3	2	2	0	0	0	0	0
Jul 1994	3	2	2	0	0	0	0	0
Jan 1995	2	2	2	0	0	0	0	0
Aug 1995	2	2	2	0	0	0	0	0
Dec 1995	2	2	2	0	0	0	0	0
Aug 1996	1	1	0	1	0	0	0	0
Feb 1997	2	1	0	1	0	0	0	0
Jan 1999	1	1	0	1	0	2	0	0
Sep 1999	1	1	1	1	0	1	0	0
Mar 2000	1	1	1	0	0	1	0	0
Jan 2001	2	2	2	0	0	2	0	0
Jun 2001	2	2	2	0	0	2	0	1
Oct 2001	1	1	1	0	0	1	0	1
May 2002	0	0	0	0	0	0	0	0
Oct 2002	0	0	0	0	0	0	0	0
May 2003	0	0	0	0	0	0	0	0
Oct 2003	2	0	0	0	0	0	2	0
Apr 2004	2	0	0	0	0	0	2	0
Dec 2004	2	0	0	0	0	0	2	0
May 2005	2	0	0	0	0	2	0	0
Nov 2005	2	0	0	0	0	2	0	0
May 2006	2	0	0	1	0	2	0	0
Dec 2006	2	0	0	0	0	0	0	0

Notes: 1 = examined as potential manipulator; 2 = policy changes recommended/conducting discussions; 3 = 'manipulating' exchange rate.

November 2005 report covers the first half of 2005, so the data corresponding to this report are for the period ending June 2005.

US bilateral goods trade balance with partner country: US goods exports minus US goods imports by country over 12 months as a ratio to US GDP. The trade data are obtained from the US Census Bureau and the GDP data from Global Financial Data. The series for Russia includes data for the USSR prior to 1993.

Partner country's current account: The current account (surplus is positive) of the partner country over 12 months as a ratio to the partner country's GDP. The current account data was obtained from the IMF's International Financial Statistics (IFS) Database. Where data were unavailable in the IFS, data from the IMF's World Economic Outlook

(WEO) Database were used. The series for Russia prior to 1992 is a Commonwealth of Independent States and Mongolia series from the WEO Database.

Partner's exchange rate relative to PPP: The PPP conversion rate to official exchange rate ratio, so a number less than one reflects undervaluation relative to PPP. The PPP conversion rate data were obtained from the WEO Database. The national currency per US dollar official exchange rate were obtained from the IFS Database. The official exchange rate for Taiwan, Province of China was obtained from Global Financial Data. Data for Argentina (prior to 1991), Brazil (prior to 1996), Ecuador (prior to 2005) and Peru (prior to 1993) are the PPP conversion factor to official exchange rate ratio from the World Bank's World Development Indicators (WDI) Database.

Partner country's change in reserves: The 12-month change in the stock of foreign exchange reserves of the partner country. The foreign exchange reserves data were obtained from the IFS Database. Data for Taiwan, Province of China are for total reserves minus gold, also from the IFS database. Data for Russia prior to 1992 are for the USSR from BIS Annual Reports 1989–1994. Data for Hong Kong SAR are unavailable prior to 1990.

Partner country's GDP and GDP (PPP): The data were obtained from the WEO Database. The series for Russia prior to 1992 is a Commonwealth of Independent States and Mongolia series from the WEO database.

Partner country's imports: Imports CIF data were obtained from the IFS database. The series for Russia prior to 1992 is a USSR/Commonwealth of Independent States merchandise imports series from the WTO.

US unemployment rate: Data obtained from BLS.

US GDP growth: Year ended growth in US real GDP. Data obtained from BEA.

Presidential election year: A dummy variable where the two reports prior to a Presidential Election Receive a one while other reports receive a zero.

REFERENCES

Adams, T. (2006). 'Working with the IMF to strengthen exchange rate surveillance', remarks by Treasury Undersecretary for International Affairs, 2 February (www.treas.gov/press/releases/js4002.htm).

Bénassy-Quéré, A. (1999). 'Exchange rate regimes and policies: An empirical analysis', in S. Collignon, J. Pisani-Ferry, and Yung Chul Park (eds.), *Exchange Rate Policies in Emerging Asian Countries*, Routledge, London, 40–64.

Bénassy-Quéré, A., B. Coeuré and V. Mignon (2004). 'On the identification of de facto currency pegs', *Journal of Japanese and International Economies*, 20(1), 112–27.

Bergsten, C. F. (1989). 'Currency manipulation? The case of Korea', Statement before the Committee on Finance, Subcommittee on International Trade', United States Senate, 12 May.

— (2006). Testimony before the Hearing on US-China Economic Relations Revisited, Committee on Finance, United States Senate, 29 March.

Boughton, J. (2001). *Silent Revolution: The International Monetary Fund 1979–1989*, International Monetary Fund, Washington.

Cooper, R. (2005). 'Living with global imbalances: A contrarian view', Policy Brief No. 05-3, Institute for International Economics, December.

De Vries, M. (1986). *The IMF in a Changing World, 1945–1985*, International Monetary Fund, Washington.

Dunaway, S., L. Leigh and Xiangming Li (2006). 'How robust are estimates of equilibrium real exchange rates? The case of China', International Monetary Fund Working Paper No. wp/06/220.

Eichengreen, B. (2006). 'China's exchange rate regime: The long and short of it', revision of paper for Columbia University's conference on Chinese money and finance held in New York on 2–3 February.

Frankel, J. (1984). 'The yen/dollar agreement: Liberalizing Japanese capital markets', *Policy Analyses in International Economics*, No. 9, MIT Press for Institute for International Economics, Washington, DC.

— (1993a). 'Foreign Exchange Policy, Monetary Policy and Capital Market Liberalization in Korea', in Chwee Huay Ow-Taylor (ed.), *Korean-US Financial Issues*, Joint Korea-US Academic Symposium Vol. 3, Korea Economic Institute of America, Washington DC, 91–107.

— (1993b). 'Liberalization of Korea's foreign exchange markets, and the role of trade relations with the United States', in Jongryn Mo and R. Myers (eds.), *Shaping a New Economic Relationship: The Republic of Korea and the United States*, Hoover Institution Press, Stanford, CA, 120–42.

— (1993c). 'Is Japan creating a yen bloc in East Asia and the Pacific?' in J. Frankel and M. Kahler (eds.), *Regionalism and Rivalry: Japan and the US in Pacific Asia*, University of Chicago Press, Chicago, 53–85.

— (2006a). 'On the yuan: The choice between adjustment under a fixed exchange rate and adjustment under a flexible rate', in G. Illing (ed.), *Understanding the Chinese Economy*, CESifo Economic Studies, Munich, NBER Working Paper No. 11274.

— (2006b). 'Global imbalances and low interest rates: An equilibrium model vs. a disequilibrium reality – comments on Caballero, Farhis and Gourinchas', BIS Annual Research Conference, Brunnen, Switzerland, 19–20 June.

Frankel, J., S. Schmukler and L. Servén (2000). 'Verifiability and the vanishing intermediate exchange rate regime', in S. Collins and D. Rodrik (eds.), *Brookings Trade Forum 2000*, Brookings Institution, Washington DC.

Frankel, J., and Shang-Jin Wei (1994). 'Yen bloc or dollar bloc? Exchange rate policies of the East Asian economies', in T. Ito and A.O. Krueger (eds.), *Macroeconomic Linkages: Savings, Exchange Rates and Capital Flows*, University of Chicago Press, Chicago, 295–329.

— (1995). 'Emerging currency blocs', in H. Genberg (ed.), *The International Monetary System: Its Institutions and its Future*, Springer, Berlin, 111–43.

— (2006), 'Currency mysteries', http://ksghome.harvard.edu/~jfrankel/CurrencyMysteriesRMB5-29-06.pdf.

— (2007). 'Assessing China's exchange rate regime', CEPR Discussion Paper 6264.

Goldstein, M. (2003). 'China's exchange rate regime', Testimony before the Subcommittee on Domestic and International Monetary Policy, Trade, and Technology, Committee on Financial Services, US House of Representatives, Washington, DC, 1 October.

— (2004). 'Adjusting China's exchange rate policies', High-Level Seminar, Dalian, China, 26–27 May. Working Paper 04-1, Petersen Institute for International Economics, Washington DC.

— (2007). 'Assessing progress on China's exchange rate policies', Testimony before the Hearing on Risks and Reform: The Role of Currency in the US-China Relationship, US Senate Finance Committee, Washington DC, 28 March.

Goldstein, M., and N. Lardy (2003). 'Two-stage currency reform for China', *Wall Street Journal*, 12 September.

— (2005). 'China's Role in the Revived Bretton Woods System: A Case of Mistaken Identity', Working Paper No. 05-2, Petersen Institute for International Economics, Washington DC.

Haldane A.G., and S.G. Hall (1991). 'Sterling's relationship with the dollar and the deutschemark: 1976–89', *The Economic Journal*, 101, 436–43.

International Monetary Fund (2006a). 'Article IV of the Fund's Articles of Agreement: An Overview of the Legal Framework', Legal Department, 28 June.

— (2006b), 'People's Republic of China: 2006 Article IV Consultation – Staff Report', IMF Country Report No. 06/394, October.

— (2006c), 'Selected decisions and selected documents of the IMF, Thirtieth Issue – Surveillance over Exchange Rate Policies, Legal Department, updated 30 June.

Jen, S. (2005). 'Chinese RMB basket still a mystery', *Global Economics Forum*, Morgan Stanley, 19 August.

King, M. (2006). 'Through the looking glass – reform of the international institutions', Inaugural Distinguished Lecture, Governor of the Bank of England, to the Melbourne Centre for Financial Studies, 21 December.

McKinnon, R. (2006). 'Comment' in response to 'Request for Public Comments on the Report to Congress on International and Exchange Rate Policies', Stanford University, April.

McKinnon, R., and G. Schnabl (2004). 'The East Asian dollar standard, fear of floating, and original sin', *Review of Development Economics*, 8(3), 331–60.

Mundell, R. (2004). 'Adjustment in China's exchange rate regime', remarks at Inaugural Seminar on Foreign Exchange System', Dalian, China, 26–27 May.

Noland, M. (1997). 'Chasing phantoms: The political economy of USTR', International Organization, Summer.

Ogawa, E. (2006). 'The Chinese yuan after the Chinese exchange rate system reform', *China & World Economy*, 14(6), 39–57.

Ohno, K. (1999). 'Exchange rate management in developing Asia', Working Paper No. 1 (January), Asian Development Bank Institute.

Prasad, E., and Shang-Jin Wei (2007). 'The Chinese approach to international capital flows: Patterns and possible explanations', NBER Working Paper 11306. Forthcoming in S. Edwards (ed.), *Capital Controls and Capital Flows in Emerging Economies*, University of Chicago Press, Chicago.

Prasad, E., T. Rumbaugh and Qing Wang (2005). 'Putting the cart before the horse? Capital account liberalization and exchange rate flexibility in China', International Monetary Fund Policy Discussion Paper No. 05/1.

Roubini, N. (2007). 'Why China should abandon its dollar peg', *RGE Monitor*, January.

Shah, A., A. Zeileis and I. Patnaik (2005). 'What is the new Chinese currency regime?' Unpublished, November.

Snow, J. (2003). Testimony of Treasury Secretary before the Senate Committee on Banking, Housing and Urban Affairs, 30 October.

Taylor, J.B. (2003). 'China's exchange rate regime and its effects on the US economy', Under Secretary of Treasury for International Affairs' Testimony before the Subcommittee on Domestic and International Monetary Policy, Trade, and Technology House Committee on Financial Services, 1 October.

US Treasury Department (2005). *Semiannual Report on International Economic and Exchange Rate Policies*, November.

— (2006). *Semiannual Report on International Economic and Exchange Rate Policies*, May.

Yamazaki, K. (2006). 'Inside the currency basket', Columbia University and Mitsubishi UFJ Trust and Banking Corp., December.

Yin-Wong Cheung, M.D. Chinn and E. Fujii (2007). 'The overvaluation of renminbi undervaluation', NBER Working Paper 12850, National Bureau of Economic Research.

Zhou, X. (2005). Governor's speech at the opening of the Shanghai headquarters of the People's Bank of China (in Chinese), www.hexun.com, 10 August 10 (accessed 25 August 2005). Speech (in English) on PBoC website: http://www.pbc.gov.cn/english//detail.asp?col=6500&ID=82.

Blackwell Publishing

Blackwell Publishing
9600 Garsington Road
Oxford
OX4 2DQ
UK

Tel: +44 (0) 1865 776868
Fax: +44 (0) 1865 714591

Scottish Journal of Political Economy

*Published on behalf of
The Scottish Economic Society*

Edited by: Robert A. Hart,
Andrew Hughes-Hallett and
Campbell Leith

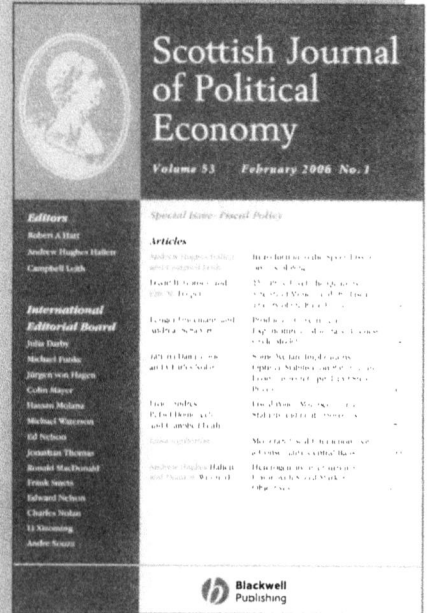

The *Scottish Journal of Political Economy* has an explicitly international reach in both authorship and readership and is dedicated to publishing the highest quality research in any field of economics, without prejudice to methodology or to the analytical technique used, to further the influence of economics within the world of practical affairs.

The official journal of the Scottish Economic Society - established in 1897 to promote the study and teaching of economics in the tradition of political economy inspired by the great Scottish economist Adam Smith - The *Scottish Journal of Political Economy* supports an approach to economic explanation which acknowledges the human, social and historical dimensions of economic activity.

For more information visit

www.blackwellpublishing.com/sjpe

Or visit www.blackwell-synergy.com/loi/sjpe for more information about accessing the journal online.

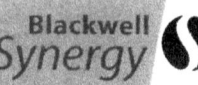 **Register FREE at Blackwell Synergy and you can:**

- Receive tables of contents e-mail alerts directly to your desktop with links to article abstracts
- Search across all full text articles for key words or phrases
- Access free sample issues from every online journal
- Browse all journal table of contents and abstracts, and save favourites on your own custom page.

Published 5 times a year, ISSN 0036-9292

www.ingramcontent.com/pod-product-compliance
Ingram Content Group UK Ltd.
Pitfield, Milton Keynes, MK11 3LW, UK
UKHW050410240426
12048UKWH00020B/1438